Ernest K. Gann

SONG OF THE SIRENS

☼

SHERIDAN HOUSE

This edition published 2000
by Sheridan House Inc.
145 Palisade Street
Dobbs Ferry, New York 10522

First published 1968 by Simon and Schuster

Library of Congress Cataloging-in-Publication Data
Gann, Ernest Kellogg, 1910–1991
Song of the sirens / Ernest K. Gann.
p. cm.
ISBN 1-57409-092-5 (alk. paper)
1. Gann, Ernest Kellogg, 1910–1991. 2. Novelists, American—20th century—Biography. 3. Ocean travel—History—20th century. 4. Sailors—United States—Biography. I. Title.

PS3513.A56 Z47 2000
813'.54—dc21
[B]

00-020668

Printed in the United States of America

ISBN 1-57409-092-5

✲

INTRODUCTION

THERE are for each of us defining moments in our lives, though their nature is rarely evident at the time we experience them. Normally we perceive them only in retrospect and are lucky, I suppose, if we manage that much. I can, however, with some certainty say that a defining instant in my own life came one afternoon in the summer of 1970, when I was poking through the shelves of a lending library in an Army hospital in Bangkok, Thailand, and came upon a paperback volume entitled *Song of the Sirens* by a man named Ernest K. Gann.

I was only 13 at the time. My mother was working at the hospital as a volunteer nurse, and I do not remember precisely what errand of the day caused me to be killing time waiting for her there, but I do recall clearly the moment in which I discovered the book. The words "muscular" and "evocative" were prominently featured in the cover blurb, beside an illustration of the face of a clean-shaven man with a square jaw. Behind the face there was a square-rigged ship under full sail. Something in this presentation spoke to me, and I immediately resolved to swipe the book.

I do hereby confess that I did just that, and that I read the book, and that I loved every word of it. I have read it again and again since then, that same purloined copy, and it is one of those rare pieces of writing that speaks to me each time I focus upon it. Sometimes it speaks softly, sometimes more loudly, but it always tugs at me somehow in a way it never managed before, so I have always come back to it. I do not exaggerate when I say my love of this book has in some part been responsible for my life as a writer and a sailor.

Ernest Gann was in his day, and among many other things, both a bestselling author and a man of some repute in the realms of film and theater. Born in Lincoln, Nebraska, in 1910 the only son of a successful telephone company executive, he could easily have settled into a life of upper-middle-class comfort and complacency, save for the fact he could not easily settle into anything.

As early as age 14, Gann was producing and screening his own films. Later, after a dose of military school, where his father had hoped to extract some measure of conformity from him, he managed to gain admission to the graduate program at the Yale School of Drama, in spite of having no undergraduate degree. After dropping out of Yale, he took a stab at a career as a Broadway stage actor. When this fell through, following a brief servitude in his father's telephone empire, he went on to establish himself in several other capacities in the entertainment industry—as an assistant director at Radio City Music Hall, a commercial movie cartoonist, a newsreel cameraman inside Nazi Germany, and as a powerful casting director for various film studios.

One would think this would be enough for any man, but Gann was only just getting started. During a period of high prosperity (Gann, throughout his life, cycled between many financial booms and busts), he took up flying as a hobby and became intensely devoted to it. When the movie studio he was working for suddenly folded out from under him, he abruptly resolved to pursue "honest work" for a change and launched a new career as a pilot. It was an auspicious move, as he found in flying a calling that both suited his restless, peripetatic nature and inspired him as a writer.

Starting in the late 1930s and all through the 1940s, Gann successfully plied his trade in the air. Mostly he flew commercial passenger planes, first for American Airlines and later, after the war, for Matson, a trans-Pacific carrier that failed. During the war, he flew cargo to the most remote corners of the globe for the U.S. Army's Air Transport Command. In 1944, he published *Island in the Sky*, a novel based on a search-and-rescue experience in which he helped save a comrade whose plane had crashed in the Arctic wilderness of northern Canada.

Island in the Sky was the first in a series of 23 books authored by Gann that engaged him until the very end of his life. His last effort, *The Black Watch*, an account of the lives of spy-plane pilots, appeared in 1989, just two years before his death of kidney failure in 1991. He first started writing full-time in the 1950s, after a very brief career as a commercial fisherman on the West Coast. It was in these early years that he scored his biggest successes. Several of his earnest, straightforward adventure novels made the bestseller lists, and six of these were made into movies, most notably perhaps *The High and the Mighty*, starring John Wayne, and *Soldier of Fortune*, starring Clark Gable.

Alongside his love of flight there ran through Gann's life the parallel thread of an abiding love of the sea. Save for his abortive fling in commercial fishing, this never explicitly expressed itself in terms of a career, but Gann's eldest son, George, shared his passion for things nautical, and Gann was deeply gratified when George made the merchant marine his profession. The sea provided subject matter for a few of Gann's many novels, but *Song of the Sirens* is the only autobiographical work recounting his experience with it at length. In that sense it is a companion to *Fate Is the Hunter*, an autobiographical account of his life as a pilot. Of all his books, it is these two that most clearly rise to the level of literature.

Fate Is the Hunter concerns itself with destiny, or, if you will, with defining moments, those split seconds so acutely defined in flight where individual lives either end or continue. Gann survived his share of these while working as a pilot, including one memorable occasion in which he almost flew a cargo plane straight into the Taj Mahal in India. He knew many other pilots, however, some quite close to him, who did not survive such moments. He was keenly aware of the fact that it was often not his skill that saved him, and in his book we see how he was both humbled and fascinated by this.

Song of the Sirens, on the other hand, is a book about relationships, a sort of adventures of Don Juan in which Gann affectionately invokes all the boats he ever ventured to sea in. Perhaps the most intriguing of these relationships are those in which he competes with other men. There is *Restless*, for example, an exquisite little steam launch usurped from under him by a band of steam power fanatics "who are not unlike early Christians in total dedication," and *Uncle Sam*, a beautiful Friendship sloop he in turn steals away from a man so thoughtless as to act as her pimp. But his "most enduring affair," as he calls it, is with the book's main character, the 117-foot schooner *Albatros*. He frankly confesses his devotion to this vessel is irrational and that he cannot afford or abide her relentless demands upon him. We note this same element of irrationality in all his relationships, even with the most modest of his sirens. As with the forces of chance that dictate his destiny from without in *Fate Is the Hunter*, these emotions ruling him from within are beyond his control.

Albatros was launched in 1921 for use in the North Sea pilot service and was one of the very last pilot schooners built in Europe. She was captured by the Germans during the war and served as a radio-station ship for U-boat operations. After the Germans were defeated, the Dutch made her a cadet training ship in their merchant marine. He purchased her in 1954 and subsequently re-rigged her as a brigantine, with square yards on her foremast.

Gann had acquired *Albatros* during a period of high prosperity, at the very peak of his success as a writer in the mid-1950s. Not only were his manuscripts being made into bestselling books, and his books into movies, but he was also being paid handsomely to write the screenplays, and it must have seemed at the time everything he touched turned to gold. Appropriately, it was Sterling Hayden, famous schooner-man turned Hollywood actor, who made the introductions. In *A Hostage to Fortune*, his 1978 autobiography, Gann describes how Hayden kept detailed files on large sailing vessels available around the world. The actor, he wrote, showed him photographs of the *Albatros*, then on the market in Holland, "with a leer I thought suitable to a sultan's procurer." And Gann confesses, "I was like a drunkard given the key to a saloon."

Though they obviously had something in common—they were both Hollywood "outsiders" who used the wealth they garnered from films to purchase large schooners and sail off to the South Seas—Hayden and Gann were at heart very different sorts of men. Hayden was a working seafarer who was lured into the film industry and despised himself for it. Gann was genuinely attracted to the business, but nevertheless was far too restless to remain content within it. These differences are reflected in their respective books. Hayden's *Wanderer*, in which he tells the tale of his life, of how he fled Hollywood, abducted his own children in defiance of a court order, and sailed off into the Pacific, is a book of angst and tension. *Song of the Sirens* is a work of love and devotion. Hayden flees to the sea as his last refuge, while Gann compulsively embraces it. We note in *Wanderer* that Gann is one of the people whom Hayden desperately wires for money when he runs out of cash in French Polynesia. But Gann must send his regrets and offers an addict's excuse: all his resources are tied up in the building of yet another vessel in Denmark. This was *Black Watch*, a large wood ketch whose construction Gann commissioned almost immediately after selling *Albatros*. (She is alive and well and is now *Mar II*, doing day charter work out of Halifax, Nova Scotia.)

In many ways, Gann's ownership of *Albatros* marked out an important defining moment in his diverse and crowded life. It was in *Albatros* that he embarked upon his most ambitious voyages—from Europe across the North Atlantic, through Panama to the West Coast, thence out to the South Pacific, and then eventually all the way back to Europe again. More intimately, it was on *Albatros* that he fell deeply in love with Dodie Post, a crew member who later became his private secretary and then his second wife. In *A Hostage to Fortune*, he described the moment in which he brought his new ship home to San Francisco Bay for the first time—with Dodie Post at his side, son George on board as crew, the ship passing in the moonlight under the Golden Gate, a landmark valued in both his prior lives as a fisherman and an airline pilot—as the most fulfilling he could hope to experience:

> My cup, I thought, is very full. . . . I could not understand how these diverse things could be, nor could I conceive how there might be more. When we broached the rum I raised my glass to Dodie Post, and said, 'To whatever comes next. Good luck.'

But Gann, better than most, understood that bad luck must come with the good, and that neither are subject to the command of human intelligence. He felt keenly the cold hand of fate passing him by to land on the shoulder of another. Never more so, perhaps, than when he learned of the loss of *Albatros* not very long after he sold her. She had been purchased by Christopher Sheldon, a theology Ph.D. with a captain's license, who with his wife, Alice, a medical doctor, ran her as a school ship for young boys. In a notorious incident most recently retold in the popular 1996 film *White Squall, Albatros,* under Sheldon's command, was suddenly caught out and overwhelmed by a freak storm in the Gulf of Mexico in the spring of 1961. Sheldon survived, but Alice, four students, and George Ptacnik, a cook who had also served under Gann, all went down with the ship. Charles Gieg, one of the students who survived, wrote a complete account of the disaster in *The Last Voyage of the Albatros.*

Gann empathized deeply with Sheldon, remembering times he himself had "wept for mercy" under the burdens and responsibilities of command. And he despaired over his inability to comprehend why he was kept safe while others suffered. He wrote in *A Hostage to Fortune*: "Now, rationalizing to the limits of my ability, I could not discover a satisfactory explanation for my repeated evasion of doom. Why Sheldon? Why all the many others I had known? Where was the balance?"

Finally, several years later, the arrow of the hunter found its mark, and the sea punished Gann in turn when George, his beloved son, the "stalwart shipmate" to whom he dedicated *Song of the Sirens*, was swept overboard from a tanker while in a storm off the coast of Alaska. "I had lost not only a son," Gann wrote later in recalling this greatest tragedy of his life, "but the dearest friend I had ever had in all my worlds."

Gann is remembered best by aviators. Among them *Fate Is the Hunter* is something of a cult classic, and not uncommonly the aerial literati will rank Gann's name with the likes of Antoine de Saint-Exupéry and Anne Morrow Lindbergh. His vision of flight as a dance with chance still rings true with pilots and holds appeal for them. Likewise, his vision of seafaring as seduction and of seagoing vessels as objects of desire will ring true, and be just as appealing to sailors. This man was one of us, a man of the sea, and, if nothing else, a fine storyteller with more than a few entertaining tales up his sleeve.

It is, on reflection, perhaps not so strange after all that he has been remembered by the pilots, but nearly forgotten by us sailors. The literature of the air has existed only briefly, its lists are still quite short, and it cannot afford to squander talent of this nature. The literature of the sea, by comparison, is as wide as its subject, and it is much easier for us to forget and neglect works that are truly worth reading. How lucky, then, to find this book that day in the hospital library. How lucky now to at last replace a well-worn copy with this new edition. How reaffirming, too, to know that a book so important to me will again have a chance to find the audience it deserves.

Charles J. Doane
Rockland, Maine
August 1999

SONG OF THE SIRENS

☼

TO SON GEORGE—

. . . true man of the sea
and stalwart shipmate

☼

CONTENTS

IN HARBOR • 11

I • THE *ALBATROS* • 15

A MIDDLE-AGED MAID OF FADING BEAUTY AND QUESTIONABLE VIRTUE

IN HARBOR • 77

II • THE *ALBATROS* • 79

ARRIVES ON THE SCENE OF PAST AFFAIRS

IN HARBOR • 139

III • THE *ALBATROS* • 141

REJUVENATED FOR HIGH SOCIETY

IN HARBOR • 171

IV • THE *ALBATROS* • 175

HER DAYS OF OCEANIC BUTTERFLIES AND RAVENS

IN HARBOR • 261

V • THE *ALBATROS* • 265

THE CHAINS OF POSSESSION . . . AND TRAGEDY

EPILOGUE • 307

IN HARBOR • 317

☼

Beyond all things is the ocean.

—SENECA

☼

THE CAST

Albatros
Li Po
Raccoon
Fred Holmes
Story II
Mike
Liberty
Restless
Henrietta
Thetis
Margarite
Uncle Sam
Diver
Caroline
Don Quixote
Butterfly
Black Watch

☼

IN HARBOR

If this series of gales does not soon relent, I have promised to bring out the Chinese firecrackers which have been cached in my secret drawer for several years. I will hang them from the bow and set them off in the best Hong Kong style and hope their influence with the wind gods will bring change. It is impossible to foresee how such a performance will be accepted by our dour neighbors except to further convince them of our insanity.

We are in a small sailing ketch in the harbor of Rønne, which is on the Danish Island of Bornholm. It is a fair-sized island of considerable natural beauty and it is surrounded by the Baltic Sea and gales.

This is October, the equinox is past, and while it is naïve to expect decent weather in the Baltic at this time of year, neither is there any record of such continuous tempests. One radio report from a station nearby has just given the wind speed at 31 meters per second, which is hurricane force. Our little vessel is bound for the port of Frederikssund on the western side of Zealand, and the total distance from where we lie to her destination is less than 150 miles.

Normally this would offer a pleasant if rather cold passage, easily accomplished because our vessel is as stalwart as the regiment whose name she bears, the incredibly gallant Black Watch. *But she would not be able to make any progress at all against the present combination of wind and Baltic current, both surging and howling almost exactly from the direction we must go.*

Every day we lean against the wind and make a pilgrimage to the breakwater. There we stand, eyes watering in the frigid blast, and solemnly study the sea. The brief visit to the breakwater is merely an affectation since we can view the whole discouraging spectacle just as well from our poop. We can see the waves exploding over the breakwater and spewing gigantic geysers of solid spray almost as high as our masts. We can see the heavy breakers on the shoal just offshore and it is enough. At night, secure in our bunks, we can hear the humming bass dirge in the rigging and know that our windsock will be further torn to bits by morning, and if our burgee is still there at all, it will be much reduced in size. We have ceased displaying our national flag. The only one we have left has flayed itself past repair.

Rønne is a small town embracing the harbor. It is deserted by tourists at this season of the year and the natives keep well within the shelter of their tile-roofed houses so that the cobbled streets are empty. It is reasonably pleasant walking along the moors which surround the town, but the sky remains a consistently dirty gray, the rain comes down in chilling cascades, and nature itself appears to have hibernated.

Yet we are far from melancholy since there is warmth aboard and good food. Through the after cabin windows which are peculiar to this ketch, a collection of fishing boats and cargo vessels, converted from sail in such a way that much of their original beauty of line remains, is visible. They are doing exactly the same thing we are doing, which is waiting. It is some comfort to know that the masters and crews of those other craft are also frustrated and appear on deck only momentarily to sniff at the sky, frown at the wind, and then retreat into the bosoms of their charges.

We avoid pure idleness and brooding, knowing the dangers of both in forced confinement. It is healthier and much more amusing to reflect on other vessels, other crews, and other times, and try to discover why it is in this day and age that any person supposedly possessed of his wits will insist on moving from one place to another under sail.

The mysterious power of oceans to attract human beings is often attributed to our genesis, but why should an ordinary rowboat on an ordinary pond generate similar fears and satisfactions? Depending on our age, the imagination can be stimulated and adventure arrive as the horizon retreats only a few yards, and it becomes quite possible to develop an unashamed affection for the most humble craft. The more sentimental mariners will not think it strange to find themselves in love with an object which floats them upon a special world.

☼

I

THE
ALBATROS

☼

. . . A MIDDLE-AGED MAID OF
FADING BEAUTY AND QUESTIONABLE VIRTUE

☼

ONE

IN Rotterdam, where perhaps my most enduring affair began, the rain is peculiarly dirty as if each droplet had brought its quota of coal debris from England across the Channel. At such times the Holland sky appears as flat as the land below so that you become the meat of a great sandwich and the cloud overcast is so thick it remains twilight even at noon. If there is but a mediocre wind the total sensation of cold is so powerful the private parts of a man shrivel and all passion hibernates until warm shelter is found or the sun shines again—which is said to be against Dutch law.

Thus it is something of a miracle that the Hollanders succeed in laughing at their April weather—as much of a miracle as my instant lusting for a dead thing found covered with grime, undressed, and altogether melancholy in spirit. She was the schooner *Albatros*.

I climbed to her main spreaders which were some 70 feet above the level of the canal, and looked down upon her sodden decks. Soon I knew that my staring had become myopic, as is usual with a man suddenly lost in desire. And it seemed to me this great dripping thing was the most beautiful of creations—a treasure to be rescued and reglorified before another day had passed. I could not define her charm, nor as yet conceive how in this age such a project would be realized. Yet I knew it was something that had to be done.

From the altitude of the spreaders I could best appreciate the lovely curve of her stern, ample without the least hint of fat, the placement of her masts in relation to her length, and the perfect proportion of her jibboom. From the perch aloft, heedless of the rain, I looked down upon a vessel much larger than I had ever thought to possess, and dreamed without shame. It was the same visionary pattern known to men for thousands of years, escapist, unsophisticated, and almost hopelessly unrealistic.

There was only one reason I could even contemplate buying a vessel like the *Albatros*. She had served as a training ship for many years, yet now her Dutch shipping proprietors sheepishly confessed they could not find enough young recruits to man her. I would have disbelieved them, since most European countries successfully maintained at least one sail-training ship, yet their asking price convinced me they were anxious to be rid of her. So when I had completed my inspection, I made an offer of even less, and all too suddenly for my financial courage, became a shipowner.

My rashness had at least the quality of the absolute. How a private individual of limited means was to maintain such a vessel when a large steamship company declined was a problem I deliberately refused to recognize until it was too late. In this manner drunkards convince themselves another drink is necessary, gluttons gorge against the day of their passing, and philanderers excuse an extra affair.

There was also the business of sailing her. I knew I could not afford to pay a crew even if true windjamming sailors could still be found.

Thus my love affair with the *Albatros* began in doubt and our subsequent marriage was governed more by passion than by reason.

The *Albatros* was of 92 tons registered gross with an overall length of 117 feet if you included her jibboom, which I preferred to do except when it came to paying dockage fees. At such moments I declared her length on the waterline, which was 84 feet. She was built in Holland just after the First World War and showed her age, particularly along those sections of her decks where people had trod for thirty-five years.

Her hull was of steel plates, riveted in the bygone fashion, and many hundreds of her rivets were now smooth-headed by the passage of waters. Her decks were of pine, which was not a good thing, and her masts were of steel, which was a very good thing.

A yard for a squares'l was crossed on her foremast, and this spar, like her boom, gaffs, and jibboom, was of spruce. All of her tackle was extraordinarily heavy, as befitted a ship intended for the muscles of eager young men. The antique anchor winch was intended to try their souls.

She was somewhat narrow of beam, being only 20 feet, 6 inches at the waist. I presumed this would make her a wet ship and I was right. Her bulwarks were waist-high and that was a very good thing.

Her accommodations were Spartan. Wash water was obtained from a pump on deck. There were eighteen hard bunks and a galley belowdecks with a coal stove which smoked regardless of the tender but which with an uncharacteristic gesture to comfort, the Dutch had piped to a series of radiators. A small electric pump circulated the heated water, and thus the interior was relatively warm and dry.

Her sails were of flax, a material with which I was totally unfamiliar, but which I later came to admire. They were in good condition and all of her running rigging was nearly new.

The engine room was full of afterthoughts. The auxiliary engine was a German M.A.N., which in the best Americanese soon became known as the "African Queen." There were four cylinders, each the size of a small beer keg, and these were startled into action by the sudden release of considerable air pressure. If all went well and the African Queen was honestly in the mood, the initial hissing of air would be followed by a horrible gasping, snorts of disgust, then some ominous thuds, and finally, as clouds of black smoke spewed from all sections of the engine, some sequence of orderly explosions prevailed and the engine was supposedly ready for duty.

There were two generating engines for charging the batteries and for pumping air so the African Queen could be started. The primary generator was a very old German Junkers which had two cylinders and puked lubricating oil all over the engine room whenever it was running. There was a standby generator of French manufacture. It had only one cylinder, very little power, and a straight exhaust which caused it to sound exactly like an old Browning machine gun and produced the same restful effect.

Beneath these various contraptions was a labyrinth of pipes, undulating, spiraling, snaking their way between, over, under, and around each other like discarded intestines in a slaughterhouse. Each year since her original launching various reforms had been made to satisfy new piping needs, so that now even the Dutch engineer who was supposed to reveal the secrets of this puzzle found himself perplexed. He was a small man with vague wisps of hair remaining on his torpedo-like head. He smoothed these hairs frequently as he tried to explain which pipe led to the sea, which to the bilges, and how this valve and that valve influenced the whole mess. During his halting lecture I sensed that his heart was not in his delivery and at first believed it was because of my mechanical stupidity.

He sighed again and again as he felt and thumped at pipe after pipe and said frequently, "I myself do not understand why this pipe is here. It leads to nothing."

Not until later when he confessed that his own true love was fiddling in a small chamber music society would I be certain that my ignorance was not his cross. He was only a man cursed with misemployment—which in some ways is more numbing than no employment at all.

The officials of the Dutch steamship line had more than kept their part of our bargain. They supplied the *Albatros* with all manner of things from blankets and dishware to extra line and charts. Yet it was the first of August before we were ready to sail.

By persuasion, cajoling, and considerable public lamenting on the pitiful state of modern man in a welfare-conscious, push-button world, I had managed to assemble a crew who had made their individual ways to Holland at their own expense and were now willing to sail back across the Atlantic without pay.

There was Bigelow, who came as First Mate. He was a man of sweeping enthusiasms and causes and shared my conviction that exposure to physical hardship and hazard tended to restore certain lost perspectives. He was altogether a handsome man, tall and spare, and the fierce set of his jaw constantly spoke of his determination. When I had first known him long before, he drank the full bowl always, and smoked incessantly. Now he drank not at all, nor smoked, finding a substitute for such indulgences by standing on his head Yogi fashion every morning and proclaiming to all who would listen that rice was the only fit food for human beings. Bigelow was almost frighteningly intelligent and very courageous both in spirit and action. He was also a first-class seaman and I blessed his coming.

McDaniel came as Second Mate. From the instant of our first meeting on the pier a strange antipathy developed between us. He stared down upon the beloved thing which I now owned in partnership with the bank and said, "Good God, what heavy gear! For damn sure we'll be a lot stronger when this voyage is over." That McDaniel happened to be absolutely right compounded my resentment, and his manner, which I mistook for deliberate surliness, seemed to ridicule my enthusiasm. He was a solid block of a man with tremendously powerful arms and legs. His cold eyes examined both my darling and me without a trace of approval, and his silence clearly suggested only pained tolerance for our enterprise. I did not realize then that his love for ships and the sea equaled my own, or that his moody silences were a consequence of an all-crushing natural shyness. I did know that he was a fine and experienced seaman, so in spite of our disappointment in each other, I welcomed him.

Oliver joined us. He was a lanky, debonair Englishman who moved with the cautious uncertainty of a parading stork. He had been a pilot with the RAF and we had long been friends. His wide grin and devil-may-care attitude were more than usually heartening after the cloud of McDaniel had passed. He marched sedately down the pier, long red hair flying about his ears, and he said when he looked at the *Albatros*, "Of one thing I am convinced. That thing will never fly."

And I treasured him more than ever because he knew nothing whatsoever about ships or the sea yet was willing to cross the ocean in my prize.

Because Oliver had been a pilot I held the illusion that he

knew something about engines. So he was instantly appointed Second Engineer.

Warren agreed to serve as First Engineer. We had sailed together before in a much smaller schooner and he really did know something about engines, particularly if only ingenuity and bailing wire must keep them functioning. He was an ebullient man with a constantly mischievous smile. He was also possessed of enormous energy and was quite fearless.

Still left his practice in California and came as doctor. He knew little of ships or the sea and so took the land with him always. But his presence aboard was comforting and his good humor never sagged.

If the *Albatros* had been an airplane she might have been better manned, for Johnson came, who had been a bomber pilot. He knew nothing of sailing and so volunteered to become a third nurse to the African Queen.

There was Yates, who was a businessman by profession. His spectacles and dignified manner were utterly deceptive. Not very far beneath his Rotarian exterior there was the soul of a true adventurer. He had sailed only in small boats, but he learned very quickly and soon became our most valued hand on deck.

There was finally a younger contingent, who variously made their way along the wharf at Rotterdam. With one exception they had been recruited by Bigelow, who suffered from a nautically common delusion that very young men make very good sailors. Because such very young men once manned the sailing ships of the world and according to the records were often enough in full command of their own ships by the time they had reached twenty-five, I also tried to believe these would prove strong, indefatigable, and would ignore discomfort. Perhaps the youths of a former time ate differently, or slept on a different side, or perhaps they were never subject to momism. But there must have been a fundamental difference in their inner texture.

These men were Brownell, Stone, Davis, and Chellis. Only Brownell emerged triumphant from his past environment and his voyage.

Steven was the youngest member of our company and he was in a perilous predicament since he was the Captain's son. Thus nepotism rather than momism might have troubled him, but he had been to sea since first teething and had become a thorough sailor. He never asked for favor of any kind, nor did he receive any.

For such a company there had to be a full-time cook, and since sea cooking is a very demanding culinary art he had to be a professional. So Rogerts, a young Dutchman, became the only paid crew member aboard. He was not plump as good cooks are supposed to be, but lean and wiry with muscular arms more suited to a topmast hand. He was fair-haired and strangely pale of complexion and his English was barely elementary. Moreover he had a weakness for geneva, which is a drink the Dutchman considers gin. And so at first we feared for what he might produce from the smoky confines of his galley, since even a leaking ship is better than one with a heedless cook. Our apprehensions were baseless. Calm or gale, Rogerts sent forth miracles from his galley.

There was nothing remarkable about our intended voyage from Holland to California. Hundreds of much smaller craft had crossed the Atlantic in safety and some comfort. A few bold individuals had even rounded Cape Horn alone—which is something like climbing Everest without oxygen. If anything, our voyage lacked the appealing ingredient of the pitifully small challenging the mighty, which has always accompanied the brave Peter Pyes, the Slocums, and the Chichesters of the oceans. Those wonderful people made their voyages in *boats,* which is a finicky matter of nautical terminology. A *boat* is a craft small enough to be carried by another craft, while a *ship* is too big for such a parasitical role. There is more to this than mere word discrimination implies, because a *boat* can usually be manned by one person or perhaps a few, financed in the same easygoing fashion, and such chores as weighing the anchor remain a simple hand-over-hand operation. (The only exceptions to this rule are submarines, which traditionally are called "boats" by those who sail in them.)

The relatively large size of the *Albatros* automatically created certain frustrations and hazards never to be encountered in smaller craft. She was not a great status yacht manned by a crew of professionals simply earning a living. She was first an anachronism because she was a true sailing ship devoid of modern comforts or navigational devices, and she was secondly an anachronism because the days when any individual, save a very few international millionaires, could keep such a ship afloat were long gone. Thus she became a common venture with the crew providing devotion and muscle while I served as Captain as well as a financial Don Quixote. It was not my first such enterprise, nor did I presume it would be the last. I was a long-confirmed addict. The sea was my opiate and I would satisfy my desire regardless of all else. And like so many slaves, I sought to justify my craving by solemn declarations of practicality; writing of the voyage would pay for this or that . . . a film would pay for everything.

The Dutch harbor regulations required a pilot to be aboard for the passage down the Maas River toward Hook of Holland. On the day of sailing he came just before noon and I was secretly relieved because there were a multitude of other things to consider without bothering about Rotterdam's maritime traffic, which is certainly the heaviest in the world. And this pilot inspired confidence at a glance. Though he was a small and elderly man, his large hands and remarkable blue eyes spoke of a lifetime at sea.

His uniform cap was tilted jauntily on his white head and his first commands were wonderfully reassuring.

Standing beside the engine telegraph, I rang down slow astern and marveled that Warren, now invisible in the engine room, could produce the necessary commotion from the African Queen. I was instantly impressed with the pilot's seamanship as the *Albatros* strained against the after spring line and the bow swung easily away from the pier.

Our Dutch friends had assembled along the pier in surprising numbers. Most put on an appropriately encouraging front, yet a few shook their heads solemnly as if they knew what awaited us over the horizon. And a few wept.

The little port of Maassluis lies far down the swirling muddy river which flows past Rotterdam into the North Sea. Here our pilot would collect the fee for his skill and knowledge and leave us to our own devices. Maassluis was his home port as it had been for a generation, and there was no reason to believe that it would present any difficulties.

The channel which leads into Maassluis is narrow, and the late afternoon sun revealed a considerable current working past the entrance. Our ancient mariner seemed to ignore it. He appeared more interested in the crowd which had gathered along the quay and he waved to them frequently. As we approached at half speed he explained that many of the people were his friends and relatives, assembled to witness his farewell performance. He was retiring and it was thought locally to be a particular and fitting honor that his last charge should be a sailing ship manned by Americans.

I stood beside the engine-room telegraph awaiting his order to slacken speed and regarding the current with growing interest. I thought how clever and wise this old salt was to carry on at good speed, thus maintaining better rudder control if the *Albatros* should be swung by the current.

I studied the quay and saw there was sufficient room just astern of a gray police boat. And I waited as the distance to the quay diminished rapidly. After a few minutes I looked questioningly into my mentor's delft-blue eyes. And again I saw a son of Neptune. The face was seasoned in salt, the wrinkles each as should be, the skin leathery from years of winds. But I ventured to say, "Maybe we'd better slow a bit?"

"No," he said, smiling at those on the quay. "Not yet."

The *Albatros* weighed over 100 tons. The distance to the stone quay was becoming very short. And still we were making 4 knots. I knew Warren would be standing by the controls in the engine room and I only hoped the African Queen would instantly answer his bidding.

We charged on, inexorably.

"We are going pretty fast," I said, directing my voice toward the sky lest I seem to presume.

It was all very well to say that a captain of a ship is her master and responsible for her destiny at all times, and a pilot merely acts in an advisory capacity. Yet in this case the relationship was uncommon. The pilot was not only a qualified captain on great commercial ships; his experience *had* to be a thousand times the weight of my own.

And this was his home port—a place I had never seen.

Of course, I reasoned, there must be a strong countercurrent flowing out of the harbor entrance. The moment we meet it our terrible progress will stop. *These are the kinds of things a pilot knows.*

I waited, my hand ready on the handle of the telegraph. Now there was some gay shouting from the quay and our pilot doffed his cap.

Surely now he will say, *"Stop!"*

But he seemed to ignore me, concentrating on the quay. He called only to McDaniel, our most experienced helmsman, who was at the wheel. "A few turns to starboard, please."

I saw that Bigelow was forward as he should be and had the crew standing by with lines and fenders.

We passed the mouth of the channel, our long jibboom pointing directly at the police boat. Soon we passed into water of great tranquility and I saw very suddenly that our speed had not diminished in the slightest. There *was* no countercurrent.

"Now?" I called anxiously.

The pilot dismissed me with a wave of his hand. And I thought to hell with protocol. I rang down "Full Speed Astern." Seconds later black smoke vomited from the exhaust and I felt the heavy throbbing of the propeller. I glanced hopelessly at our pilot and saw that he stood as if bewitched. The smile had left his face and his eyes were strange and unseeing. His lips remained compressed.

The people on the quay became ominously silent. Three uniformed men scrambled from the police boat.

Our propeller was now thrashing industriously, but it might as well have been activated by a rubber band. We continued to rush through the water like a berserk elephant. My own feeling of helplessness was profound and our dazed pilot remained utterly silent.

I could only think that if I had acted sooner we could have stopped in good time.

We had slowed to perhaps half a knot when the tip of our jibboom speared the mahogany pilot house of the police boat exactly in its center. As the spar skewered the house there was a sickening crash of glass and a prolonged splintering of wood. The habit of quick prayer acquired during a considerable flying career now reasserted itself. I asked that the three men I had seen abandon the patrol boat were the total of her crew, and I immediately appended a second request. Please, let our steel bow stop before we slice this wooden boat in half.

My prayer was partially answered, for our dolphin striker bent and came to rest against the police boat hull. And that was all. When our striving propeller at last overcame kinetic force, our cutwater was still some six feet from the wooden planking. Then very slowly we began making sternway and the great phallus of our jibboom withdrew from the shambles.

No one, either on the quay or the *Albatros,* said anything. The appalling silence was broken only by the further rending of wood and the labored thrashing of our propeller.

In anger my cruelty was terrible. I shoved the old man away roughly, as if he were capable of resisting. And I swore to his bewildered and hurt blue eyes that he was an absolute fool. Now I would take full command.

Not until later, when the preliminary details of our embarrassment were done and we were well secured alongside the quay, did I think to look again at the little man who had been our pilot. He was still standing near the charthouse where the force of my shove had sent him. He seemed to be hiding from his friends and relatives, who were waiting out their own embarrassment. And I saw that he was weeping, as only a man could grieve at disgrace in his heart.

As I approached he looked at me in resignation. He seemed to say, If you strike me now, you will hit only the dead.

I wanted to tell him of my own shame, how unclean it felt to physically overwhelm a much older and frailer man. But I could not find the words to redeem myself to him.

At least I must try atonement to myself. So I lied to him. "Something must have gone wrong with our reverse gear," I said. "Or the rudder, perhaps. We'll investigate."

He looked at me a moment, the wisdom in his face lost in despair. Then he turned away silently, refusing my hypocrisy. He walked slowly to the rail, where he reached upward and accepted a helping hand from the quay. He did not deign to look back before he vanished in the circle of his friends and I never saw his pathetic little figure again. But during the next few years at sea I sometimes saw his face—whenever arrogance and pride began to whisper that I was an intrepid captain.

The inquiry was perfunctory, and for some reason I have never understood, those in charge of the police boat made no claim. The crew of the police boat professed to be not in the least displeased at the shambles wrought to their deckhouse, since they would certainly have at least a month off while repairs were made. Nor was any explanation offered for the pilot's remarkable behavior. I said to the officials that he seemed to be in a trance during the critical moments and had ignored my suggestions. And they simply replied that he was very old and perhaps the excitement of the occasion had been too much for him. It was an inquiry which everyone present seemed anxious to conclude before it really began. No one was blamed for anything. Indeed, did anything happen?

As long as no claims were to be made against the *Albatros,* I willingly went along with this generous philosophy and accepted the idea that our approach to the port of Maassluis had been perfectly normal. It was *their* police boat. The Dutch officials took a statement from me and from qualified witnesses who had been standing on the quay. And that was all. I paid the pilot's fee even though it was not demanded. Somehow, I thought, the gesture might help to further persuade all concerned that the ghastly wreckage just ahead of us did not exist. And perhaps if the little man received his final professional reward he might feel he had earned it.

We sailed the next morning, not without certain new misgivings among our crew. It had hardly been a perfect voyage in the first hours. And some of my reverence for pilots had been washed away. I could not know it would be further diluted by pilots as far separated as the islands of Polynesia and the Kiel Canal.

☼

TWO

MAN goes down to the sea in many ways, the least common of which is actually going to sea. Yet there are and always have been relatively few sailors. It is said we came from the sea, beginning as unicells; our sperm tastes of the sea, our tears are of salt water. As embryos we resemble fish, and the mammals of the oceans are our underdeveloped cousins. Noah rescued our species by putting to sea, and only at sea may the complete mixture of all the grand elements best be sensed and comprehended.

To all of the many theories there are counterarguments, sometimes scientific and sometimes quasi-religious. There is no true satisfaction in either the arguments or the theories, and the real key seems to have been lost or deliberately hidden somewhere in the beginning of man's time.

The hour of day seems to have little effect on the magnetic power of the sea. It makes no difference if you bring a vessel into port at three o'clock in the afternoon or three o'clock in the morning. It matters not if the sun is shining or if it is pouring rain. *Someone,* at *least* one human being, will appear and take your heaving line or just stand watching while the vessel is secured alongside the dock. Weather and time influence only the number of people so compelled, and the same silent supervision applies to any vessel departing, whether previous notice has been given or not. Whether it be Oslo or Nassau, Piraeus or Honolulu, Papeete or Curaçao, Travemünde, La Coruña, San Francisco, Stockholm, Balboa, Christiansø, or Milos—fair weather or foul, you may depend absolutely that at least one human being will be standing on the wharf in silent welcome or farewell.

Man seems to have an instinct for such moments.

The people who engage themselves in this activity are of every race and environment. They appear from nowhere and are known collectively as the "Dock Committee" though their numbers may vary from one to a thousand. No one can say where or when those who oblige themselves to greet a vessel at three o'clock in the morning, sleep. They never appear to have dressed in haste. No one is certain where those who wait patiently for hours until a vessel sails, work. People serving on Dock Committees seem to have no other business. Yet the committees are not composed of mere loungers or even retired mariners down for a nostalgic moment with the sea. There are women who stand as transfixed as any man; there are well-dressed businessmen, entire families, lovers, and the lonely. All behave in exactly the same way regardless of their geographical location. They watch in a kind of reverent silence, seldom moving, and when either the arrival or sailing has been completed they continue to hold their positions. Only their eyes move, hungrily, as if they fear missing the slightest detail of a vessel or her rig. They stare at those aboard, observing every activity in a manner which becomes infuriating until you meet their eyes and understand they are really not seeing you but themselves. For their eyes are glazed with the faraway and they are totally unconscious of their rudeness.

Probably those who come down to the wharves and harbors of the world are ultimately driven by a stronger force than may be discovered in science or religion. Perhaps they come because a ship is a tangible representation of their romantic dreaming, a mental indulgence shared in one fashion or another by all but beasts. The solitude of an empty sea viewed from shore is one thing: euphoric, or for dark brooding according to the will. The sea *and* a ship complement each other in the imagination, and the urge is to become as closely identified with both as may be possible. Thus people of Dock Committees will not stand back on the wharf, but will move to the very edge of it and sometimes in their eagerness nearly fall into the sea. And perhaps when a vessel arrives or leaves, the long-stifled dreams of the spectators respond accordingly, for sailings invariably create visible sadness, while arrivals provoke a certain excitement and cryptic joy. At such times a wharf is a place where these emotions can be shared with strangers. Even sailors forget that the horizon observed from 10 feet above the water is a mere 3½ miles away. To Dock Committees, and to others who only linger on a lonely beach, the sea horizon has forever been limitless. Beyond it is adventure and romance, mystery—the swirling kingdoms of every man's imagination. These are essentials beyond the ocean horizon not to be found in daily life, neither in books, nor music, nor art in any form, and as modern existence becomes more and more protected those essentials become increasingly more difficult to enjoy.

So it could be that the members of Dock Comittees are starving. Only by coming down to the sea can they suck up morsels of adventure, which is essential to full life.

Basically these were the reasons for which each one of us found himself in the *Albatros* bound west from Hook of Holland into a fresh northwest wind. Schooner fashion, we set the mainsail first, then foresail, staysail, and jibs. We sheeted everything home with a maximum of unnecessary effort and fell away on course down the channel at the thrilling speed of 4 knots. Even to those aboard who knew nothing of sailing it soon became obvious that under her present rig the *Albatros* was not going to break any records.

Soon after the low shore of Holland sank into the mud-colored water, our complement of younger men, with the exception of Steve, became ill. They longed for their mothers, and all desire for adventure left them. This curse of all small vessels was to be expected, since for some reason youthful bellies are notoriously tender. But the illness is really nonselective, striking down every manner of person in the most capricious fashion. Apparently there is no way to discover whether a person is prone to seasickness; you are or you are not, a fact which the exaggerated motion of small craft reveals almost at once. *Probably* physical condition has something to do with it although it is invariably the splendid younger specimens who are stricken first. I know a Frenchwoman who is an ultimate example of frail femininity and has never allowed even the thought of exercise to sully her mind. I once took her to sea expecting disaster only to find she had the appetite of a cormorant. The most physically powerful man I have ever known is a professional fisherman who has suffered agonies every day of the many years he has put to sea. The duration of the affliction is unpredictable. Many people recover after a few hours, yet one man who would later join the *Albatros* succumbed for eleven days and lost twenty-five pounds as a consequence. He showed no signs of recovering until at last he set foot on land, whereupon his salvation was instantaneous. There are also those fortunates who simply do not become seasick regardless of weather. I lay cautious claim to such fortune, knowing that for causes past comprehension, one day, one night, very suddenly, my immunity may be challenged.

As for pills, diet, psychological persuasions, prayers, fetishes, and magic spells, they never seem to spare a person who is simply going to be seasick.

We had set our course for the Royal Sovereign Lightship which is off the south coast of England. Late in the afternoon the wind came around to the north so that we were tempted to set our Slaapmutts, which in Dutch means "sleeping caps." This was the name given long ago to the twin sails set above the single yard we crossed on the foremast. We were quite unfamiliar with them although they functioned as a raffee. They were set one at a time by an awkward combination of lines to the deck. If we had thought the younger men aboard were going to climb to the yard and free the Slaapmutts for hoisting, we were mistaken. It was entirely too far above the safety of the deck for their taste, so it was Bigelow and McDaniel who did the first chore. I studied the faces of Stone, Chellis, Davis, and Brownell as they watched their considerable elders working aloft and could not detect the slightest indication of shame. Which somehow made me ashamed. I only hoped they might become bolder with time.

Halfway down the Channel more serious matters began to reveal themselves one at a time, as if their gremlin masters would wait until we were far enough at sea to make repairs either inconvenient or impossible. The first was discovered during one of the ship inspections we carried out with each change of watch. There were two heads in the forepart of the ship, both relics of European marine plumbing. Though the toilet bowls were side by side, a steel bulkhead separated them for privacy. This gesture to delicacy had apparently been judged enough, because there was but a single pump which flushed both bowls simultaneously and it was located outside the cubicles. Thus if there were two men engaged, the first to finish often flooded his neighbor prematurely, or, just as annoyingly, left the entire disposal problem to his shipmate. There were some very unkind words said about this crazy arrangement by all concerned, and our disgust became complete when we discovered that the valve which led to the sea had come apart, allowing the ocean access through the bowls. We bailed out the mess and Bigelow was lowered overside and submerged in the cold Channel sea until he could insert a wooden plug in the inlet. Afterward we found that the guilty valve, which should have prevented water from entering inadvertently, was frozen open. The expert who had surveyed the ship had obviously missed something. We began to wonder what other items he might have missed.

The classic sailing-ship route to the Americas from England begins at the Lizard and bears southwest past Ushant, thence to Madeira or the Canaries when the southeast trade winds are carried across the Atlantic. Once out of the Channel itself any convenient course may be shaped to take advantage of the prevailing northwesterly winds, which are sometimes called the Portuguese Trades. At first we were lucky and the winds blew according to the books. For five days we surged along making as much as 9 knots and seldom below 7. Finally I was able to observe this new love in her element, and my pride was so infectious McDaniel smiled frequently, Bigelow exulted, and our younger men temporarily ceased their monotonous rehash of what they were going to do next semester and actually looked at the sea. Which was glorious. The water stole color from the sky, thickening it until the blue became a heavy, thrilling cobalt. Porpoises, sheerwaters, and stormy petrels performed separately and ensemble as if they were determined to contribute their special act to the whole show and perhaps achieve stardom. There was very little noise because we were going with the force-6 wind—only a gentle ploshing as the *Albatros* rolled, occasionally the squawked protest of a block under strain, and sometimes a soft fluttering when a larger wave would heave the ship slightly off course and so ease the pressure on the inner jib. Our voices became subdued as sailing men's voices should be and there were long periods when no one spoke at all.

These were the times when all the concern and labor involved in moving from one place to another under sail became worth while. So had Nelson sailed these waters, and Columbus; here the immigrant ships had passed to America and Australia, the tea clippers, the Vikings who had invaded the Mediterranean, and the Africans who had invaded Scandinavia. Under sail we knew a strong affinity for all who had relied upon the wind alone, and we agreed there were very few sensations which could satisfy both mind and body in this way. It is remarkable how quickly a good and favorable wind can sweep away the maddening frustrations of shore living. During the starlit nights I would sometimes turn on the radio and listen to position reports from transatlantic airplanes. Some were being piloted by old comrades and I was amused at the contrast in our speeds. But I did not envy them. They could not appreciate the environment of which we were now a part.

Our serenity was spoiled each day by the need for charging our batteries. The process took but two hours yet it seemed forever, and in moments of special annoyance we occasionally resolved to throw everything electrical overboard and rely entirely on the kerosene lamps which were still in place about the ship. Then I would remember a Chinese junk I had chartered in Hong Kong and I became less sentimental. The junk's real Chinese name had been absolutely unpronounceable to my Occidental tongue, so I had christened her the *Li Po* after my favorite poet.

I learned a great many things while sailing in the *Li Po* and reached the conclusion that a Chinese junk can be a highly overrated species of marine architecture. There are people who speak in near reverence of Chinese junks although it is doubtful how many of those enthusiasts have actually sailed in them. "Look!" they will say, "See how swift they are . . . how comfortable . . . and above all seaworthy! Ah, there is nothing like the clever Oriental in matters nautical! They even invented the compass!"

The *Li Po* was indeed swift, and for a very good reason. She was a typical small cargo junk of the Hong Kong-Canton area. She was approximately 60 feet long with spars to match and drew exactly 3½ feet. Any craft of such dimensions, including a large wooden tub, is bound to sail fast—downwind. She will also capsize with the greatest of ease, which is why numerous junks are lost every typhoon season, and which may also have been the reason the owner-captain of the *Li Po* was such a devout Seventh Day Adventist. He guaranteed his peace with God by fashioning a cross of copper stripping over the tiny doorway which led to the wooden igloo which was his cabin, and he doubled his insurance by having his brother stand constantly at the mainsail halyard—to lower same instantly if it blew more than a gentle breeze.

The *Li Po* would not sail anywhere near the wind, showing even less style than a square-rigger, and when on a reach she made appalling leeway. Her ridiculous draft gave her one advantage. During calms the Captain's entire family, including his six-year-old daughter, lay to on the sweeps and we progressed sedately at about half a knot.

Seen from a distance, however, the *Li Po* presented an appearance to satisfy the most determined romantic. What was not apparent was the shocking inefficiency of her gear, which was the fault of stubborn adherence to ancient design rather than economics. Nor was it possible to imagine the cramped discomfort of my "cabin," which was best entered on all fours and in which it was impossible to stand. Also invisible from a distance was the variety of insects which prowled the decks every night in such an indefatigable manner I was certain they changed watches. All of the *Li Po*'s faults and discomforts might have been less irritating if one modern luxury had been available. An oil lamp may be romantic, but if you must live with oil light more than a few nights you develop a strong appreciation of electricity. Which is probably why people throughout the world who have recently acquired electric light display their prize without adorning its bare beauty and hang it like a household god in the center of everything.

This same appreciation caused us to tolerate the noise of a generator in the *Albatros*. Only when no racket was forthcoming did we fret, and this was beginning to happen with ominous regularity. Soon we knew that the behavior of our two generators had more serious implications than merely losing electric lights.

Warren, whose lot it was to keep some measure of government in the engine-room zoo, did his utmost to postpone complete anarchy. He diagnosed the elderly Junkers' refusal to start as a complete lack of compression, tore it to pieces and fashioned a crude head gasket of tin cans. Then he put the Junkers back together again, cursed and cajoled, and when he ran out of breath, Oliver the Englishman tried lyrical incantations. And still the Junkers would not start.

We needed the Junkers because it performed two very important rites in addition to providing electric light. It gave power to a pump which would remove any water from the bilge. It also drove a separate pump which filled the starting tanks of the African Queen with air. Both needs now became of great interest to us all. For the wind had fallen away to nothing and we were left slopping and banging about in a convulsive, obviously embittered sea. The vast liquid which had been so enchanting only the day before now threw a continuous series of tantrums as if responding to the movements of an undersea monster taken with epilepsy. The resulting strain on all our sailing gear as the ship rolled viciously was terrible.

And suddenly, for no apparent reason, we had developed a leak. The engine-room bilge was full of water nearly to the deck plates. Fortunately it was isolated from the rest of the ship by watertight bulkheads.

The secondary generator—which we called "Lucky Alphonse" because of its French manufacture—now chose to rebel, and the shouts of frustration from the engine room became increasingly passionate. In aviation such situations are known as "snowballing"—a convenient way to describe how one very minor failure has a remarkable tendency to attach others to itself and in multiplication compound inconvenience into real trouble.

Lucky Alphonse would start, bark in its savage machine-gun fashion until it was asked to do anything useful, whereupon it would stop. Perhaps it resented its afterthought position, which was one of relative obscurity in the engine room. It had been placed far up along the hull just beneath the decking, so that in colliding with the adjacent beams Warren now added blood to his mixture of oil and sweat. Fortunately he was never seasick, nor was Oliver, nor Johnson, for as we rolled our scuppers under, they labored in a stinking, very unstable purgatory. Bigelow and I were also of strong stomach so that we were able to make frequent trips to the engine room and hinder Warren with utterly useless advice. McDaniel did not even bother to peer down the engine-room hatch. For him, the engine room and all that happened there did not exist.

There are numerous tortures designed especially for sailing men—perhaps to keep them humble. One is the pure physical torture of being becalmed in a rolling sea. The sailor then exists in a world about which nothing is predictable except that all of his physical senses will be insulted constantly and he must eat, sleep, work, and eliminate if he can, while sprawled. He cannot sit, stand, or even lie down in any of the positions normally habitual with human beings, because the relationship between himself and whatever object he uses for support is constantly changing. So that for one moment in his bunk he may become nearly weightless and the next seem to double his weight. It is worse than being in a storm and even more exhausting. And while his body cries in protest, the ship cries with him because a sailing ship becalmed is a world of tortured noises.

Another torment is mainly mental. It is initiated by a leaking ship and when the cause cannot be discovered, the uneasiness achieves true refinement. At such times the sailor asks of himself, "Why am I?"

Even in robust health Lucky Alphonse was not capable of powering the bilge pump or filling the air tanks. So after kicking it a few times to ease his spleen, Warren abandoned it. There was, he said, enough air left in the tanks for one normal start of the African Queen. Although there was no generator on the monster, it did have a bilge pump and it was conceivable that in spite of its limited capacity we could at least remove the water from the engine room and so discover why we were leaking.

The Dutch had been very proud of the mechanical insurance in the engine room. They had carefully pointed out how everything that might go wrong was protected by something else which would not go wrong. If one generator failed, then the other would take over; if the electric bilge pump malfunctioned, then the main engine would do the job; and if the air compressor failed, then there was a hand pump to cover its loss. We tried the hand pump, wishing to place more air in the tanks because in spite of Warren's optimism the African Queen had yet to make a normal start. It was supposed to start on five atmospheres of pressure. It normally took fifteen, and sometimes twenty was not enough.

The gauges told us we had only ten atmospheres, which meant we were nearly bankrupt.

We tried the air pump, which was activated by a heavy steel bar. The strongest of us could barely move it. We sat down with our hands dangling between our legs, seeking comfort in lame humor, but nothing would change the true situation. To satisfy the greed of the African Queen would take a minimum of three days' hard pumping. Warren *must* make the Junkers function, and for this project he was forgiven all other duty, fawned upon and encouraged by everyone including Charlie, who baked him a personal cake.

Not that we minded sailing our way entirely across the Atlantic, eventually the wind would return and eventually, as thousands of wind ships had done before, we would reach the Barbados. But we dared not tarry along the way. Hurricanes destined for seasonal parade were already forming on the southern horizon.

Among modern mariners there is a cult of purists who sneer at any means of propulsion except the wind. They will not install an engine in their boats, or if one is already there, they refuse to use it, and therefore qualify as this era's master masochists. It is all very well and pleasant to drift about on a Sunday afternoon chatting across flat and silent water with a friend similarly in irons, but if your intention is to voyage to a given destination, the denial of power becomes nonsense. Racing under sail is of course a sport with consequent rules to heighten competition, but since the beginning of time *good* sailors have taken advantage of every known means to complete their voyages with efficiency and dispatch.

Rolling our guts out was frustrating enough, but now our real concern was for the leak and the removal of the water from the bilge. Lacking machine muscles, we now turned to the pair of hand bilge pumps on deck. They were curious contraptions unlike any we had ever seen before, and it immediately became doubtful if they had ever been used in the entire history of the *Albatros*. The pumps were of cast iron. An assembly of levers and arms was activated by a steel bar long enough for two men to move up and down. The contraption caused a hollow wooden cup, which was bound in leather, to rise and descend inside a pipe leading to the bilge. With each stroke of the pump approximately two coffee mugs of water would be brought spewing over the deck. If we were to clear the entire bilge we realized it would be like bailing a bathtub with a thimble. And we found the effort required to move the pump was out of all proportion to the amount of water achieved.

It was the second time I had been at sea in a ship cursed with a mysterious leak and again I found it difficult to smile.

If the small craft possessed during my youth were counted, then the *Albatros* was my sixteenth command. It seemed that I had never been without a vessel of some kind, yet only once had I known the relative luxury of owning a new boat. The remainder of my voyaging had been accomplished in some other sailors' castoffs—elderly yachts so scrofulous with rot they were a hazard at a wharf, or commercial fishing boats haggard and sore from work.

Perhaps the most disastrous was the *Raccoon*—a sloop-rigged day sailer which had seen far too many years on Cape Cod. But she was the first real boat I had ever acquired with my own earnings and thus I loved her more than any of her predecessors. She had a little cuddy with an entry hatch amidships and below there was enough room for a man to sit although not quite stretch his length. It was my intent to saw a hole in the after bulkhead through which my feet could project so I could spend a comfortable night aboard. I would cover the hole with a salty little louver, hinged to drop down.

Such was my excitement in acquiring the *Raccoon* for only one hundred and fifty dollars which had taken me all of a summer's work to earn, that I neglected to see if her gear included any means of emptying the bilge. And for the first week there was no need of concern, for she was remarkably stable and not a drop of water came aboard. There was also practically no wind.

All of the first week I was absorbed in setting minor rigging details to rights, and the winds were so light I had little temptation to venture far offshore. Soon however, in the way of Cape Cod, the weather became more boisterous. Charged with pride, enthusiasm, and the special stimulus of a first autumn wind, I sailed the little *Raccoon* out of a narrow estuary which backed up into a tidal pool near South Falmouth. We were alone because that is the way I thought things should be on this nuptial voyage.

Once clear of the beach, I put the *Raccoon* on an easy reach and we danced over the glittering seas. It was such a fine and jolly wind that I was compelled to render a song about one Trixie, a harlot of some reputation in Boston. I was so pleased with the *Raccoon* and the radiant day that I forgot time and distance until long after the land had dropped below the horizon. At last I decided it was time to come about on the opposite tack and head back to the estuary, and a moment later we were stepping gingerly on the path of the sun. I had resumed my review of Trixie's colorful adventures when my voice wilted. For there, before my eyes, the entire high side of the *Raccoon*'s deck was parting from the hull.

I watched the expanding division between deck and hull as if mesmerized, as if standing absolutely still while a rattlesnake gave full warning and struck my leg. It just could not happen, yet there it was, an open wound in the side of my vessel some 8 feet long and about 6 inches wide. And there, just below its open mouth, were several billion gallons of water waiting to be swallowed.

I saw that the chain plates of the two mast shrouds had pulled out of the *Raccoon*'s ancient frames in response to the pressures on the mast, and had lifted the deck with them. She is rotten, I thought, she is as rotten as Trixie's anatomy and now we are all three far from any salvation.

Just on the horizon I could see a thin yellowish line above the blue of the sea. The shore. It would take at least an hour to make it.

I held the same course we had taken after coming about and hardly dared breathe while I considered the possibilities. Prudence first declared I should douse the sail immediately lest the mast go over the side. What then? The *Raccoon* would return to an even keel and I would be in a dubious race with the oncoming seas, because in the evil manner of all unmanaged craft she would certainly lie broadside in the troughs. I would have only a minute or so to douse the jib, remove it from the forestay, and keep the seas from the opening by a method known as "fothering." I would have to pass one end of the jib completely under the *Raccoon*, heave up taut and secure it in seconds. It just couldn't be done. The impatient seas would slosh through the gap betwixt deck and hull, her little cuddy cabin would start to fill, and the *Raccoon* would sink ever deeper into the water with depth and weight of water being rapidly compounded. Even now, with the gap as high as it could ever be, some spray spewed through the opening. I resolved to hold straight for the beach under full sail and pray the wind would not change in either direction or force, or the chain plates give way another fraction of an inch.

There were moments during the next hour when my stomach muscles lifted the *Raccoon* gently over the larger than ordinary seas, and the mast was additionally supported by invisible cords of my desire. I tried not to stare at the mast or the hideous gash in the side of my so recent love. There was something indecent about her appearance now, as if on a wedding night a bride had revealed a frightful disease and was now boasting of her deception. And for the first time I discovered that it was easy enough to be brave for momentary intervals, but being alone with danger tried a man in direct proportion to the time involved.

The hazy, yellow line of the shore seemed to recede rather than rise, and all about us the ocean was deserted.

Occasionally I caught myself measuring the space between the deck and hull. Had it widened? . . . Perhaps half an inch. No. It was my fear influencing the messages to my eyes. There was no visible change. The deck seemed to have torn away just so far and stopped and was now being held by fastenings which were presumably sound.

The uneasy truce continued until the beach became well defined. Then I knew that the deck was rising again, little by little, yet inexorably; the space between hull and deck had enlarged from 6 inches to 8. Soon it appeared to be almost a foot. There was no sound resulting from this subtle change and the very silence made the total effect more unnerving. There was only the hissing of the sea, the soft vibrato of the wind and a burst of sharp crackling from the leech of the main as an odd wave threw us a trifle too close on the wind.

Wounded, we charged on. I yearned for some mighty hand to reach down and press my crippled little craft back in shape again, for I was certain the gap was now over 12 inches.

There were the pilings at the entrance to the estuary. A mile yet, perhaps a mile and a half. I could hear the deep and menacing rustle of the surf.

That ballad about the versatile Trixie. I tried to raise my voice in praise of her, but the croak was false and even flatter than usual so I became silent again and listened to the sea sounds and watched the gap. By leaning slightly to windward I could now suffer the unique experience of looking at the interior of the *Raccoon*'s little cabin from the outside. The view was rapidly enlarging because as we approached the beach and shallower water the seas became greater and the *Raccoon* rolled more into the wind.

Although the land was very flat there was a house perched on a slight rise which made it easy to line up with the entrance to the estuary. A line of close-set pilings served as a breakwater on the opposite side of the channel, and now I could just make out their tops as we rose upon the seas.

Another ten minutes, I thought, will see us safely inside the tidal pool. I clapped my hand to my forehead. The tide! I had forgotten about it! I rose slightly in the cockpit and waited for a lift from the sea. I could see the base of the piles. The tide had turned foul, just at these crucial moments when the *Raccoon* could hear the whisper of salvation.

We had perhaps 100 yards to go until I could ease her into the mouth of the narrow channel, and in spite of the tide there was enough wind to carry us through to safety.

Suddenly, skidding along the tops of the pilings, I saw the mast and yard of a power cruiser. He was outbound with the tide, and I knew at once there was not a chance that he could turn around in the channel or risk his own vessel trying to go astern against the tide. He was still behind the pilings and therefore could not see me bearing down on the entrance. Yet if I held the *Raccoon* to our present course, a collision was inevitable just as he emerged from the entrance.

Of all the hours of the day and night why did this man have to put to sea at just this hour? He could not possibly know that my own ability to maneuver was severely limited, and when he did see me he would be shocked to observe a sailing craft bearing down hard upon him. Although he probably knew a sailing craft had the right of way, what good was a rule when one party was unable to comply? He could not be expected to stray from the channel short of a hundred yards farther out or he would go aground. He would expect me to use common sense instead of standing fast on rules, and either luff up and wait or go on the opposite tack until he was clear. Yet I could not attempt either maneuver and survive. The moment I changed the degree of heel toward the wind, the *Raccoon* would swallow the ocean and sink forthwith. My course was as fixed as his, and unless some miracle occurred we would collide, precisely at the estuary mouth. I prayed that he might be a very fast cruiser and would suddenly decide to use all his power. Then I lost hope. The sea was too rough for even the most determined exhibitionist.

There were now no further seconds for hesitation. I could smash into the cruiser's bow or perhaps hit him amidships if he gathered speed. Or I could stab the pilings with the *Raccoon*'s puny little bowsprit. And of course sink a few seconds later. Or . . .

I heaved in on the mainsheet and allowed the *Raccoon* to fall slightly off the wind. Thus strapped down, she achieved her maximum angle of heel and simultaneously her minimum draft. We were headed directly for the beach.

Moments later I felt a sickening thump as we sank with a wave. We had touched bottom. Another thumping, another hesitation as we rose on a wave, and then we hit at a good 6 knots. The mast and sail and all of the *Raccoon*'s gear kept right on going. And so did the body of her master.

I waded ashore trailing blood from my knee and carrying the anchor which was still made fast to the shambles behind me. It was mostly awash, but I thought the tide would take it out to sea again and it was not in me to part with the little *Raccoon* so easily.

After I watched the cruiser hold firm for the horizon as if

nothing had happened, I stuck the anchor in the sand and, when the tide turned that evening, sold the remains of the *Raccoon* for fifty dollars. We had sailed together a total of three times.

Altogether my nautical affairs had been laced with structural embarrassments and I had often been near despair while nursing one marine cripple after another from port to port. Perhaps this rather hectic history was my excuse for establishing a custom in all those vessels where circumstance arranged for me to make the laws. So it was that in the *Albatros* as in most of her predecessors, regardless of the weather, gale or calm, regardless of *any* difficulties or circumstance, the bar was open for one hour each day. Normally that hour was before the evening meal and a shipmate could drink as much as he desired during that time. Only once had this privilege been abused so that the guilty one became taken-down-drunk, but now a certain check had been established which made such catastrophes highly improbable. If anyone drank so much that his capacity for duty was impaired, the bar was closed for *all* and would remain closed for an indefinite period. It was astonishing how perfectly the system worked and amusing to observe the baleful stares focused upon a shipmate who showed signs of totally satisfying his thirst. The time was known as "Bardinet Hour" after the rum of my own devotion, and it was always held on deck. Sometimes we stood in water up to our knees as seas swept across the deck, and sometimes we were at great pains to prevent rain or flying salt spray from diluting our refreshment, and sometimes we had to pause momentarily to hand a sail or come about on a different tack, but *always* the hour of Bardinet was observed. It was a time equivalent to the old sailors' "smoking-lamp-is-lit," a time for relaxation and conversation, a sharing of ship and sea and shipmates not to be known under any other circumstances. There once appeared a newspaper article concerning our Bardinet Hour. It was a long interview with one of our shipmates who was quoted: "He made us drink that awful stuff at the point of a gun."

This was a lie. I never displayed a gun at such times. I simply said abstainers would be thrown to the sharks.

It was an hour filled with minor surprises, all pleasing to teetotalers and the thirsty alike. Men washed their hands before Bardinet and sometimes shaved, although there was nothing in the custom which even suggested they should. Those who did not drink took over the lookout or the helm for those who did, and petty bickerings, such as who had whose wet socks in whose bunk, were settled with laughter.

Men thought of each other.

It was at this time that Warren came to me and said, "What are we waiting for?"

"The wind."

"We have an iron wind."

"You mean—? Are you sure?"

He nodded his head and smiled in a most superior way.

"But you have only ten atmospheres."

"I have willed it," he said. "Take courage in your Bardinet."

Soon after sunset, when our exasperation with all of the rattling and banging of a helpless sailing ship had reached near madness, Warren had retired to the engine room and faced the cold assembly of machinery with fierce determination.

He had taken a long iron bar and turned the heavy flywheel of the African Queen until it was positioned exactly so that the number-two cylinder would first explode, which he explained was the only conceivable hope of success. And when this was done he reached resolutely for the large wheel which when turned would release air to the Queen and by a dependent alternation of sucking and blowing, start the reaction we so much desired.

Now he boldly turned the great wheel. The Queen hissed, farted obscenely, and returned to death with a sigh of finality.

"One more!" Warren said, looking at the remaining atmospheres on the gauges. "One more and we've had it!"

Again he inserted the iron bar in the flywheel and heaved on it until the valves were in exactly the position he desired. And again he assumed his position at the air-release wheel. All of us who stood as witnesses prayed. We regarded him as a high priest about to begin a Black Mass.

"Count your blessings!" yelled Warren as he yanked on the wheel.

Once more there was the awful hissing. There followed a familiar gasp, and blue smoke exuded from every pore of the African Queen. At last there was an evil snorting followed by a great and primeval grunting which could only mean that the African Queen was alive.

Our triumphant shouts rang against the steel bulkheads and we watched in wonder as the monster regurgitated oil, smoke, a light fallout of graphite grease and composite soot, and at last settled into a marvelously rhythmic pulsation.

Warren moved to the throttle, which was a small wheel turned like a grind organ. He cranked it to and fro judiciously, for there was no governor to the fuel supply and if the clanking and thumping subsided in the least, the Queen would certainly die.

"Voilà!" he said. "You sailors may play with your rags and ropes. But if you want to get there—"

For two days we wrote in the logbook: "Carrying on with rock crushing."

The Queen pumped the bilge dry enough so we could find the cause of our leaking. We discovered a second pipe that had rusted through, and we said many uncomplimentary things about the Dutch inspector.

Voyaging beyond the horizon in a small vessel is knowing removal from all the superfluous vexations and tribulations which have brought modern man to a platform upon which he stands naked and alone in his secret terror, not quite sure whether he is rich or poor, or young or old, inspired or despairing, or what his sale price should be. Then the sea becomes a nirvana for the dedicated escapist, but it may also serve as a powerful restorative to the most inhibited realists. The removal begins soon after the land drops out of sight and all of the horizon marking the frontiers of the voyager's world becomes ocean. Soon afterward he discovers that one of the most painful ills which has abscessed his system and obsessed his brain has almost entirely disappeared. As soon as he realizes that whatever he wants is not to be had, and moreover that even if it was available he could not use it, he loses the pox of desire and its inevitable scabs of greed. To observe human beings without pressing desire is to rediscover mankind, and is at times so encouraging that one is not ashamed to walk on two legs.

The death of desire is linked directly to deepwater needs which are very simple. Soap is needed for cleanliness, and desire is born again if it is long unavailable. Some passing thought must be given the matter of clothing, an odd piece of cloth here and there for modesty and, according to the vessel's latitude, some costume to retain body warmth. Since high fashion of any description is hopelessly impractical at sea, a vicious pair of human frailties is dropped overboard. Vanity and envy will not be retrieved until the sailor steps ashore again.

Soon more subtle influences commence to make themselves known and further soothe the unavoidably troubled personality who only a few days previously had striven to survive in the complex of shoreside existence. According to his political persuasion, status, or social conscience, the voyager may have been distressed by racial problems, international threats, or merely by the gyrations of the stock market; now suddenly he realizes they are continuing without his vicarious supervision, and while at first he may experience a sense of futility and uselessness, these frustrations will soon be canceled by the citizen duties of his new world, which is now measured in feet and inches. The abandonment of worry about the course of history is particularly noticeable among habitual newspaper readers. To ease the pangs of withdrawal aboard the *Albatros* we followed a policy of turning on the radio news for the first three days out of port—after which we found that no one bothered to listen. And then there was peace.

Once rid of such debilitating influences, man stands in the new danger of discovering himself, and for a while the cure can be as ravaging as the disease. The average underprivileged human being, bearing a minimum of shore-nourished afflictions, may expect to pass through the metamorphosis in a few days and emerge to discover he is basically a friendly creature rarely inclined to hatred in spite of his thirst for argument and, when the occasion arises, surprisingly considerate of his shipmates. A part of this is due to a new sense of mutual security—"Here we are alone in the middle of the ocean and we must stick together if we are ever to reach the safety of shore again."

There are other fundamentals involved in this undercurrent of well-being. Money has ceased to be a necessity and is not even a useful commodity, so that the handling, counting, thinking and discussion of it is reduced to a minimum. And if the voyage has been properly planned the voyager knows he will not starve; if doubts still haunt him, he can always find some excuse to inspect the reserve. This total security, coupled with the draining of his poison juices, promotes long life; which may be why people persist in going to sea in small vessels. In good weather the contentment simulates a return to the womb.

☼

THREE

THE Portuguese island of Madeira is an easygoing tourist trap overrun with stuffed Englishmen and their partridge wives. All of the good wine is hoarded by the locals and the second best is exported. The residue, most of which is barely fit for human consumption, is served to casual visitors.

We put into Funchal, the principal port of Madeira, for provisions and to feel once more the stability of land. And we thought with so many lusty youths aboard who had been long deprived of true personal freedom and carnal pleasures, the traditional rites of sailors briefly in port would be automatically observed.

Yet those of us who had been to sea before waited in vain for signals of debauchery. Funchal is no Marseille or Hamburg, but there are a few whorehouses and the usual sprinkling of female opportunists ready in any port to cheer a hungry sailor.

At first we thought our young men were merely showing admirable restraint while they made a preliminary reconnaissance of the situation. Hours passed and we saw them still wandering aimlessly through the streets without so much as a bawdy chorus of song. Surely this must be the first time since long before Ulysses, since the first venturesome souls voyaged beyond their familiar horizon, that sailors did not quickly respond to shore temptations.

It was midafternoon before we realized our young sailors were doing exactly what they wanted to do, and somehow the visible confirmation was all the more shattering to our senses of what was right and what was wrong in the maritime world. It was as if a ship had been launched without a name, or a mast stepped without a coin at its heel, or a broadside fired with a popgun.

They sat in a park eating ice-cream cones—one after the other. While their mothers might have been proud of them, two of our older shipmates were so deeply shocked at the spectacle that they sought reassurance in the bad wine for the rest of the day. When they were eventually dumped aboard by obliging police, they claimed to have rescued our honor. The *Albatros*, they shouted triumphantly, would not leave Madeira with a reputation of being sailed by ice-cream eaters.

The Portuguese training ship *Sagras* lay near us at anchor and our intention was to salute her smartly as we sailed away. The raucous howls of our wine-filled shipmates somewhat marred our dignity, but a fouled anchor chain made the scene much worse. The *Albatros* carried a type of anchor chain long since sent to scrap by most vessels since its design allowed it to twist around itself, forming a great iron knot which jammed firmly in the hawse pipe. Thus the anchor itself hung obstinately several feet below the surface of the water. We struggled for an hour with the consequent tangle to the amusement of the Portuguese, and it was not until McDaniel managed to reeve a line around the anchor itself that we eventually brought it home.

At last we shaped a course to the southwest with the intention of intercepting the Trades as soon as possible. Once we had reached them we anticipated a traditionally easy downwind passage to Barbados.

It was the seventeenth of August and we knew there was no time to waste. In early September the hurricane season would begin. Before we cleared the harbor I was satisfied that all tradition had not left the seas. For I was soon challenged by a classical tirade of mutinous remarks from our two drunks. Their wobbly antagonism and threats of what would happen if we did not put back at once pleased me enormously. I reluctantly doused their enthusiasm with a blast from the deck hose.

All was well. The Junkers had been repaired, although Oliver said it was and always would be a collection of spare parts flying in loose formation. And we could have begun this long passage in a canoe. The *Albatros* seemed to float on a mirage. There was not a breath of wind as the island of Madeira purpled in the evening haze and slowly descended into the sea. The African Queen thumped along with surprising determination and we were content in the firm belief that two days hence, perhaps three at the most, we should find the Trades.

My own conception of Trade Winds, wherever they may blow over the seas, was of an everlasting breeze of just the right intensity and of constant direction. Under such benign influence a sailing ship might bowl along gracefully, cutwater frothing, mile after mile, day after day, exactly as depicted in so many books and marine paintings. The wind charts show that such winds are indeed reliable and their geographical area is as clearly defined as a freeway. You have only to make a certain latitude, turn away before the trades, and practically go to sleep until you arrive at your destination.

Anyone who believes this to be the true state of things is a landlubber. Perhaps in the time of Columbus and his successors there was more wind in general, or for some meteorological reason the Trade areas were of much wider proportions; or perhaps there were even secondary Trades. Examination of old sailing logs will prove the ships made reasonably smart passages in spite of their sowlike design. Something drove them other than hope.

For us, one thing soon became very obvious. Without the African Queen we might be a very long time reaching wherever it was the Trades were supposed to be blowing. We thumped along for nine days without a whisper of wind. A ship without an engine would have drifted in her own garbage for the same length of time. The sea remained a vast mocking mirror, and at night the stars were as clear in the water below as they were in the sky above. We poked our grubby fingers again and again at the wind chart and cursed its falsifications. Because our navigational fixes proved we should be there—right *there,* well within the indicated boundaries of the faithful Trades. But there was no wind at all and vulgar things were written in the logbook about doldrums.

Not long after we left Madeira the African Queen began losing oil pressure. It was now almost zero and not even the resourceful Warren could diagnose the reason. Its thirst for lubricating oil was enormous and our reserve supply was already gone. On the eighth day one of the intake valves stuck and the Queen lost much of her power. Then a fuel pump lost all interest in its duty, the thrust bearing overheated and caught fire, and a majority of the fuses on the switchboard blew out. Laboring in the suffocating heat Warren and his dazed assistants managed to keep us moving with only temporary pauses. But it was like fighting a dragon. Every time they lopped off a head, a new one grew in its place.

We managed to bumble and grumble along for another day, whereupon the pipe which was designed to bring cooling water to the African Queen fractured from the excessive vibration or perhaps simple exhaustion. So instead of soothing the Queen's ever-rising fever, the water poured into the bilge, filling it until the lubricating-oil tank was completely submerged. And our oil was diluted with sea water, which is the mechanical equivalent of putting strychnine in the soup. We had no choice but to shut down.

We stared up at our limp sails and someone wrote in the log-book, "There is not a breath of air . . . so it is possible to piss over either side—straight down."

Now with the bilge full of ocean, the Junkers refused to start, so in the heat we labored again at the ridiculous deck pumps. The stronger of us, working in pairs, could endure ten continuous minutes at the task before we fell flat on the deck, not caring whether we floated or sank. When we were not pumping we stared moodily at the sea for signs of wind and at the sky for signs of wind and saw not the slightest indication of release. When enough water had been removed from the bilge so he could see what he was doing, Warren devised an alternate cooling system of bailing wire and pieces of pipe he had found throughout the ship. He said he was sure it would work, but his confidence was meaningless, since certainly the Queen would survive only a very short time on such polluted oil and we thought best to save it for an extreme emergency—"Like someone falling overboard."

If anyone had fallen overboard we need not have been concerned about leaving him. For yet another day the *Albatros* waved her sails casually at the bald sky like some elderly dowager greeting a distant relative. We did not move except to swing slowly around sometimes and face the direction from which we had come.

We were not in any danger except the remote possibility of cannibalism if the calm continued. We persevered at the pumps mainly because it was something to do.

Still, our doctor, who had been a stalwart at the pumps, now came down with the affliction known as the GI's. We nursed him with tender sarcasms about physicians healing themselves, and I instructed Charlie to clean his galley lest we all be stricken. There was honest hurt in his eyes when I insisted he stop using the deck rag for a pot wiper.

We were consuming approximately half a gallon of water for each man per day, which was very good indeed, since every expedient to bring wind failed to produce any visible result. Profanity was forbidden in the hope that higher verbal morality might have some effect, and we yearned for the intestines of a hyena, which, according to legend, would bring wind if reeved through the starboard brace block.

A considerable delegation of sharks came to call, one of which McDaniel managed to catch. Before we hauled him aboard with a block and tackle I emptied two magazines of .38-caliber bullets into his revolting head. The abuse had very little apparent effect, so when we finally dumped him aboard we clobbered him mercilessly with a heavy maul. To us he seemed a very large shark, measuring over 9 feet, and we guessed his weight at well over 200 pounds. Even before he was entirely still, McDaniel and I, seemingly possessed of the same savage instinct, fell upon him with our knives. I do not know why we sliced at him in such a frenzied way that our shipmates stood back in embarrassment. We behaved like animals, wreaking our vengeance and frustration at our lack of wind on this wretched symbol of evil. We covered ourselves with the shark's blood and the deck was like a slaughterhouse. Even Bigelow, who was not an especially fastidious man, stood far away and regarding our regression to the primeval with a mixture of horror and wonder. Some people lose all civilized restraint when they kill a snake, chopping and hitting at it a hundred times more than is necessary to assure its death. Perhaps McDaniel and I were similarly compelled, for we hated sharks beyond all reason. They are the age-old enemy of sailors, and we wanted to kill them all.

The pointlessness of our bloody orgy was clear even to us when our passions cooled. We simply heaved the torn carcass back into the sea. We saved only the tail, which I ceremoniously carried forward and lashed to the end of the jibboom. Such an offering, as any old salt knew, was a guarantee of wind.

That night it rained. And the next day there were rain squalls everywhere about, and each stirred up a little wind so that we progressed 49½ miles.

And the next day and the next there was wind enough to make 16 miles, and the next day enough to log an inspiring 83. Then it fell calm again and we decided the shark's tail, which now stank appropriately, had nonetheless lost its powers.

We had yet to see a real Trade Wind and we were fourteen days out of Madeira.

Our optimists nursed the hope we might encounter another ship and perhaps borrow enough lubricating oil to satisfy the African Queen for at least a few days. Our pessimists paid increasing attention to the calendar and gloomily pointed out that our position corresponded very nicely with the area in which West Indian hurricanes are known to be born. This concern was not unwarranted. Only a fool would deny that during the past two days the ocean had become ominously alive. The swells had begun very gradually as if some monster far over the horizon was moving about on tiptoe, but now it seemed he must be marching.

For the horizon disappeared completely when the *Albatros* sank between the swells, and we rolled very heavily.

We longed to start the African Queen and flee the area.

As for meeting a ship, the normal commercial routes were far to the north and we were past the area where ships bound for South America might cross the Trade belts. It was extremely doubtful if another sailing ship would or could overtake us, let alone happen to be carrying enough lubricating oil to fulfill our need.

So we waited in growing anxiety and looked at the sinister swells, and Oliver was nearly beheaded by the vang, a line intended to reduce the violent whipping of the main gaff in such conditions, and Steve, who had dunked over the side to escape the heat momentarily, was struck by a Portuguese man-of-war, which is one of the most deceptively beautiful creatures of the sea. Its tendrils, dangling innocently beneath its miniature sail of gorgeous purple, emit such a terrible poison that the pain is excruciating and its victim often passes into shock. In an instant Steve's leg appeared to have been lashed with red-hot whips, and though he had ample cause to howl, he did not. Still gave him a merciful injection, but it was two days before he could hobble from his bunk.

Bigelow came to me soon after dawn with the surprising news that a ship had been sighted on the horizon. It looked like a tanker, and if he could be hailed and persuaded to stop, certainly he could spare a drum of oil.

I went at once to our radio, in which I had a minimum of confidence. I put out a general call, giving our position. "C.Q. . . . C.Q. . . . If an eastbound tanker now has a becalmed sailing ship in sight on her starboard bow, please acknowledge."

I paused and was about to give the *Albatros* call letters and repeat the message. Most of the crew had quietly gathered behind me. I envied their faith. They had not been betrayed so many times by radios.

Then, to my complete astonishment there came a voice loud and clear. The accent was unmistakably British and my own hopes rose.

"Tanker *Arndale* here. We thought we were looking at a flying Dutchman. Good morning."

In ten minutes the *Arndale* hove to less than half a mile from us. Though we were rolling our scuppers under, McDaniel, commanding eight of our crew at the falls, managed to launch one of our heavy boats without a fault. He chose oarsmen and they pulled away for the *Arndale*. Much of the time they were lost to our vision as they descended between the still-increasing swells, and there were moments when only half of the tanker's stack could be seen.

After an hour had passed, our boat was seen to be pulling away from the *Arndale*. We cheered when we saw they were towing a 50-gallon drum of oil.

When both oil and boat were safely heaved aboard and not a person or a thing had suffered so much as a scratch, our relief was matched by true pride. For even well- and long-trained professionals could make a mess of things under such conditions of the sea.

While the others wrestled the drum into position so that its contents could be drained into the African Queen, I returned to the radio and thanked the *Arndale* profusely. They refused any payment and merely wished us well. It was a gesture carried off with the best of English sea gallantry. In minutes they were gone beyond the horizon.

The heat of the day had not really begun when there came a series of tentative sneezings from the engine room, blue smoke rose from the open hatches, and black smoke gushed from the exhaust. The African Queen was alive! At once I rang down Full

Ahead on the telegraph and we turned on course for the Barbados. Einstein's theory of relativity ignores a rare human sensation. It does not trouble to describe what it is like to proceed in a long-dormant sailing ship at the thrilling speed of 6 knots.

Less than two hours after the *Arndale* had vanished we felt a gentle breeze on the back of our necks. And before we could set square sail, Schlopmutts, and free the mainsheet, the breeze became a wind. Popcorn-like frills of wavelets appeared everywhere on top of the swells. A few very gay nimbus clouds swept past overhead and in another half-hour it became obvious that we no longer needed the African Queen.

At last, when we were not so dependent on them, we had caught the Trades. By noon it was blowing a sensuous force-5 and we were bowling along at a fancy 8 knots. During that day we made 147 miles and on the next 187, which was nearly our record for any noon to noon.

All was as it should be and on the twenty-first day of our voyage we made port at Barbados. It seemed that on the morning of our rendezvous with the *Arndale* our luck had changed in the only way it could.

We did not as yet realize how very sweet our fortune could be.

When the full displeasure of the elements falls upon a man, he is temporarily overwhelmed and permanently changed within. After the trial he is ether dead or forever afterward humble and discreet. Thus my own relief at reaching Barbados was tempered by a new and unaccountable foreboding.

As in every port, it was my obligation to call upon the harbor-master and sign various papers. On this bright picture-postcard morning I said to him, "I wish it wasn't so muggy. This smells like hurricane weather."

His patronizing smile was comforting and he said, "You are not to worry."

"We had some big swells a few days before we came in. I wonder . . . do you think it meant anything? We rolled our brains out"—and I saw that he was only half listening.

"What happens outside I do not know." He yawned. "But be sure of one thing. You are quite safe here. We have not had the slightest trouble from hurricanes in over fifty years. The last one was in 1898."

The next day we sailed from Barbados.

Three days after our departure the building which contained the harbormaster's office was destroyed by a hurricane and the entire island was so devastated it was necessary to send in a considerable force of the U.S. Caribbean fleet, food relief, and units of the Red Cross.

If it had not been for the blessed *Arndale* . . .

☼

FOUR

We knew nothing of the disaster at Barbados until we reached Curaçao, which is a hot and airless little island in the middle of a crude-oil-scented nowhere. Curaçao is a free port, so it holds certain attractions for covetous tourists, but the island king is oil, brought from Venezuela to be refined. For us it offered a shipyard where various clumsy repairs were attempted on the miserable Junkers and a brief lease on life was given to Lucky Alphonse.

Bigelow, ever driven by a thousand inner fires, left us in Curaçao. He had always taken the world and its troubles as a personal responsibility, and now it seemed he was bent on sailing into the Pacific atom-bomb area and by exposing himself draw attention to the hideous and even greater folly now in progress. We wished him the freedom of the seas, which he was destined not to enjoy. I was very sorry to say farewell. He was my friend and had been a splendid First Mate. McDaniel took his place and the indefatigable Warren doubled as Engineer and Second Mate. Our younger contingent had hurried off to their campuses and there was mighty relief on both sides. Of them, only Brownell remained. He had begun his sea career in complete innocence and had become a most promising sailor.

Our losses were made up by the arrival of a man named Helprin, who was forever afterward to be known as "Peter Dawson" because of his choice of whisky. We were destined to make many voyages together. Peter Dawson's head was covered with a heavy thatching of white hair and he was not a very big man. His merry, brilliant eyes appeared to loop the loop whenever he was up to some mischief, which was almost all of his waking hours. He was a delightful rogue who sometimes masqueraded as a dignified citizen. He had a magic facility for making bosom friends of total strangers in ports all over the world. He was an "expediter" beyond compare. Foreign languages did not exist to him. He would address a Portuguese, a Tahitian, or a Norwegian in his special brand of Brooklynese and somehow they understood him. The world was his natural friend. He was frequently invited to the home of whatever merchant he dealt with, where God only knew what kind of communication was established with the rest of the family. Peter Dawson was an inventor, a sage and a knave, a poet, a self-named ignoramus and a scholar, a gentleman and a roughneck who was openly adored by all of the hundreds of shipmates and shore people who ever had anything to do with him. He was, most of all, passionately devoted to ships and the sea.

In Curaçao our deck force was further replenished by the arrival of Post and Henderson, two young ladies who were also destined to sail long in the *Albatros*. Gratiot, a handsome, wonderfully gentle and meditative man, took Still's place as doctor, and Cordrey completed our complement.

The African Queen took us from Curaçao to the Panama Canal. It was a flat calm the entire way.

The Panama Canal is a capsule state enjoying all the benefits bureaucratic socialism can provide. It is an incredible project, at once efficient and marvelously accomplished and at the same time so imperious and monastic that the passerby has only two choices. He can fight it, which is futile, or he can say, "I am a nothing. I do not really exist except as a number. I am at the complete mercy of the all-powerful, omniscient, magnificent, never-to-be-contested Panama Canal Company and all of their arrogance and extortions as ordained by God."

The food charges are outrageous compared to those in any other port. Fuel bought from the Panama Canal Company costs over twice as much as the going rate all over the world.

When I tried to have repairs made to the ever-ailing Junkers, I was flatly advised to go away. "Not even the United States Navy can afford us," the official explained with no attempt to conceal his pride. "If they have trouble, they do their best to limp along to any other place."

This curious monopoly, operated by the shy left hand of the United States Government, is possibly one of the most zealously guarded and secret despotisms of all time. It is ruled rather than managed by an appointed president who carefully avoids all publicity lest his absolute kingdom be revealed. Only the purely technical operations of the Panama Canal Company deserve any praise, yet even that admiration is soured by watching and listening to the near slaves who carry out the physical work of passing vessels from the Atlantic to the Pacific or vice versa.

I took our papers to be processed and at the crucial moment the arm on the official's stamping machine broke. The poor man was dumfounded at the tragedy, then he slumped forlornly in his chair. He did not weep visibly, but he did put his head in his hands and he shook it slowly as if to drive away his despair. He seemed to be probing the depths of his soul for some answer as to what man should do when his machine failed him.

"Maybe you can fix it," I said, hoping to console him.

"I don't think there's another one in the stockroom." He sighed. "It's never happened before."

Finally our hero rose and went away for a long time. He returned eventually and there was no sign of improvement in his mood. His superior had advised him that without a stamp properly executed, our anachronistic, inoffensive, quite useless sailing ship simply could not proceed.

"I cannot help you. My hands are tied," the official said.

Then with unforgivable lack of compassion I replied that his hands had been bound by his umbilical cord in a granny knot since birth, and I swore we would spurn his miserable canal and sail around Cape Horn. And for the moment, I meant it.

My face was saved by the clock. Even as I was mentally calculating how many months it would take to round the Horn, an almost instantaneous change occurred. What little interest there had been in the *Albatros* evaporated and there was a great banging of desk drawers.

The unstamped papers were thrust in my hand and I was told to be gone. It was exactly four o'clock. It was quitting time.

If there were an ideal ocean in which to sail, the ingredients would have to be gathered from all of the seas. We could start with the blue-green depths of the Aegean, to which should be added the softer winds of the Caribbean, the lagoons of the South Pacific, and the smooth waters and passing scenery of the Swedish Archipelago. The bald, lifeless skies of both the Aegean and the Mediterranean should be avoided. Instead, Bahamian man-o'-war birds should be called upon to glide across the moon, pelicans and cormorants should be recruited from the California coast, albatrosses and stormy petrels from either the Atlantic or the Pacific. Of mammals, the great barnacle-encrusted whales bound for breeding in Mexico's Scammon Lagoon are always impressive, turtles from the same region display just the proper dignity, and of all porpoises in all the seas none seem to match the exuberant exhibitionism of those to be joined off the Pacific coast of Nicaragua. To this Valhalla we should add the long twilights of the Hebrides, the bourgeois temperatures of Portuguese waters, and since sailing creates a ravenous appetite, most certainly the abundance of fish to be caught almost anywhere between the western approaches to the Panama Canal and Alaska.

We should exclude from this assembly those steep and nasty little seas of the Adriatic, the hot and boring haze of the Ionian, Tyrrhenian, and summertime Mediterranean, and the fogs of the North Atlantic. Let us also forbid the "chubascos" to be met off Central America and lower Mexico, the mistrals and levanters, and meltemis, and boras, all of which, in spite of their fancy names, are winds which can make life miserable for sailors.

Lest we become mere voluptuaries it will be well to include a few annoyances—if only for variety. Occasional Gulf Stream thunderstorms can be interesting and they always provide enough spectacle to frighten the timid, but usually they are all water and noise. Provided your boat is reasonably seaworthy and your stomach not too tender, a "norther" in either the Bahamas or the West Indies can provide special excitement because while the winds are hard they only occasionally reach gale force. Some rain from the coasts of Norway might be refreshing if we do not permit it to continue as long as it really does. Norwegian rain is a sort of permanent heavy mist, but it does not greatly hinder navigation since it falls against a backdrop of black mountains, and in the daytime you at least know where the shore is.

Now for shipmates. We might include at least two women, although it is extremely difficult to specify their numerical proportion to the rest of the crew. One woman aboard is an unhandy situation for a variety of reasons and she must be of heroic metal if she can avoid becoming either the star of the show, which is sickening, or an embarrassing nuisance. Three or more women seem to make the proportion topheavy, and some instinctive urging compels them to collect about the decks in chattering groups more suitable to the back fences of suburbia. And sooner or later they gang up on the least conforming of their group and not even God or the Captain can save her.

Once resolved to prove she can be as good a sailor as any man, a woman competes with prejudice, and her very determination results in benefits to both the ship and her shipmates.

Most deepwater sailors true to the name highly disapprove of women in or even about a ship except for occasional carousals in ports. They are thinking of ordinary women and to their objections I herewith agree. But I have been shipmates with some extraordinary women. If they are selected with extraordinary care, the results can be astonishing.

Although we put into port only once, we were forty-nine days making our way from the Panama Canal to San Diego. Gidley, a handsome, dashing man who could easily have been the reincarnation of Hawkins or Drake or any of the more spirited privateers, had replaced McDaniel. He was an old friend and by trade a professional fisherman. Hence I slept soundly when he had the watch. Brownell, too, had made such progress that he was promoted to Second Mate.

Gidley brought with him a parrot called Rebecca, after a notorious Mexican whore. She was a crotchety bird so continuously at odds with captivity that she bit anyone who ventured near her cage, including her master. Rebecca was foul-mouthed, and except when her cage was covered she kept up a continuous insulting commentary on her shipmates and, if ignored, angrily kicked seeds and general parrot debris all over her area of the saloon.

Rebecca was a female better left ashore, yet by comparison she was only a minor annoyance.

Our troubles with the African Queen continued whenever the wind failed and we needed its assistance. Francis Drake in his lump of a *Golden Hind* often made better progress, for the winds were finicky and the opposing currents strong. No matter what we tried, we could never seem to average more than 100 miles per day and too often it was 25. During one twenty-four-hour period we lost 5 miles.

We passed through a violently antisocial chubasco which left great damage along the Guatemalan coast and none to us. We slobbed unromantically along for days through leaden seas more suited to Scandinavia and would have been vastly more discouraged at our progress without Peter Dawson's unique personality. He was like an impish troll constantly engaged in some project of which no one could predict the result. His wonderfully inventive mind was applied full tilt to our toiletry problem, which had begun in the English Channel and had now reached such a state that the actual safety of the ship was involved. Use of the one head which we could reasonably trust not to come apart and sink the ship was reserved for the two girls aboard. This presented certain embarrassments, and for a time shyness was everywhere.

Peter Dawson loathed anything mechanical and in particular all machinery which might have found its way into a sailing ship. He pretended that he did not know where the engine room in the *Albatros* was located, and his smug serves-you-right expression at each succeeding mechanical disaster almost made us ashamed to attempt repairs. While we sweated, pounded, twisted, and cursed below, Peter Dawson remained strictly aloof. He was a sailing man. The winds would be his only servant. He was utterly devoted to everything above the waterline and busied himself constantly with minute changes of sheets whether there was wind or not.

"We'll get a little more out of her if I ease that fores'l sheet just a touch," he would say after solemnly studying the situation. Our speed at the moment might be a wallowing 2 knots or even less, but Peter Dawson was an optimist in his own constant regatta. He was never content that our sails were doing their flaxen best, and though the adjustments he made rarely increased our speed a particle, it never seemed to discourage him.

He brooded long on our lavatory situation and at last one morning reported the solution had come to him in his dreams. Out of old bits of canvas, a pair of oars, and a few bits of board, he constructed a boothlike arrangement on either side of the ship. Regardless of our heeling with the wind, one or the other was always available.

Occupants of Peter Dawson's crude accommodations were shielded from public view, though once inside they were entirely exposed to the elements. We found this more than refreshing under certain conditions of wind and sea, and as we progressed northward to colder weather there were frequent remarks about brass monkeys. Yet Peter Dawson had planned well. The oars were lashed at the exact height to provide a comfortable footrest, a lifeline was handy lest his clients be swept away by heavy seas, and after considerable trouble with spray and rain rendering the paper unusable, he devised a protective system consisting of a tin can with removable top, all secured Bristol fashion to a convenient rope. The structures were offensive to the eye, but we soon grew to like their facility so much that none of us ever wanted anything to do with the confinement of normal ship heads again.

We had not been able to take a navigational sight for days, but somewhere at least 100 miles off Costa Rica we were beset by a plague of gnats. We thought it marvelous that such microscopic insects could venture so far to sea, and we were even more impressed when a squadron of grasshoppers arrived, presumably to eat the gnats. We could think of no other explanation.

We had more reasonable explanations for the rats which had now become so bold that our mutual habitation of the *Albatros* threatened to become a battle of survival. I claimed they were obviously Panama Canal officials in true uniform, and others thought they might be Panama Canal officials who had lived with tyranny long enough and had defected. Whatever they were, our potato supply, which was stored in the boats, had been ravaged, and what was left of the miserable vegetables bought in the Canal, plundered.

We were not sure if we were host to a single industrious rat or several, since when observed crossing a deck at normal speed one rat looks very much like another. We were on rat patrol day and night, hoping to exhaust the marauding bastards. Immediately on sighting our antagonist a hue and cry was raised and the chase began. Those off watch found it difficult to sleep below the pounding of feet and the poking with sticks at every possible hiding place. Once in desperation we tried luring the rats into the engine room. If by placing bits of food at strategic points we could trick them into the maze of the Dutch piping system, then we were certain any rat would go insane. Or if one found his way out, then we agreed peace should be declared and the rodent appointed Captain.

During this time a new annoyance developed. It began so gradually that the more we listened and looked throughout the ship, the less certain we were of the cause. It commenced on a relatively still night when all about the ship was at peace. Our rats had retired after gorging without injury at the several traps we had set. We were rolling easily along at about 3 knots. Somewhere within or alongside the ship metal was banging against metal. The sound was erratic in rhythm so that the sequence of clangings could never be depended upon. We thought one of the anchors might have worked loose in its hawse, but found them secure. Perhaps it was something aloft transmitting the sound down one of the steel masts. A thorough inspection all through the rigging revealed nothing amiss. We pressed our ears to the cold and dormant African Queen, wondering if perhaps her crankshaft had at last gone adrift, but the sound was not there. Fire extinguishers and even the pots in Charlie's galley were listened to and observed, and if they made the slightest tinking were further secured with bits of marlin. Yet the noise continued day and night, and even at mealtimes we would fall silent and listen.

It was the sort of repetitious sound which in time must certainly drive us crazy. There prevailed a certain mass nervousness even during Bardinet hour.

It took several days before we isolated the noise. We discovered it came from a fuel tank located in the forward bilges, where no one had thought to look. One of the baffle plates inside the tank had broken loose from its moorings, and as the *Albatros* rolled, it slid on a miniature sea of oil back and forth—back and forth. Since the tank was half full of oil and the plate much bigger than the inspection hole, there was absolutely nothing we could do about it at sea. We had no choice but to wait many thousand more times for an invisible second shoe to drop, enduring the suspense all the way to San Diego.

After having been so long in warmer latitudes, we were now very cold much of the time. The African Queen chose to behave in the opposite fashion. If it functioned for over half an hour it would overheat so that the cylinder-head temperatures rose out of sight. Warren had been obliged to leave us in a Mexican port and perhaps it resented his absence; certainly Gidley and I, now charged with its care in addition to our deck duties, were less sympathetic. We tried everything we could think of to force more water through its water pump, which was constructed on the same basic principle used in ancient Egyptian wells. Gidley's hands were powerful and my fury gave me too much strength. Together we managed to overtighten all the hold-down bolts, and as a consequence fractured the water-pump housing. We knew at once that we had finally murdered the African Queen.

More than six weeks out of the Panama Canal we crept toward the harbor of San Diego on a feeble morning breeze that expired just at the entrance. In true old sailing-ship fashion a tug chanced by and we bargained for a tow to a shipyard. When inquiries were made as to the speed of our passage, we immediately changed the subject.

My worst and so far secret fears of keeping the *Albatros* were confirmed in San Diego, for the shipyard repair bill was staggering. Just over the horizon I could hear the familiar sound of wolves howling, but now it was somehow an uglier sound because it came from the sea.

Yet the costly repairs did nothing to improve the disposition of the African Queen. During the relatively short passage between San Diego and San Francisco she ran only long enough to develop two fires, again suffer a water-pump collapse, and somehow feed diesel oil into her crankcase, which absolutely forbade any extensive use.

One hundred and eighteen days out of Rotterdam we groped through heavy fog to find the Golden Gate. Only remnants of the original crew had remained aboard. They were easily forgiven if they wondered why.

☼

IN HARBOR

Here, in the Danish harbor of Rønne which is so different from subtropical Barbados, we can stand shivering on top of the deckhouse and see over the breakwater to the Baltic. It is covered with white froth spewed on a gray base. We are another world away from the sweat of too hot suns, the fetid odors of stagnant West Indian harbors, and the soft sound of black sailors gossiping in the night. We can think of such an environment and fancy we can remember exactly what it was like, but all memories are sauced with time. It was another life. We cannot return to it any more than we can exchange this confinement for the moment when we will once again sail from this place. Two of our lines parted today. That is already history, and if asked I could not make an accurate guess as to exactly when it happened. Our present security consists of four stern lines, four bow, and three spring lines. So we have both present and future available in one sweep of the eye. If one of the lines snaps, its employment will instantly become history yet the future will remain visible in the others.

Our hull-to-hull neighbor, who is so obviously unhappy about our climbing over his sewer pipe en route to the wharf on one mission or another, is also present and future—until we sail away. Then he too will fall into the sauce of memory and perhaps never be resurrected again. If I could only understand Danish! I think he might be asking that we wear rubber-soled shoes. But we are. Certainly he can see our boots. Perhaps now, with the waiting plus all the endless travail of loading the pipe and securing it just so, his cargo of molded clay has become a very rich and precious thing, and if it must be damaged he prefers it be done by the seas. Or he knows that he is fighting a last-stand battle. Such a ship as his, so elderly, converted from what once had to be a graceful windjammer, cannot compete even in good weather with the soulless steel hulls which are also awaiting the merest chance to perform their missions.

Even that chance is not yet. The future is not here. It is still howling outside.

☼

II

THE *ALBATROS*

☼

. . . ARRIVES ON THE SCENE OF PAST AFFAIRS

☼

FIVE

RARELY have I heard the magnificent foghorns which surround and orchestrate the Golden Gate, or read of them, or even thought of them, without zooming away as if blasted by their sheer volume to the roistering, absurdly poignant life of a commercial fisherman which I pursued for somewhat more than three years. It is a pity that all who would follow the sea, whether as professionals or amateurs or as purely vicarious adventurers, cannot experience the vicissitudes and triumphs of the men whose livelihood lies hidden in the depths. There is no formal school given to instruction in this curious trade or even a guide to its mysterious curriculum; the hours of study are agonizingly long and laborious, the campus usually uncomfortable and often dangerous, and the honoraries of very unworldly value. Yet I know of no other separate endeavor involved with salt water which so consumes a man, making of him both servant and master, demanding nearly all of the facets of good seamanship along with a special loathing of organized security.

Every day and every night in fine weather and foul, commercial fishermen pass beneath the great bridge which spans the Golden Gate, and now as the *Albatros* slipped by the last great horn, which sounds like a gored bull, I could easily visualize two boats, here somewhere in the murk, their silhouettes vague and transparent, but all else about them vivid and true. I am once more comrades with the kindest, dumbest, most gallant and generous, sympathetic, and incurably optimistic men in the world—men who take in strangers, who lapse into bitterness only when the odds are utterly overwhelming and who are so tough they do their best not to appear tough; men who dress like evangelists on Sundays and are so dazed with fatigue all the balance of the week that they have energies remaining for only one passion—fish.

There, unloading in the rain, water cascading from his sou'wester when he tilts his head to look up at San Francisco's Fisherman's Wharf, will be Viscovich, who was my first professor. He is a Yugoslav and master of a very old and matronly figured dragger named the *Florence*. In her decaying bowels there is an ancient asthmatic Atlas diesel which drives the *Florence* halfheartedly through the Golden Gate and to the sea beyond, where both she and her master and crew are supposed to justify themselves. That they are not always successful is an embarrassment Viscovich wears with gentlemanly resignation.

No one who goes to sea in the *Florence* makes much money. It is possibly the fault of the Atlas engine which pukes oil all over the engine room when it is running, and probably, because of its acrid stench, drives most self-respecting fish away from our net. But you do not say anything derogatory about the Atlas to Viscovich, since it is beloved of him and he spends as much time below tinkering with it and fondling it and patting it in an almost obscene fashion as he does actively seeking fish. Viscovich is a handsome man of the solid mahogany mode, and his wind-sore eyes seem always on the point of capitulation to our misfortunes. But he is a fine and dedicated skipper, and even though the *Florence* is known as a hard-luck vessel, his crewmen are loyal to him. They know and he knows that his war with the fish buyers can only end in defeat because among other handicaps Viscovich is not a Sicilian and the poor man's Mafia takes sensuous pleasure in toying with Adriatic neighbors before emasculating them.

Rattigan, the skipper of a smaller but newer boat named the *Westerly,* is my second professor. He is an Irishman from his curly ocher hair to his Belfast face which is copiously adorned in freckles of impressive diameter. He speaks with a slight south-of-Market-Street accent which enhances his rather tough-guy demeanor, and it is true that it is unwise to offend Rattigan. It is also true that Rattigan is a marvelous fisherman, possessed of that esoteric sense which allows one man to make port with a full load while others do less than half as well. Along Fisherman's Wharf he is considered something of a genius. And like many geniuses he is sometimes given to overindulgence which causes particular anguish among the fish buyers, for they would vastly prefer more docile and predictable victims to their usury. They are inclined to spit on the dock and say, "Who da hell wantsta lend Rattigan bread or a boat when da bum is liable to concentrate for a coupla weeks and come in with the payoff?"

☼

There are four main types of fishing conducted outside the Golden Gate—salmon in the spring, tuna (albacore) in the summer, crab and long-lining in the winter. Even the fish buyers admit that Rattigan is master of them all. The Irishman has sworn he will make a long-liner of me, which is fishing the hard way. The *Westerly* is 50 feet in length and of typical West Coast design with the pilothouse well forward, a flying bridge, and a full open afterdeck for working any of the four kinds of gear.

In the mist, at three o'clock in the morning, we leave the wharf bound for that indefinite spot some 11 miles offshore where Rattigan knows there is an abundance of black cod. Finding it originally must have drawn the utmost from Rattigan's near-magical resources, yet equally remarkable is his ability to return to the exact spot again and again although there is nothing whatever in sea or sky to mark it. The Fathometer is more likely to deceive mere mortal man than guide him, for there are several other 60-fathom holes in the immediate vicinity and none of them have any cod.

On the way to the hole we chop frozen bait and squeeze the hard chunks on hooks. Two thousand two hundred and fifty hooks. Our hands become so numb that we err occasionally and insert the hook in a finger instead of the bait.

It makes little difference. We cannot feel anything at all below our wrists.

Just after the metallic December dawn we arrive over the general area and Rattigan starts cocking his head like a bird dog. Now the only sound is the low purring of the idling diesel. Silence! The master is going into a trance. Silence. I can hear my own breathing. This is a very important few moments. If Rattigan should turn human and choose the wrong hole, then all of our labor and discomfort from long before dawn until long after sunset will have been for naught. Now, yearning for sleep, sore in limb and mind from our previous day's efforts, I almost wish Rattigan would make a mistake.

As we proceed very slowly in a circle Rattigan continues to

posture, slamming his fists against his sides and sniffing as if he could actually smell cod 360 feet beneath the surface. At last he shivers and wipes at his nose and announces, as if he had received a message from some divine source, that this is the place. We will now proceed with the business of making a "set," which is both tricky and dangerous because economics forbids more than two men aboard and so many things happen simultaneously that four hands are not always enough. Because of the anarchistic nature of our gear, which is very similar to that employed by Joseph and his brethren, Rattigan must now choose a course for our set which will be in harmony with the light wind he senses will increase, the tide he senses will swing, and the current he senses will change. He cannot see any of these forces any better than he can see the cod.

Now he is satisfied. He turns the *Westerly* over to the automatic pilot, rams on almost full throttle to the diesel and we leap for the afterdeck. The day has begun with the usual flourish.

The baited hooks have been lightly hooked around the perimeters of ten rather flat wicker baskets. This must be done just so and the hooks canted just so, and Rattigan has carefully inspected my work, because neither his nerves nor spirit can stand the frightful chaos which only a few fouled hooks can create. The percentage odds are high since there are 225 hooks to each basket and the end of one basket main line is secured to the end of the next until the whole assembly forms a continuous line more than a mile long.

First an anchor and a flag buoy are dropped to mark one end of the line. Then as the *Westerly* plunges at 6 knots through the chill morning mist, Rattigan stands in the stern holding one basket after another—tilting each one and swirling it so the hooks will fly away clean. If they tangle at such speed, it is like having set loose ten baskets of angry supercharged snakes. And the hooks have been known to catch a man, which is why a heavy knife is always kept close at hand. I must learn a great deal more before I dare change places with Rattigan. Now my job is simply passing the ready baskets to him and setting the empty ones aside. At 6 knots in a rolling sea even this servile task can become demanding.

With the first marking buoy away, Rattigan devotes himself utterly to disciplining the ten peevish baskets which now seem to have actually taken on life. He shouts at them and dances as he turns out their contents. He swears at the occasional group of hooks swept away afoul of one another, yet mostly, as if recognizing their master, the hooks fly astern like tiny darts, whistling by Rattigan's demanding face. When all the hooks have gone over the stern, Rattigan tosses an anchor with a flag after them. It marks the final end of the line.

We shut down and drift. We will have some breakfast and then sleep for two hours or so. During this time the two anchors will take the long line and the hooks down to the fish. My sleep will be but a fitful and intermittent escape. For my hands keep trying to cry.

Noon. The cramped cabin of the *Westerly* is below in the bows and smells powerfully of diesel oil, cod livers, stale cigarettes, moldy blankets, rubber, wet clothing, and the peculiarly animal scent of men unable to fit regular bathing into their routine. Rattigan is snoring and the hatch above my head swings back and forth across the sun.

We must rouse ourselves and eat again. Then the long day will really begin. According to the weather the *Westerly* will have drifted a mile or even 5 miles from her original position, and if the visibility is poor, it will not be easy to find our flags. We must return to the first buoy, haul it aboard; then will come the anchor and with it the beginning of the mile-long line.

Once the hauling begins Rattigan becomes a one-man band, for he must handle his boat so cleverly against wind and sea that the long and heavy line which curves so far to the bottom always remains at the proper angle to the winch.

This is the ultimate of "boat handling." No other saltwater endeavor, with the possible exception of tugboat maneuvering *within a harbor,* requires such finesse. No excess strain will be tolerated by the main line, which is now so burdened with fish. Yet it must come up, and its weight must fight the pull of the vessel plus wind, current, and tide. There are engine controls and a wheel near the bulwark so he can manage this task and at the same time reach frequently for the main line and heave the larger fish aboard. In the clear water the cod seem to be on parade, one after another, their white bellies twisting upward from the depths until some thirty or forty fish are visible arriving from limbo all at the same time.

The main line passes over a roller set in the bulwarks and then through a pair of metal shives placed a few inches apart. When the cod's head collides with the shives, the hook is torn from his mouth and he flops to the deck. The line continues to me and I re-coil it as best I can into an empty basket. When each length of line fills a basket, Rattigan stops the winch while I untie the ends and take up a new empty basket. Then the hauling starts all over again and continues until the next basket is needed. When the fish are piled too high Rattigan will stop, and working together we will throw them into bins set on deck.

The hole is not in the shipping lanes and there is no reason for other fishing boats to frequent the area, so it often seems that Rattigan and I are the last two men in the world, with only a few gulls and too many fish for company. Then there are times during the long afternoon when I remember there are other men over the horizon exercising their brains in new and clever ways and with only trifling strain on their backs and their world is filled with noise, the abysmal under-hum of a great city, and the whistles and bleats and screeches which are unheard because they are accustomed to them. Here our world is entirely surrounded by water, and the line which continues its inexorable rise from another world must be served, making us quite as much slaves to our labors as the men over the horizon.

It is the last of twilight before we are finished. We turn for port and make a bowl of soup, gnaw on some bread and salami, and warm our guts with heavy red wine. We eat and drink in haste because our day's work is really not done.

As we roll for home the deck lights reveal a host of sea gulls following above our stern, screaming and whining like poor relations demanding their share of a rich man's spoils. Cod! Mountains of cod . . . more goddamned codfish than anyone will ever need, and they all have to be cleaned. We will drop their livers into cans, although the synthetic oils have made it hardly worth the trouble, and finally when the goddamned cod are all laid in the boxes and we have scrubbed and washed down thoroughly, then we will still have much more to do. The only way to stop profaning our bounty is to remember that these fish did not voluntarily leap to our deck and that there were times in the not-so-long-ago when more honest and simple men *thanked* God for such a catch.

When we are finished with the fish we begin on the baskets and make them ready for baiting on the coming morning. Many of the hooks have been bent as the shives forced the cod's head away from it, and some are missing. The thin lines which unite the hooks with the main line and are called "gangions" are sometimes frayed or torn away altogether. A few of the baskets hold wet tangles which will crumble a man's patience and finally pulverize it.

It is madness. No one eats black cod these days except cats. Delivered to the unenthusiastic buyers they are worth only eleven cents a pound.

If anything, the night cold always seems more penetrating

than on the outward-bound passage, so that after an hour or so it seems we have no fingers left at all, only red stumps with white ends which move clumsily according to our command, but which really belong to someone else.

I yell at Rattigan, "Are your hands cold?"

"Always."

"I thought it was just me because I'm new."

"You show me a fisherman says everything that sticks out from him, including his prick, ain't frozen most the time, and I'll show you a liar."

Rattigan is a born educator.

I did not spend enough time with Rattigan. Instead I took what little money I had available and with the eloquence born of enthusiastic ignorance persuaded LaFrenier, who should have known better, to part with some of his savings and embark on a totally new adventure. To compound the foolishness I induced one of the finest men who ever failed to live long enough that our enterprise could triumph over inexperience. His name was Fred Holmes and he was slowly dying when he "lent" me the money, and I doubt if he believed a word I said, but he was that sort of a man.

It was not because of the money that I named our first fishing boat the *Fred Holmes*. I loved the man. During his last year, when his body was wracked with myeloma, we at least brought him some joyful distraction with radio calls to his hospital bed from the vessel of his name. We lied sometimes about the amount of fish we had on board and he knew we were lying and even so it was said he laughed in spite of his excruciating pain—which was enough to make the whole project worth while.

LaFrenier and I went to Seattle, where we climbed over half a hundred boats for sale. Finally we chose a brand-new troller built by a Swede who was reputed to be the best builder of all.

I discovered that he was also a miser, so dedicated to pennies that he had leaned the carburetor mixture on his car until the engine stopped every time he paused at an intersection. He revealed himself one day when we were picking up final supplies just before sailing.

"Yah," he explained as he pressed the starter button on his immaculate prewar Chevrolet. "Gas costs lots of money. No sense to use it ven you vait for traffic."

I could not convince him that he actually used more fuel by restarting his engine each time.

In spite of his penury the Swede had built this little vessel well. She was 40 feet in length and her frames were of oak with planking of Port Orford cedar. So she smelled marvelous below. The bow was bold, the stem unusually straight and determined for this era, and she had a pleasant sheer which extended sweetly all the way aft. Her stern was not beautiful, the transom being absolutely vertical above the water, and at first I was concerned lest she present too much flat surface to a following sea. There was a deep trolling pit aft, which was comfortable although the reach over her counter was a bit long for our arms. There were two sets of salmon gurdies on either side aft, which we later discovered were worse than useless.

She could carry 8 tons of iced fish, which was considerable for a boat of her length, and this capacity was pointed out to us as a great attribute. Unfortunately, no one ever explained how we might catch 8 tons of fish on a single voyage.

The pilothouse was small though neatly done, and all the interior woodwork was varnished. There was a fold-down chart table on the starboard bulkhead, an autopilot, and an enclosed head, a luxury enjoyed by few fishing craft. Below the pilothouse was the engine, a Buda gasoline, brand-new. It was in the open, sharing the space available with whatever men occupied the two bunks on either side. Next to the engine was a kerosene stove and opposite a fold-down table large enough for serving two persons.

The whole vessel was comely, efficient, and strangely appealing, like a well-scrubbed Scandinavian girl of modest beauty. So even though the Swede refused to reduce his price a penny, we bought her.

The Swede knew pigeons as well as fish.

The snow was still on the surrounding mountains when we sailed from Puget Sound bound for San Francisco. It was March, which is a tricky month for all mariners, but the seas were smooth, and since the exhaust of the *Fred Holmes*'s engine passed through a stack inside the pilothouse, we were always warm. Even Cape Flattery, which is at the tip of the Olympic Peninsula and can be quite as brutish as Finisterre or Hatteras, was kind to us, and for a day and a night the *Fred Holmes* proceeded smoothly southward. This was the best of luck because the northwestern coast is desolate, devoid of decent shelter, and the winds can be as vicious as anywhere in the world. Thus we were in tremendous spirits and exalted at the prospect of making our living in a new and exciting fashion. And the *Fred Holmes* had already taken our hearts. The Buda engine worked with a minimum of noise and on checking our fuel consumption we were amazed at its economy. The autopilot worked. The bunks were comfortable and we dreamed the hold was full of fish instead of a mere 2 tons of ice which we had taken as ballast.

☼

SIX

LaFrenier knew nothing of fishing. So my fragmentary knowledge, absorbed so recently from Viscovich and Rattigan and a man named Gidley, allowed me to swagger a bit as I explained just how we would do this and that. We played at navigation, which was old hat to both of us, ate, and slept. And at evening LaFrenier would slip briefly away to be by himself. He would stand gazing at the darkening sky and I knew that he was praying. He was the perfect Catholic, believing all that he was told to believe. I respected him for his unswerving faith, having seen it put to frightful test. The only mystery was why he so believed in me, and I was determined to deserve it. I could not know how soon my pagan prayers would rise with his own.

The wind did not approach with any subtlety. There had been none and then in ten or fifteen minutes there was a great deal of wind. It came from directly ahead. But we had both been in many winds before, principally in the little schooner *Story II,* and so we were not concerned. The seas built more slowly than the wind and soon they were of a size to test the behavior of the *Fred Holmes* in what could be fairly termed rough waters. We were enormously pleased. Occasional spray made a ripping sound across the pilothouse windows, but there was never a pound from the hull. She rose to meet each sea most gracefully, her roll was easy, and so without whip we had no difficulty in standing anywhere without holding on. Indeed, the Swede had built well and from a sound design.

Since LaFrenier had the evening watch I went to my bunk. Except for the sensation of partial weightlessness as we rose and fell with the seas, I could not have been more comfortable and utterly content with our tiny isolated world. I was reading Chinese poetry, which is like smoking opium, and I was half listening to the steady thrumming of the Buda engine a mere 8 feet from where I lay. All very well for yachtsmen to fiddle with their sails, I thought. Give me, on a night like this, a good and reliable engine. How secure we were! How so very much our own masters in a business where a man could breathe daily of the sea, never wear a tie, never develop a paunch, or be measured by lettering on his office door. Congenital optimists drift quickly into slumber when counting profits from new enterprise, so I was barely half awake when I resolved that next year when we had things well in hand, we would buy a second boat and thus insure a catch by one or the other. Fishermen were dumb. They didn't understand mass production or diversification. We would show them how we protected ourselves when one type of fishing proved futile. Two boats would be the beginning of a fleet, which would lead to another and another until we commanded a full task force.

I was dozing upon these matters when the engine coughed and stopped. Immediately I felt the *Fred Holmes* swing away from the seas. I half rose in my bunk and called to LaFrenier.

"Hey?"

"Dunno! Stand by!"

He pressed the starter button and the engine caught immediately. And it ran perfectly. My faith in new engines, which had always been devout, could again crawl back into the cocoon of innocence.

"I guess we had some dirt in the fuel," LaFrenier called down. I closed my eyes again. Of course. We knew about such things. They happened. At sea there is a tremendous difference between night and day alarms, and relief from the nocturnal frights is all the sweeter.

It was not more than ten minutes before the engine coughed again and slowed to almost idling speed. I swung down from my bunk and went quickly to the pilothouse. LaFrenier was steering, his face unhappy in the dim yellow light from the binnacle.

"The autopilot won't handle her at this slow speed," he said.

"Then ram on some power! What are we waiting for?"

"I have full power on. This is as fast as she wants to go."

It was too black beyond the pilothouse windows to judge the state of the sea, but the door on the after side of the pilothouse was open and I could hear the wind. I didn't like the sound of it.

LaFrenier knew more about engines than I did in about the same proportion I knew more of fishing. Which was hardly a recommendation. I told him I would steer while he slipped below for a conference with the engine. He vanished in the darkness beyond the short ladder leading below and I wondered what our next step would be if the engine quit altogether. We were about 50 miles off the Oregon coast, which was comforting. At least we wouldn't be blown on the rocks for a long time.

Soon the engine took proper hold again and surged forward. I yelled in triumph and when LaFrenier reappeared I gave him an appreciative swat on the head.

"You're a genius. What did you do to it?"

"*Nada.*" LaFrenier was very fond of Spanish.

"Nothing?"

He shook his head.

"But—?"

"I just went down and looked at it."

We laughed and I asked him just what kind of a look he had given it.

"Like *please* . . ."

I turned on the autopilot and lingered near the wheel, waiting for another slowdown. I stepped out on deck to look at the sea and moved from the shelter of the pilothouse so I could feel the wind. It was now blowing hard, perhaps 30 to 40 miles an hour, and the sky was crypt-black. I returned to the protection of the pilothouse.

"We won't make much progress against this."

LaFrenier, always the optimist, now reminded me of our sail. It was a small leg-of-mutton affair, intended to ease the rolling of the *Fred Holmes* in beam seas. Downwind in a gale it might give us 1 knot. "We could always turn around and sail back to Seattle," he said.

I wondered.

There was something about the way this wind had come on and the way it was increasing that made me apprehensive.

I went below reluctantly, since if I was to relieve LaFrenier at midnight I should have some sleep.

I turned in "all standing" and closed my eyes. Now I could

hear the seas smashing with ever more determination against the hull, and our motion was not always as even and controlled as it had been. I was almost asleep when there was a great *carrump* on deck and I knew we had taken an abnormally large sea. Then after a time there was another and another, and I heard LaFrenier slow the engine to about half speed. Good. No sense in beating our new boat to pieces.

I heard LaFrenier singing and I wondered if it was his way of shrugging off fear. He was particularly devoted to popular ballads, and worse, knew every word of the insipid lyrics.

I tried to sleep. There was more heavy thumping on deck and I found it soothing to reflect on the marvelous strength of all well-built boats. Suppose you took a house and tossed it in the air, then twisted it back and forth after it had slammed back in its original position, then tipped it from 30 to 40 degrees or even more from side to side and constantly pounded it with tons of force while propelling it through a resistant mass. And you repeated this torture at least once a minute, hour after hour, day after day, year after year. How long would a house last before it collapsed?

With a few exceptions all of my vessels had been positive Brunhildes for strength . . . and yet there had been the apparently stout little schooner *Story II* which had almost driven us out of our wits with her secret malaise. With that same hopelessly brave man who now stood in the pilothouse whortling away so merrily, on a night of somewhat less wind though much heavier rain, the *Story II* nearly foundered right from under our weary feet. I was disturbed now to recall that that voyage had also been in March, and sleepily resolved to stay well anchored ashore throughout all Marches to come. In the *Story II* we had been bound from New York to Nassau and had managed to remain mostly in the "inside pasage" until we were south of Hatteras, which had been a very prudent choice because one gale after another punished the Cape. We had gone aground a few times in the sketchily worked sloughs and shallow bays, but none of our groundings were severe and we thought nothing of them until further shallows to the south obliged us to make for the open sea at Morehead City.

Soon after we dropped the land, the *Story II* developed a persistent leak. We were under sail in tolerable weather, although the glass was on its way down, and I anticipated a good bashing when we tried to cross the Gulf Stream.

Now, only half hearing LaFrenier's saccharine singing, I could not be sure which night it had been that had nearly finished us. We had sailed through a series of spectacular thunderstorms which proved to be more bombast than agony except for the torrential rains which each one dumped on our decks. I knew we must be on the fringe of the Gulf Stream, because the air had suddenly become very warm and the seas were short, sharp, and brilliantly phosphorescent. With so much accumulated water in the bilge I decided to start the diesel which would operate the very efficient mechanical pump. But the diesel would not start because all our tumbling about had created an air lock in the main fuel system and all our clumsy efforts to eliminate it proved in vain. About this time another pair of thunderstorms preoccupied us until dawn and we found it convenient to forget about the leak, until someone reported there was water over the cabin floorboards. Then, already exhausted from our night's work, we set to continuous labor at the hand pump on deck. It was a standard "fisherman's" pump, a large affair with a bowl the size of a soup tureen and a great steel bar for activating the bellows. It had always been very efficient, and if it is possible for an object of hard labor to inspire affection, then that heavy chunk of iron casting could be said to qualify.

We had not pumped more than a few minutes before the impossible happened. The whole casting fractured. After the dull clink we simply stood and stared at it for a time as men gaze upon something evil and detestable which they do not entirely believe. Without a foundry and machine shop we were nearly helpless, and what crude replacements we fashioned out of wood broke after only a few strokes.

By noon the water below had risen ominously and we resorted to a bucket brigade, which proved awkward and almost futile. It was so far from bailing point below to the hatch on deck, where a man waited to empty each bucket, that the total chain required three men. Since the wind was capriciously shifting all over the compass, two other men were occupied just sailing the vessel. With six aboard, that left one to navigate, cook, or lend a hand wherever required. That interminable day we all discovered a truth of the sea: A man will bail for his life if he is reasonably rested and well fed, but when these blessings are long denied there comes a time when he just doesn't care. By second nightfall, with *Story II* wallowing like a sick hog, we had nearly achieved such an attitude. We had ceased speculating on the cause of the *Story*'s leak and LaFrenier had forsaken his perpetual concert.

The weather was obviously deteriorating again, and my thinking was, in turn, sluggish, petulant, and irresolute. So I resorted to something I had never tried before. I went to the medicine chest and swallowed a large Benzedrine tablet, and in five minutes was transformed from a confused and bone-weary Mr. Hyde to a marvelously energetic Dr. Jekyll. Moreover, our whole situation with its overtones of desperation became perfectly clear. I knew we must do our utmost to make the very nearest land even if we had to beach the poor *Story II*, and no other activity regardless of temptation must divert us.

The nearest port was Charleston. Even with our lame and reeling gait we could make it in ten or twelve hours provided the wind held. And if we bailed only part of that time we could keep her afloat.

So we had employed ourselves, and sometime before dawn we came upon the outer breakwater at Charleston. It was raining very hard. What little I could see between the arms of the breakwaters would have brought only despair had I not still been driven by artificial chemistry. As it was, I saw that we could squeak through the entrance on a very close reach and with a wind of such force probably make our way right up the rockbound void to the harbor's shelter.

We succeeded; and for long I was proud of the vessel, and even of myself, for neatly accomplishing a difficult sailing task. In the pre-dawn we deliberately ran *Story II* on the mud in Charleston Harbor to keep her from sinking. And after thirty-six hours I lay down with thanks to God—but almost at once came near to panic. For then the reaction to the Benzedrine came upon me and my heart pounded until I twisted in terror. This, I was certain, was how one dies; and I wondered if the energy and clarity of thought it had so temporarily lent me must now be paid off in full.

Now here in the roaring Pacific night was LaFrenier singing away again some idiotic ditty about a sleepy lagoon and a tropical moon. I listened patiently, remembering how the next morning *Story II* had been towed to a Charleston shipyard where we discovered that the leak was the fault of her keelson. It had been constructed in two sister pieces, which when working heavily in the seas had allowed water to enter through the long division.

My esteem as a sailor also took a drubbing. When would I ever learn that vessels were as deceptive as people and that pounding and slapping one on her rump and declaring what a stout craft she seemed to be by no means confirmed her structural health.

☼

Just as LaFrenier finished a particularly banal lyric about his tropical moon, the engine came down with a terrible fit of coughing and slowed until it was barely clicking over.

In seconds I had rejoined LaFrenier in the pilothouse. With so little power available he was having a hard time trying to keep the *Fred Holmes* head to wind.

"This is not good!"

"Sí!"

"It can't be dirt in the fuel. The tanks are new!"

"It can still be dirt."

LaFrenier said he could remove the fuel filter and clean it, but to do so we would have to shut down completely.

I told him we could not shut down, or we would swing broadside to the waves and their tops were breaking. The right crest could roll us over.

"We can loaf along like this," LaFrenier said. "We couldn't go much faster without breaking something anyway."

LaFrenier's labors at the wheel were becoming more energetic. "She's a handful!" he yelled. "Every time we come up on a crest the wind grabs her bow and she almost gets away from me!"

I relieved him at the wheel. He sat down on the floor and braced himself against the bulkhead. "It's going to be a long night," he sighed.

It began to rain much harder. Water spewed against the pilothouse windows as if someone were playing a fire hose. There was considerable lightning. We reached a crest just as a prolonged flashing occurred and I was appalled to see how the entire horizon was formed by a wall of water perhaps 50 feet ahead. Then everything became black. We waited for the crash and it came. I remembered that we had forgotten to ask the Swede if he had used safety glass in the pilothouse windows. I looked aft through the pilothouse door. The water was up to the thigh-high bulwarks. It glistened with phosphorus and some of the luminescent globules slopped into the pilothouse. I glanced at the St. Christopher medal which LaFrenier had screwed in place over the compass and hoped it would exert more influence. There were times when I thought the *Fred Holmes* would never come back on course.

"It's just a warm front moving in," I said, knowing my voice had a small-boy sound. "Equinoctial." I savored the fancy term for such a brute and somehow felt better.

"*Sí. . . .*"

"When it gets light we'll wait for a smooth, then turn downwind and sail until we can fix the engine . . . but not now."

"No. Not now for sure." I recognized real concern in LaFrenier's voice and it made my own fears return. He was such a hard man to scare.

We were silent for a long time.

The engine came down with nerve-racking coughing spells more frequently as the next hour passed. We both noticed that it happened whenever we fell off a particularly violent sea.

"Sounds like a sticking carburetor float," LaFrenier said. "But that doesn't make sense with a brand new engine that's been running perfectly—"

"Until tonight."

We found that a full hour at the wheel made us both very slow to react, so we relieved each other at half-hour intervals. Sitting on the floor in our off-duty spells, we managed to doze. I had my head cradled on my knees and was trying to sleep when I fell to thinking about the Swede. And suddenly I knew.

I jumped to my feet. "That damned Swede!" I yelled. "That square-headed tightwad! That cheap bastard!"

"How now," said LaFrenier, who spoke ill of no man and was annoyed when others did. "He was a very nice guy."

"Nice he may be, but a Scrooge. Before we came along he used this boat a few times himself."

I slipped below and stared at the engine. I found the carburetor adjustment, took a deep breath, and hoped I was turning it the right way because if I did not, the engine would certainly stop. I turned it to the left, which is the normal way to open most valves. Lo!

The engine came to life with a thrilling surge.

"Olé!" yelled LaFrenier.

I crawled back to the pilothouse thinking about kingdoms lost for the want of nails. I told LaFrenier of my trip with the Swede in his car and how he had leaned the carburetor past the maximum to save gasoline. And I could not resist a somewhat patronizing tone when I declared my cleverness. "In smooth water it would run mostly on air, which pleased the Swede, but with a little bouncing around . . . the poor, miserable engine was starving to death."

"Why that son of a bitch!" LaFrenier said slowly and quietly, which from such a compassionate man sounded like the anger of the gods.

It was a furious dawn and we thought it would never come. Even with our new weapon of power we had the greatest difficulty holding the *Fred Holmes*'s head to sea. The waves were hills obliterating everything beyond themselves. They were by far the greatest waves I had ever seen and so very long from crest to crest that our motion ascending or descending each one was wonderfully smooth. There were no subsidiary waves to toss us about—they had been blown flat. So the little *Fred Holmes* rode smoothly, even at the bottom of each trough. A big ship would have had a very hard time of it, but our diminutive 40-footer was lifted and let down like a fat duckling.

Our trial came each time we achieved the summit of a wave, for then the wind would catch our bow and spin us aside so that our wild descent into the valley was made half lying abeam no matter how we worked with helm and engine. And almost every wave now presented a breaking top—true combers at least 3 to 5 feet high. We knew that if any one of them should catch us just wrong we would be completely engulfed and rolled over on our beam ends.

It was blowing ever harder. Time and again it seemed certain that we would be overwhelmed and capsize. We frequently experienced the eerie, vertigo-producing sensation of sliding backwards with the engine roaring at full ahead. Yet without the engine it would have been all over in a very short time. Everywhere the sea was white except for the valleys, which were a sickly pea-green laced with gray froth. I had not been so thoroughly frightened in years.

"Our Father is really mad this morning," LaFrenier said wearily.

We had both seen Him irate before, but never so totally unforgiving. There was not one minute's respite, no lull, no momentary clearing, when we might catch our breaths and fleeting courage. Only the rain had ceased, but the wind came on stronger than ever, creating the sound of a thousand kettledrums.

The morning dragged in spite of the constant alarms and moments of sheer quiet terror. We could not heave to, as we might have in a sailing vessel, or turn downwind and run before such seas with lines astern to slow our speed. The first breaking comber would sweep us clean, fill the pilothouse and space below, and so would end this voyage. We could think of nothing to do except what we were doing. Utterly dependent on our engine, we must continue to present the bold *Fred Holmes*'s bow pugnaciously to each succeeding monster. Once every twenty seconds . . . every twenty-five . . . every thirty.

We were so very small.

We chewed on chunks of plain bread to drive away our fatigue. LaFrenier no longer sang, although I wished he would. Any distraction. Any cheer, for even at noon it was hardly brighter than at dawn. We talked of the *Story II,* and making Charleston in the rain and darkness, and of how it had been LaFrenier's birthday so we had stood around for an interminable ten minutes reeling with exhaustion and sipping at a congratulatory drink no one wanted. And we spoke of the soggy cookie with three matches stuck in it which was his birthday cake.

The drumming noise outside was awful.

Now again our weariness was great and we asked each other why we would never learn. We dared not use the autopilot since every sea had to be taken just right. Then how long must we endure this continuous vigil? I decided to try calling the Coast Guard and find out. They should have a weather report and we could make some plans.

Response to my call was almost instantaneous as if they had been waiting. And the voice was wonderfully loud and clear.

"Here is the Coast Guard cutter *Itasca.* What can we do for you? Over."

I gave our assumed position, which was indeed a presumption. And I asked if they knew how long this blow would last. The voice intoned a brief report which was ambiguous and vague, but in which we found some encouragement. Sometime this night or early tomorrow morning the wind should moderate.

Then the voice said cheerfully, "If you require assistance we are not far from your assumed position."

"We are all right, but one thing more. What is it blowing in this area?"

"Stand by. . . ." There was a long silence, then the voice returned. "At the present time our anemometer reads seventy . . . seventy-two . . . now dropping to about sixty knots."

"Thank you very much." I signed off. LaFrenier and I looked

at each other. We were not sure if confirmation of our wind estimates was pleasing or shocking. Now we knew what the little *Fred Holmes* could take. There remained the question of our own point of surrender.

The storm continued all through that day and into the night. Not once did the engine falter. We slept in quick snatches, huddled on the floor, braced between the exhaust stack and bulkhead. We were now past fear, semiparalyzed and numb to every normal sensation except a compelling need to urinate frequently although we drank no liquid. We remembered how it is always so when deep fright and nervous fatigue arrive together.

When we spoke it was in monosyllables. "Okay?"

"Yeah. I'm okay!"

Our voices were little cries against the tumult outside.

About midnight we sensed the wind had moderated even as the Coast Guard had predicted. But the seas remained enormous and our work unrelieved. Not until the second dawn was there any real improvement and by noon there was no wind at all. Scars appeared in the overcast. There were passing moments when sunbeams stabbed at the sea. And we slept in turn. The combers were gone although the basic seas had subsided very little. We took a series of very rough radio bearings and discovered we were off Astoria, Oregon. During all of the time since the night before we had not progressed ten miles toward our destination.

Now we needed fuel and so it was mandatory that we endure a final test. We had never been to Astoria, but we knew about the notorious bar which guarded the seaward entrance to the port. Even in a mild blow the bar often became impassable. In anything except fine weather it was as dangerous a place as any on the western coast of North America, and all vessels, whatever their size, approached it with caution.

We did not. We were too tired. A sort of nonchalance possessed us, a feeling that we had seen the worst we were likely to see for a long time. The passing of the wind hell had left us in such a state of dazed euphoria that we were ready to believe that both boat and our lives were charmed. We even put the *Fred Holmes* on the autopilot and proceeded at full speed for the bar.

We came upon it in the yellow of late afternoon. A freighter was hove to off the bar waiting for the swells to diminish and we had the temerity to pass close beneath her massive stern, wave at her crew, who obviously thought us insane, and finally watch her sink down between the swells until only her stack could be seen. There was still no wind, only the yellow, evil light and the distraught thundering of seas pounding across the bar ahead. Those seas would be behind us, and for a moment we discussed the foolishness of attempting a crossing in a boat with so flat a stern. Then I yawned and LaFrenier repeated the gesture. We were just too tired to care.

God . . . and babes and fools. On this yellow afternoon, with dark, mud-colored seas rising so high they entirely obscured the land, perhaps the miserly Swede was also working in our interest. Our normal cruising speed was 6 knots. Now we planed down the bar swells at 10 and at times perhaps 12. The autopilot groaned as it spun the helm from hard over to hard over. But the autopilot did not worry or panic. There was no switch marked "fear" on it. As each swell overtook us, the little *Fred Holmes* lifted her stout butt just enough and just in time to avoid being pooped. A cunning, knowing hand had fashioned her well below the water where style really counted. And we knew that never again would we worry about the more apparent hazard of her square stern.

We slithered down the last great swell and entered calm water. We proceeded up the river and at last moored alongside a sweet-smelling pier of fresh-cut pine.

Later we learned we were the only craft of any size or description to cross the bar that day. And we learned that at Cape Blanco, which was not far to the south, the wind during the time of our greatest weariness had reached a maximum of 110 miles per hour.

☼

SEVEN

IN April we went for salmon, which was disastrous. It seemed that whatever we tried brought the sour taste of failure to our mouths. The gurdies, which are essentially large-diameter reels fixed to the boat, were of bastard manufacture and the brass of such poor quality that the integral parts constantly broke down. Again the Swede had economized most stupidly. We would have salmon on our lines and be unable to raise them, or we could not ease the brakes so our wire line and heavy weights would go down properly even when we were lucky enough to find a few fish. While we wasted precious time struggling with the gurdies, most of the salmon in the ocean laughed themselves into unawareness and were caught by other boats.

Nor could we afford new gurdies, for our average catch was less than six salmon a day.

Instead of ridiculing these presumptuous beginners, or smugly remaining aloof while we sank in our own despair, many fishermen did what they could to help us. Even so, we were soon obliged to face reality. We had begun with the most difficult commercial fishing of all, one that required perfect gear carefully set by men of vast experience. We had not understood how deservedly salmon fishermen were the honored technical aristocracy of commercial fishing beyond the Golden Gate. With San Francisco as their hailing port, Gidley could deliver; and Red Rosselli, Rattigan, Fonce, and Tunisan and Hoy and Freckles LaVella were expert enough to ice down enough salmon for a profitable season, but there were not many others.

Thus it was as much in humiliation as in hope that before June we conveniently came down with tuna fever. It is a head-spinning disease which strikes the waterfront of most Pacific Coast ports each year, and only the most resolute and healthy-minded fisherman can escape dreaming of the riches which await him if his luck will be just a shade better this year.

In June the rumor starts. A boat (seldom exactly identified) has caught the first albacore. Where? Cedros Island—twenty miles west. . . . No, it weren't: Right off the Coronados, by God! . . . Oh no! Just west of the Pioneer Seamount. . . . Two hundred miles southwest of San Diego. . . . San Nicolas Island. . . . Fifty miles west by north of San Clemente! Always the location of that first albacore caught is a matter of conjecture and debate, and always there are those who believe his capture marks the beginning of the season—now will begin the miraculous arrival of tuna hordes.

Not even the ichthyologists claim to know whither the albacore are bound. It seems they are not intent on spawning or apparently anything else. They just come. They come and they stay until mid-October and then they are gone. Nor does anyone know where they go. And the next year they may come in even greater numbers and be found close inshore instead of out where they belong. No one knows very much about albacore except their speed, which is great, and their market value to the canneries, which is subject to instant change.

Every year the crews of most boats fishing out of San Francisco have the same difficult choice to make. As the preposterous albacore rumors start blazing up and down the waterfront they can stay with the salmon, which is playing things conservatively, or succumb to their inherent gambling instinct, which will drive them for albacore and possible riches or ruin in the season. The two fish are never in the same waters and the gear is entirely different, so they cannot choose both at the same time.

For an American, commercial albacore fishing is a certain form of insanity and the asylum is those waters which extend from Lower California to northern Oregon. This is a great deal of ocean. The men and boats engaged are unofficially divided into separate fleets, as distinct in style and character as the ports from which they hail. There are the first- and second-generation Portuguese and Yugoslavs, who put out mostly from San Pedro and San Diego. There is a predominantly Italian fleet out of San Francisco, sprinkled with a mixture of apple-pie American refugees from Kansas, Texas, and anywhere where salt water is an unknown quantity. There is a smaller contingent of assorted personalities from Fort Bragg, Crescent City, and Point Orford, and finally when their halibuting is done, a mighty invasion of the "squarehead" fleet from Seattle and adjacent ports.

The squareheads work their way south in fine big vessels designed to match the toughness of the quasi Vikings who man them. These sturdy craft originated in the Scandinavian home waters and their lines were transferred to American builders with little change. The hulls are essentially of European schooner conformation and many still carry two masts and at least a steadying sail. Both bow and stern are relatively bold and high, but an easy sheer gives even the grubbiest a look of grace and elegance. They are deep of draft and seem to roll like so many drunken whores when they first approach over the horizon, but they are splendid sea boats and able to fish in weather that must cancel all action except survival aboard their southerly competitors. It is pitiful to witness this fine and well-kept armada sail majestically through the questionable assortment of flotsam which comprises much of the southerly fleet. The schooners range from a minimum of 50 feet to an average of 70, while the southerner may be as small as 30 and rarely exceeds 50. The squareheads carry at least two or three career fishermen, while the southerner is variously crewed by two men or a man and his doughty wife, or often by one man alone. There is simply no comparison between albacore fishing and the big-business affair of East Coast draggers, or the great Southern California tuna clippers which range as far south as Peru. It is one thing to wrest a living from the sea when a true and well-found ship of more than 300 tons is beneath your boots and you have the company and assistance of many men. It is another life to range 100 miles offshore or even more, and stay there taking whatever may come for weeks at a time in a craft which is really no more than a small motorboat. Every year several such craft are lost and the wonder is that anyone persists in chasing after a few tons of fish which are practically inedible until after they have been canned. The financial reward, unless the fisherman is most skillful, determined, and extraordinarily lucky, is far below what the same people could earn ashore. Moreover, there are no pensions for American fishermen, no tariff protection of any kind, no system of stable pricing, no recompense if he is injured, and no security for his widow if he is drowned. There is not even a suggestion of security of *any* kind; in fact it seems that landsmen, government, and sometimes God are all in league to make life difficult for albacore fishermen.

Fishing for salmon is a slow and methodical business with the boat barely moving through the water. And a salmon fisherman spends every night at anchor or in port. His relatively comfortable life gives him an air of sedateness and he is not much given to careless talk. Albacore fishing in trollers is done at a normal speed of about 5 knots, and at night the boat is allowed to drift anywhere from 50 to 150 miles offshore while the fisherman fights for what little sleep the weather and seas permit him. The albacore boat remains far offshore until the hold is full, until there remains just enough fuel to make port, until the fisherman runs out of "groceries" (they are never called "stores" in commercial fishing craft), or until the fisherman himself becomes so weary and discouraged or in need of sexual intercourse he simply cannot bear his isolation any longer. Storms do not drive him to port. Usually shelter is so far away the storm would have passed long before he could arrive. Because of this environment, dedicated albacore fishermen are inclined to temperament, exaggeration of their catches, and the wearing of flamboyant shirts.

All of this was known to LaFrenier and myself, but our miserable record with the salmon made the decision easy for us. We had to gamble. We heaved our useless salmon gurdies onto the dock and left them there. We took on 6 tons of ice and set forth through the Golden Gate to break our hearts in a new way. Our destination, Cedros Island—some 700 miles to the south. We were "prospecting," as some men search for oil and others for gold. Where, in all the sea about us were the *albacore?*

Although we were beginning to suspect there were large areas of ocean that were devoid of fish, we did not as yet choose to admit that fish traveled in herds, grazing like cattle or sheep across the widely separated fields of this enormous ranch. Passing through the empty regions a fisherman might as well save wear and tear on his lines, for there is simply nothing to take his hooks no matter how cleverly baited. As a consequence the location of the ever-changing grazing grounds becomes a laborious and patience-wearing task of exploration, which is one reason why many West Coast fishing boats work in pairs or even trios. Not only can they cover a greater area; in a lonely ocean it is also comforting to know a friend is nearby even if he is over the horizon. If fishing is bad you can always gossip over the radio. If it is merely fair you can discuss ways and means to improve it. When the modern fisherman's radio is long silent you can be certain of one thing. He is very busy actually catching fish. Even when he is "in the fish," hauling for all he is worth, a loudspeaker on deck keeps him informed of the latest news, although if asked the progress of the latest international tragedy he would only look bewildered. It is not the failures of diplomats that worry him, but who is doing what to the fish. Interpreting what is said on the fish-band is an art in itself and cunning fishermen soon learn to detect the truth according to the intonations of another man's voice. Gidley in the *Wayfarer* will say, "I dunno," which is the fisherman's introductory *"Alors"* or *"Entonces"* to *any* statement. "I dunno . . . things are pretty dull. I have a few on board, but they won't school up. Guess I'll try making a long tack east."

Depending on how long Gidley actually stays on the microphone, his report can mean that he really has only a few fish on board, or he may have sixty. Since he has not given his actual position, his notion of proceeding to the east is meaningless. He is probably telling the truth about the fish not forming a school, because if they were, he would be much too busy hauling them aboard to talk to anyone.

Listen now to Freckles LaVella in the *St. John Bosco*. His voice is high-pitched and weary. "Dunno . . . I dunno. I dunno what a guy can do. I been east, west, south, all over the god-damn ocean . . . an' I pick up a few stragglers here, another one there . . . but I dunno."

This means that Freckles indeed does not know what to do next and he is reporting the catch of a few "stragglers" only to save his face. He is just waiting for some colleague to come on the air who is unable to conceal the joy in his voice; who might report that "things are not too bad this morning." Before the man has finished his sentence, Freckles will have a bearing on him and be proceeding at full speed to share his fortune.

It is well to keep an ear always attentive for the voice of Hoy in the *Quest*. Listen to him call a soft invitation to an unidentified friend.

"Hey, Manuel . . . you might make a pass over here."

No more. That is quite enough. When you hear Hoy speak so, pick everything up and go like hell for wherever your bearing shows Hoy to be. He is unquestionably up to his powerful shoulders in fish.

But there were no voices to interpret as LaFrenier and I rolled southward in the brave little *Fred Holmes*. It was much too early in the season for the more experienced hands. They would wait and see because, they said, fish could not read a calendar. So except for an occasional bird or a delegation of porpoises the ocean was ours alone. We moved through utter desolation day after day, night after night. We were far outside of the steamer lanes, so not even a ship relieved the monotony. We set our lines at dawn each morning and we hauled them in when it was dark. Occasionally we caught some seaweed.

On the eleventh day in the vicinity of Cedros Island we were obliged to turn for port because our fuel was running short. And on the eleventh day we caught one albacore. He weighed about 20 pounds and was very beautiful. He was also one of the world's most expensive fish, representing the cost of 6 tons of ice, 400 gallons of fuel, plus groceries and sundries for two men for fifteen days, which would be the total before we actually delivered him to a buyer in San Diego. We could not bring ourselves to allocate his share of boat cost and gear.

Before we iced him down in the hold LaFrenier petted our prize and spoke to him sweetly. "Please," he murmured, "introduce us to your family."

Our one fish brought us a special reward when we arrived in San Diego. Our treasure was indeed the first the fish buyer had seen, so we had officially opened his season. Delirious with the prospect of a new year's easy profit, he momentarily betrayed his calling. He not only bought our single fish at the going price without haggling or prophecies of his own financial doom, he *gave* us a bottle of cheap whisky.

Boldness was our chief weapon in the war we had now joined. In the little *Fred Holmes* we ranged thousands of miles over the waters where albacore were to be found. And gradually, by good fortune, imitation of our betters, and a certain stubborn persistence, we began to catch a few fish.

When we returned to San Diego at the end of our second trip (never called a voyage in the fishing fleet), we had iced down a ton and a half of albacore. In our opinion this was something more like the way things should be and we were variously influenced by our accomplishment. LaFrenier developed a certain mannerism of speech, which combined a rather pleasant melody with studied carelessness. The majority of his sentences were preceded by "I dunno's," which did not really signify that he was in true ignorance of the subject at hand, but marked him as a genuine fisherman.

My affectation was a swagger better suited to Captain Ahab and a way of sticking my thumbs behind my belt and standing with my feet spread wide that suggested Bully Hayes.

In addition to our enthusiasm and seamanship we had a good

boat, which was more than many fishermen had. Thus we might have stood a good chance for the season if only because the technique of fishing albacore is uncomplicated. A troller such as the *Fred Holmes* carries two heavy outrigger poles about 30 feet in length. These are set on port and starboard cap-rails just abaft the pilothouse. When the boat is under way, they are normally hauled inboard and secured in a near-vertical position against spreaders which extend from each side of the mast. When the boat is actually fishing or prospecting, the poles are carried at an angle of about 45 degrees to the deck and five fishing lines trail aft from each pole. Because of their different lengths the lines can be hauled inboard one over the other, normally without entanglement.

In addition to the ten outer pole lines, three or four short lines are streamed directly aft over the transom, and a single long line from the truck of the mast. Very often it picks up the first fish of a school.

All of the lines are in four sections, the rubber which absorbs the initial shock of the fish hitting the bait, the line itself, which is normally heavy cod line, then a length of nylon varying from 6 to 18 feet, and finally 6 feet of wire leader. At its end is a double barbless hook concealed and presumably made tempting by various colorful jigs. The number of opinions on just what these lures should be and how they should follow the leader is exactly equal to the population of fishermen.

Yet we were honestly learning. Our long workdays had always been rewarding even when fish were few and far between. There was always the hunt. Where? *There,* maybe. . . . A hundred miles to the south? Fifty miles to the west? And we had, by sheer chance, stumbled into a school when no other vessel was in the vicinity to interfere. Suddenly all fourteen lines were straining with fish, and at once we put the *Fred Holmes* in a tight circle. For over an hour we hauled, heaved, and threw back our lines. Our arms ached and the lines cut through our wet canvas gloves until the blood of our hands mixed with the bright red albacore blood. We took sixty-one fish from the school before they sounded and we were covered with slime, blood, and pride. We did not realize that good fishermen, working faster and much more skillfully, would probably have taken at least twice sixty-one, for when a school of albacore decides to commit mass suicide, their frenzy is awesome. They will take your finger if you are so foolish as to dangle it overside. A school so maddened will deliberately follow a boat around and around in a circle, roiling the water just beneath the stern, voracious, fighting, it seems, for the first chance to be caught. Then as suddenly and mysteriously as the attack begins, everything is over. Some finned policeman halts the panic and the entire school plunges for the depths. You may fish the identical area for the rest of the day and not have a single strike. To prolong the fray, wise fishermen constantly "chum" the circle even as they haul. They carry a stock of salted bait in a stinking barrel and toss tidbits into the wake of their vessel, which works wonders.

We made three trips before we knew about such refinements. Yet little by little we had absorbed a great many things. Seek water of the right temperature. Fifty-eight degrees is ideal. "Jap Heads" are by far the most reliable lure although it is well to carry a few "bones" on the longest lines for invitation. Wash the blood from the albacore's mouth with the deck hose because bloody fish are more likely to spoil and the buyers are just waiting for any excuse to cut their price. Beware of boats from the squarehead fleet. They are seldom looking where they are going, and they are bigger and may run you down, especially if they've been hitting the aquavit. Clear your lines constantly, because fish are not as dumb as you think and they know dragging seaweed when they see it. Work in any kind of weather. The fish don't give a damn how hard it's blowing. Be sure you're ready to start the day's fishing long before dawn, since the "morning bite" is often the most productive of all and you may spend the rest of the day trolling hopelessly across a liquid desert. Keep fishing until you can't see what you're doing or observe the lines. The "evening bite" may save your day. Install refrigeration as soon as you can afford it and meanwhile conserve your ice. It is almost a certainty that the day your ice is nearly gone, which will force you to make port, there will be the greatest run of albacore in history. Distrust 99 per cent of the fish buyers no matter how friendly their smiles. Look at their soft hands, then at your own, and admit they are smarter. So stand by the scale and watch them as you would a cobra. Be certain they consider you a congenital idiot for doing what you're doing. Don't prove them right. Don't start the season too soon and don't work it too late. The honor of catching the first albacore won't pay your fuel bill, and autumn storms can slay you. Know that when there are few fish the price will be high, and when there are many fish to be caught by any fool the price will be low. Have your emotional apparatus tuned to accept this law or your weeping glands will soon run dry.

We completed our first albacore season with a profit. When all of the expenses had been counted and our last fish had been sold, simple arithmetic proved to us we had taken in three hundred and twelve dollars more than we had spent. Such was the grand total for two men working fifteen hours a day for almost four months. Such was our first year's harvest of the sea.

The following year we did much better and after one memorable trip made port with 6½ tons of albacore. Our profit for the season was over five thousand dollars, and we began to think —which for fishermen is dangerous. I revived those dreams I had found comforting on that wild night off Oregon in the *Fred Holmes.* Surely, I reasoned, it is bad business that repairs and crew rest must keep a boat in port a certain number of days during the height of the fishing season. If we had two boats, at least one would always be working—and obviously two times five thousand dollars was ten thousand. So? "I dunno."

We were so engaged in the financial legerdemain necessary to buy a *second* boat that we ignored certain ugly rumors already worrying the waterfront. The cupidity of fish buyers was such a long-established fact that the customary drop in price as each season waned neither surprised nor discouraged us. It had always been so. Yet now the price of albacore had fallen to four hundred dollars a ton although everything else necessary to the fisherman's existence had risen. Only the squareheads up north had the wisdom to establish cooperatives and put their catches up for bids. Along the California coast things financial remained the same as they had been when the Italians first fished out of San Francisco under lateen sail.

"Okay, Joe. Ya need money for gear? Ya got it. Because your old pal here is gonna advance it. Just be sure you sell your fish here. Then we'll knock what you owe off your account slow."

Slow? So slow the fisherman was never out of debt—quite. It was planned that way. Buyers might hate each other, but they knew better than to violate the system. Never let the fisherman off the hook. Thus, like our comrades, we remained at the complete mercy of the buyers. They would stand on their docks like characters out of the cheapest melodrama, chewing on huge cigars and studying their manicured nails and allowing the sun to glisten on their cuff links and rings of gold. I kept looking about for the cameras; certainly these caricatures of capitalistic evil must be acting in an underground movie produced by the Communist party. Or it might be an avant-garde comedy? But our disbelief soon melted before their shocking actuality. They did not consider themselves caricatures at all, but realists to whom the display of sparkling baubles was the herald of a successful man's triumph over his dumber brethren. The majority were performers of impressive histrionic talents and were well rehearsed in their snortings and whining and prosy vulgarities and anxious preening of the oiled hair while they told us how they were glutted with tuna, but out of sheer charity would condescend to buy our fish. They knew that not one fisherman in a thousand had the courage to throw his catch back in the sea.

"Okay, fella. Ya don' wanna sell? Eat 'em yoursel? Only you're gonna look mighty fuckin' funny with a ton of tuna in your belly."

And they would amble away.

They knew something we did not know and sensed a coming change. They knew the Japanese were planning to deliver frozen tuna on their docks at three hundred and twenty-five dollars a ton. And since among other idiosyncrasies they were all confirmed cynics at heart, they were reasonably certain the American Government would do nothing to protect a thousand-odd fishermen who were seldom in port on Election Day.

Along the wharf in San Francisco there was a man whose name was most easily pronounced by grasping the throat with both hands and squeezing hard so that it came out to sound something like Gargenella. He was a kind man and an honest fish buyer.

He was the only one.

☼

EIGHT

It seems to make little difference where the American commercial fisherman labors; be he a Gulf Coast shrimper, a Chesapeake scalloper, a New England halibuter, or a California tunaman, he is inclined to believe in good-luck tokens and fairies and that no man's luck can be continuously bad. And most of them have a lack of guile often combined with a childlike, rather winsome view of economics. We were now totally dedicated to the life. So in the euphoric manner of fishermen whose season has not been catastrophic we decided all was well forever. My favorite theme of expansion prevailed over LaFrenier's common sense, and once more we returned to Seattle, where the best used boats were known to be. There is of course a very fundamental reason why any commercial boat is for sale. She has failed to make money for her previous owner. And there are endless rationalizations which will assist a prospective buyer to convincing himself that he can reverse the record.

Almost the first boat we inspected was named the *Mike*. After the mockery of a further search, in the course of which we clambered over all the hyenas of the northern ocean, we returned to her in a mood any seller would recognize as eager. She was middle-aged and smelled of shark liver and oil, in which specialty she had been engaged until synthetics made the trade as extinct as buffalo hunting and brought her owners to near ruin. She was 10 feet longer than the *Fred Holmes,* powered by a Mack diesel engine which appeared not to have been overly abused, and had a flying bridge atop her wheelhouse which gave us a heady feeling of importance. She was painted green with a white wale stripe nearly the full length of her hull, and the angle of her wheelhouse against the sweeping line of her deck was such that when viewed in profile she presented a very formidable appearance. There was also something indefinable about her heaviness, a muscular peasant quality, suggesting the necessary stubbornness to match our mood. The total effect was powerful enough to make us ignore the sundry legal papers which festooned her deckhouse, and we became the mortgagees. We later learned how the sharkers, at last released from their bondage, were so elated they stayed drunk for four days.

The *Mike* could carry 11 tons of iced fish, although we were no longer so naïve as to believe we would ever use her total capacity.

Again it was in March (and exactly two years after sailing south in the *Fred Holmes*) that we left the waters of Puget Sound. The *Mike* was now the number-two vessel of the Western Ocean Fishing Company, a firm whose assets consisted almost entirely of stationery which we had ordered in a moment of grandiose planning. How it might increase our catch of fish remained forever a mystery.

At a meeting of the board of directors it had been resolved that I should be master of the *Mike* while LaFrenier would take over the *Fred Holmes* when we arrived in San Francisco.

Soon after passing Cape Flattery we discovered something about the *Mike* which shocked us. It was like slipping into bed with an ardent woman and suddenly discovering she was a syphilitic leper. For she rolled like no boat we had ever known. She rolled in the slightest sea, farther and faster without actually capsizing than our eyes and stomachs could believe. And there was a vicious whip to her roll which could send a man reeling across her deck and plaster him hard against whatever object or bulkhead stood in his way. No man who worked her ever became entirely accustomed to the *Mike*'s incredible motion and in time she was destined to become known as the most uncomfortable boat in the albacore fleet. Taking a meal in the *Mike* was always a problem if there was any sea at all, so smart diners kept one foot braced high against the opposite bulkhead. Yet in spite of her miserable affliction she was to prove an unusually seaworthy craft and was particularly distinguished when proceeding against head seas. She seemed able to ignore them, and though she might be rolling her fat ass off, she would plunge steadily forward and rarely lose any way.

We soon had reason to admire her talents, for a day after passing Cape Flattery, in almost the exact area where we had been so beset in the *Fred Holmes,* we were challenged by another storm. The entire pattern of wind and sea and concern was repeated with depressing similitude except that this time the trial began more easily because we were in a larger boat and had an engine which never faltered. Nor did the wind blow quite so hard, although it was certainly a full gale. And it snowed. And we had a man aboard I thought might be dying.

His name was Kimball and he had joined us for the passage down to San Francisco because he thought it would be an adventure. Alas.

He was a very big and agreeable man renowned for his athletic prowess, concerning which he was pleasingly deprecatory. There was about him some bluster but no more than is natural to big and hearty men suddenly released from their city desks and allowed to prance around in the fresh air. While we were still in the smooth waters of Puget Sound with the *Mike* gliding along like a respectable matron on her way to church, Kimball would look up at the surrounding snow-capped mountains, be compelled to breathe deeply, then hammer his chest with his fists, and then breathe deeply again. And between thumpings and inhalations he would exclaim, "Magnificent! . . . Magnificent!" And I thought how true and tragic that a man of *his* magnificent dimensions was not in some way daily concerned with those mountains rather than employing his muscles to shuffle papers.

As the hours passed I found Kimball's enthusiasm touching, for everything that he saw and sensed excited him to new parades of jubilant adjectives. Even the wretched stew which I cooked and stirred with the handle of a crescent wrench because I was simultaneously engaged in repairing the stove, Kimball pronounced as absolutely *cordon bleu!* He was everywhere about the *Mike,* trying to find spoons and plates so we could eat my indigestible goulash, cleaning the port debris off deck, exclaiming over the chart as if it would momentarily reveal some pirate treasure, and climbing up and down the ladder leading to the flying bridge like an amiable gorilla. We were pleased that our guest was so enjoying himself.

Before the gale had more than announced its coming Kimball began to crumble. We were preoccupied with the *Mike*'s astonishing style of rolling, and the wind was nearly full upon us before I realized that Kimball, who apparently thought all boats rolled like the *Mike,* had been following me around like a worried puppy. We were still so freshly out of port that there were many things to be attended and wherever I went—to the engine room to secure tools and oil against the rolling, or on my hands and knees checking the bilges and the stern bearing, or in the pilothouse greasing the automatic-pilot chain, or fussing with the oil control to the stove, which leaked and stank more than it should—there was Kimball panting at my heels. I wanted to tell him to go away and read some of the magazines he had brought, but then I saw his eyes and they were not at all the same eyes I had observed before.

We were in the deckhouse, which was compact but comfortable enough during those few seconds of each minute when it assumed an angle of less than 30 degrees. The galley occupied the after part of the deckhouse, my bunk and the sink took up the port side, and a bench and table—which served as a catch-all for tools, tobacco, personal possessions of every description—and dining area took what space was left. There was not much room between anything, which was good since the distance a man could be catapulted before coming up against something solid was all the less. Beyond the forward bulkhead was the wheelhouse, which was entered via a narrow swinging door. A heavy sliding door next to the odiferous diesel stove led aft to the open deck. It was closed now against the considerable commotion outside.

With the wind had come an abrupt lowering of the overcast and then even lower scud which raced across the water at masthead height. There was little left of the afternoon light, yet I could see that Kimball's eyes had become dilated and there was a look of wildness and dismay behind them that concerned me even more than the *Mike*'s ridiculous gymnastics. Hoping to revive his exuberant spirits, I tried a few lame jollities about the carefree life of a sailor, to which he failed to respond.

Soon LaFrenier called to me from the wheelhouse, where he had been on watch, and said he had a fine radio bearing on Astoria. During the few minutes it required to pull out the chart and plot it I forgot about Kimball and the increasing wind. To counter our disappointment in the *Mike*'s motion there was now revealed an attribute which we could not have discovered in port. The separate engine room below confined the noise of the Mack engine, so that in the deckhouse only a rather pleasant and throaty humming was audible, and its extraordinarily heavy construction quite isolated the occupants from the outside weather. Now, with sea and wind making up a symphony of nasty noise, the *Mike* plowed onward like a liner. Only her rolling marked the turmoil outside; it was so quiet in the deckhouse I could distinctly hear the rattle of two dishes motivated by the slight engine vibration. When I turned to the dish locker with a bit of rag to silence them, there was Kimball again.

He was standing between the stove and the locker with his back to the sink and I saw that he was shivering. I refused to believe my eyes, which insisted that somehow he had shrunk two feet, but there was no question about his attempt to communicate. His mouth opened and closed several times without a sound and his arms were linked across his mighty chest as if to squeeze air for his voice. I asked him, foolishly, if he was feeling all right.

He tried to reply but failed, and churlishly I left him to stand in his muteness while I went forward to LaFrenier. If possible I wanted him to obtain another radio bearing to cross with the one from Astoria and thus fix our position nicely before other events intruded, as in such weather they were bound to do. When I returned to the deckhouse after a few minutes I was rather surprised to see Kimball still there—in my preoccupation I had actually forgotten he was aboard. He had not loosed the embrace of himself with his powerful arms, and his eyes had become dead agates. He had found his voice.

"Did you know it was snowing outside?" he asked in a monotone.

"Sure. It's just a little squall."

"Is it going to be worse?"

"Probably."

LaFrenier called back a new bearing—this time from the lightship at Cape Flattery. I bent over the chart immediately, as much to avoid Kimball's fisheyes as in my desire to plot the bearing.

"There are thousands of hailstones on deck," Kimball said. "You can't stand up. Can't you call the Coast Guard?"

"For what?"

"To come help us?"

Crossing the new bearing didn't agree with my dead-reckoning position very well and I was annoyed at my apparent error. But before I could find it and justify the accuracy of the lightship bearing I had to be rid of Kimball and his beseechings. My impatience festered as I explained we were perfectly all right and had no need of any assistance and the *Mike* could ride out this little blow with the greatest of ease, and the very best thing he could do now was climb in his nice warm bunk with some magazines and forget where he was. I glanced suggestively at the hatch hole, which was in the deck at the forward end of the deckhouse. Descent through it was made via a straight steel ladder to the engine room and also the fo'c'sle, where there were six bunks.

Kimball shook his head. "I couldn't go down there," he said slowly. In a way I couldn't blame him. It was much noisier below because the bulkhead between the fo'c'sle and engine room was only plywood and the seas meeting the *Mike*'s steady progress did not divide without protest. And there was the psychological block of going *down* into extremely unstable confinement—the primitive sense of being trapped.

Kimball's eyes had returned from the dead and I suddenly became aware of what I should have recognized long before. He was utterly terrified.

I foresaw little prospect of using my own bunk this night, so I suggested Kimball might like to try it for size even though its height above the waterline in comparison with his own greatly multiplied the force generated by the *Mike*'s rolling. He moved slowly toward it, grabbing at everything he could reach for balance. He seemed to be in a trance and again I had the distinct impression that he had diminished remarkably in stature.

I put the bunk's fiddle board in place for him so he wouldn't roll out and drop the 5 feet to the deck and gave him a heist when the *Mike* rolled in the bunk's favor. When he was in and secure at last, I found I was panting with the exertion of fighting the roll of the *Mike* against the eccentric tumbling of his lump-like mass. I smiled at him while I caught my breath and said, "Now, rockaby, baby . . . when the wind blows—" then I stopped. For there were his eyes searching me out, and I tried to pity him, yet ashamedly found myself hating him. His behavior was all the more distressing because he had been such a noble physical specimen and now I could only think that he was letting us down; he was letting the entire human race down, exposing by his miserable exhibition how vulnerable to fear we all are. His abject eyes spoke plainly enough to me and they said, You are a fraud with your careless air. There is nothing genuine about the way you pretend to dismiss this gale, there is nothing honest about the phrases you employ to convince either yourself or me that all is well, or anything true in your heart. Because you are also afraid and simply lack the courage to admit it.

I did not like what his eyes seemed to say. I wanted to throw him overboard.

Now that he was lying down he reminded me of a battle painting in the Louvre which included a fallen warrior whose eyes were so rendered that they followed every movement of the viewer and seemed to censure his survival. Now it seemed to me that here between us totally different men there was on his part a frightening advantage, because having abandoned all pride he no longer had need to pose and could at his own pleasure mock all who would pretend they were strong.

As had its predecessor of two years before, the gale continued all through that night and the next day. LaFrenier and I had relieved each other so that one or the other of us could slip down into the fo'c'sle for a few hours' rest, such as it was. By the third exchange of watch neither of us heard the cacophony of noises below; hence we were fatigued yet still far from exhausted. Even so a taut anxiety seemed to possess me and in time I knew it was not due to the storm. It was Kimball's eyes and body, both of which seemed inescapable. He lay flat on his back with a peculiar corpselike rigidity and his big hands were clasped firmly across his chest as in death. His face appeared to be carved in wax and at first I wondered if men, like birds and certain animals, could die of fright.

If Kimball was dead his eyes were certainly not. From time to time it was necessary to pass through the deckhouse on one duty or another, which meant passing him reposed in my bunk. And always it would be the same—there were Kimball's eyes following me though his head remained absolutely motionless. Now, however, his eyes had ceased their beseeching and become openly contemptuous, saying without any apparent assistance whatever from Kimball himself, Ahoy, faker! When will your stiff back bend and your intestines ravel. When will you scream silently for mercy and grovel in your own indignities, since it must come to all men.

I could not tell Kimball how I was a veteran of his catechism, so during one unavoidable encounter with his eyes I paused long enough to ask, "Why the hell don't you close your eyes and go to sleep?"

To my surprise the dead Kimball answered me: "How can I?"

"How can't you?" I said, bitter with envy because my own body yearned for sleep. "You've got the best bunk in the ship."

At least his eyes protested my cruelty, which was much better than if he had simply accepted it. I thought of asking LaFrenier to come back and perhaps convince Kimball I was not deliberately punishing him with the whips of wind and sea and that his torment would soon end. Then I remembered LaFrenier's bedside manner, which was that of a priest administering Extreme Unction, and decided against it.

Just as I started away from Kimball, the *Mike* twisted over a larger than average wave and took such a violent roll I was thrown against the lockers below the bunk. When I rose, rubbing at my bruised rib cage, I heard Kimball say as if he were asking the time, "Aren't you ever afraid?"

"No," I lied. Fear in confined areas is like typhus, for it can infect the population so fast that mere worry can become panic in minutes. I knew I must not speak to Kimball again or remain in his vicinity, so I fled to the wheelhouse and slammed the door after me.

The indomitable LaFrenier was perched on the small seat which folded up from the bulkhead. His eyes were half closed and he was crooning softly. When I entered he paused, then went on to finish his rendition before he said, "I think it will be dawn soon."

"It better be. Our friend is giving me the willies."

LaFrenier nodded his head. *"Sí."*

We watched the angry light arrive like the first day of Creation, and either awe or fatigue forced LaFrenier into silence, so there were only the moaning of the autopilot in labor, the metallic hiss of spray when it struck the pilothouse windows, and the subdued rumble of the wind.

"Let's swear all over again we will never go to sea in March."

"Sí."

LaFrenier's predilection for Spanish had only increased since our albacore trips in Mexican waters, and now I found it irritating. Why in God's name couldn't he stick to his native language? I was about to ask him caustically for an explanation of his fancy when I realized that if I was angry with such a staunch shipmate, then indeed I must be on the verge of breaking, and the true cause was not to be found in him but in my own waning endurance and a childish envy of the man-shell who had usurped my bunk.

"And in the future let's not invite strangers to share our lot."

"Sí."

Having said my piece and conveniently forgotten that I had invited Kimball to use my bunk, my pique had scattered as quickly as it had joined, and we were content and relatively comfortable until the edge of dawn revealed the sharp-gouged summits of the seas and rising beyond them a sky of prison-gray. In the heavier squalls it was still snowing, but the cozy little wheelhouse had become a soothing oasis, not only from the elements but from the defeat which lurked in the gloom behind us.

As the *Mike*'s pugnacious bow became more clearly outlined and we saw how easily she tackled each sea, we developed a new and almost maudlin affection for her. Roll she might, but here in the wheelhouse there was a sense of doughty power and even a feeling of inherent stability.

By nine o'clock the wind had diminished until it was only blowing a fresh force-6. It was providential, because in contrast to the sea room we had had in the *Fred Holmes* two years before, we were now less than 10 miles offshore.

There were times when, rising on a great swell, we thought we could see the land stretching darkly along the eastern horizon. At other times, particularly in the squalls, there was not more than a few yards' visibility. Our "patient," as we now called Kimball, seemed to have achieved a state of mental and physical suspension so that he had managed to deny even the basic needs. He had not relieved himself for at least a day and a half. Perhaps we should have let him rest in peace if our own longing for land had not been so powerful.

We used Kimball as our principal excuse and persuaded ourselves that a port known as Umpqua River was close at hand and offered quick shelter. We were very tired or we would never have made such a foolish decision, for during a blow the safest place for any seaworthy boat *is* at sea—not messing about with the dangers of shallow water. If we had ever attempted entrance to the Umpqua River before, we would most certainly have remained as far offshore as possible.

It was actually no more than a wound in the beach and we approached it just before noon with good visibility. We could see a dark line of pine trees marking the shore and from the wildly careening flying bridge we could make out a pair of stone breakwaters extending seaward perhaps five hundred yards. Outside the breakwaters the seas were jagged with gray beards foaming along their tops. When they charged the breakwaters, they exploded mightily, yet there were moments in between when a smartly handled boat might pass.

We held off for almost an hour, easing up and down, our engine deliberately slowed so that its drive matched the wind and we would hold position. We studied the sequence of the larger waves and judged the intervals between their crashing on the bar which served as a dangerous threshold to the breakwaters.

And we decided it could be done—if we were to approach boldly and not equivocate. Demurring, even for a moment, would find us overtaken just as we were in the narrow entrance; caught wrong by a pursuing wave and we must be cast against the stones no matter how we or the *Mike* labored to escape.

Unless we were extraordinarily lucky. It was very obvious that once we were committed to the entrance of the Umpqua River on such a morning there could be no turning back.

The *Mike*'s helm was very stiff and her rudder not as large as it should be, hence steering was plain work, even in relatively smooth water. There were two wheels, one in the wheelhouse at deck level, and one on the flying bridge. Watching the seas scamper between the breakwaters, I realized steering was going to be a wrestling match and so sent LaFrenier down to follow me through on the lower wheel. Working together, I hoped we could spin the helm faster.

We stood just off the entrance, still waiting for what I knew not except a possible recharge of daring. From my elevated position I had a clear view of the slot between the breakwaters and the action of the seas around them. The legend of the "seventh wave" is almost true. For some mysterious reason *about* every seventh wave is larger than all those before and after, and frequently when the seventh wave has passed there is a relatively flat area during which the seas appear to subside and gather themselves for the next major assault. This area is known as a "smooth." You wait for such a time if you are going to come about in a sailing ship or bear around on the opposite tack. You look for a smooth when you must maneuver a powerboat in difficult ocean conditions. The time duration of a smooth is rarely more than a minute or so, although fortunately the greater the major seas, the longer the interval of relative peace.

Now I waited, the wheel firm in my hands, my rubber boots placed wide apart to counter the *Mike*'s wild rolling, and I wondered if Kimball had called upon his personal devils to set this stage for my ordeal.

The wind had eased again and scud no longer flew off the waves. I could not see or talk to LaFrenier, but I could feel his extra strength flowing through the helm whenever I turned the rudder. Also just behind me was the exhaust stack, and in it I could hear the reassuring grumbling of the Mack diesel.

I warned myself that I must be patient. Now, now? No. Nor now. Wait!

I saw a granddaddy wave approaching, which is a fisherman's way of saying a wave is enormous. The *Mike*'s flying bridge was approximately 15 feet above the water, yet I could not see over this wave. It was a pigmy compared to those we had seen in the *Fred Holmes,* but locally it was everything.

The *Mike* rose swiftly upward with its approach, lifting like a toy. The crest slipped beneath and I gasped at the realization of its speed. At the summit of the wave I could see for miles: the curved inlet beyond the breakwaters, and the rumpled sea slicing across the distant horizon to the west. And nowhere could I observe any sea to compare with this granddaddy.

As we skidded down its black backside I glanced once again to seaward and saw that the smooth matched its creator. Now!

Even as I jammed on full throttle and spun the wheel I heard the thunder of the granddaddy colliding with the breakwater. For an instant everything was lost in spray and foam; then the two ends of the breakwater came squirting upward like surfacing submarines. We were plowing full speed for the narrow separation between them.

I was pleased with my timing. For a few minutes we rode perfectly steady in the huge smooth valley. Steering was easy.

But it soon became apparent that my estimate of our distance to the breakwater had not been so shrewd; I had thought it would take us two minutes, perhaps three, to reach the entrance at full speed. Now it looked as if it would be closer to five minutes.

And a new granddaddy was making up to seaward.

We could not turn away and try again. We would be caught broadside to both seas and wind in shallow water. We had to hold course for the entrance.

We almost made it. Thirty seconds in an airplane can be an eternity. It can also become a very long time in a boat if it makes the difference between entering a harbor under control or being hurled into it.

I glanced over my shoulder, saw it coming, and whispered the name of Jesus. I slammed at the throttle lever to make sure it was full on, which it had been anyway, and the futile gesture made me feel all the more helpless. Our maximum speed was 9 knots. How could we hope to escape a wave that was coming on at 18 or better?

I felt the initial lift just before the *Mike*'s bow was even with the breakwaters' heads. We rose rapidly and the breakwaters seemed to sink.

The *Mike* paused as if to gather her maximum strength. The engine maintained its heaving snoring, yet we made no apparent progress. Instinctively I hunched my shoulders.

We rose still farther until I thought the very bottom of our keel must actually be several feet above the breakwaters. Then the crest hit our stern with a great sickening thump and we were propelled forward so fast I could feel our self-created wind against my face. The *Mike* slewed to port and drove straight for the northern breakwater. I spun the helm hard over, pushed hopelessly at the throttle again and tried to tell myself there was still space enough for the *Mike* to respond and turn away from the pile of great stones.

I jammed down on the wheel with all my strength. It made no difference. The wheel was already hard against the stops.

The change came very suddenly. The wave passed on down

the channel, leaving us again at a standstill in the following trough. In spite of the queasy sensation of being trapped, I now thought we stood a chance. We wallowed helplessly for a moment; then our propeller regained authority and with the helm hard over we charged toward the opposite breakwater.

The wrestling match I had anticipated had begun. It lasted for perhaps three minutes. We fought and hung on. Once the *Mike* rolled over so far I seemed to be looking straight down at the water, and though I stood high on the flying bridge, I had the crazy notion that I could reach out and plunge my hand in the sea.

Gradually, like a spawning salmon fighting upstream, we made our way far enough into the channel so that there was some protection from the breakwaters. We made a final controlled surf down a rapidly expiring granddaddy, and with the engine still growling full out, slid into smooth water.

I sighed, and the *Mike* seemed to join me.

Our decision to enter at all had been bad seamanship. Given a trifling less luck and we would certainly have been tossed upon one breakwater or the other.

Kimball appeared on deck soon after we entered Umpqua River. He had found his voice, and after some overpolite inquiries as to our whereabouts announced that he had made a mistake in his original estimate of his free time. He must return to his job at once. We understood and we were grateful for his consistency, for it would have been deeply disturbing if he had suddenly found courage to say he was leaving because he was afraid of being afraid.

He swung his impressive bulk up to the dock with the grace of a true athlete, and his smile and hand wave were hearty, as befitted a sailor home from the sea. Not until he turned his broad shoulders and strode jauntily toward the bus station did we find our relief turning to pity. What was it like to live in a perpetual masquerade? What tales he must contrive when friends inquire of his great adventure.

The Western Ocean Fishing Company was now sailing under a policy based on my conviction that two productive units are better than one. The theory has certain drawbacks in the fishing business. Perhaps the fish refused to cooperate because they were not made privy to our overall program; the only certainty was two nearly empty units wandering about the ocean rather than one. There was a consequent doubling of expense and twice as many shares to be divided.

A season passed during which LaFrenier fished the *Fred Holmes,* and I the *Mike.* Dinehart and McDowall were our mates and none of us prospered. Meals aboard became so frugal we began to eat our catch, which is not considered a good omen among professional fishermen, or even good manners. At last, in the windswept, chill-blue shadow of a San Francisco Fisherman's Wharf warehouse, we were able to make wages cooking crab. The work lasted until the local supply of crabs was exhausted. We longed for the high seas where a man could make his yearly fortune in a few days if only . . .

In desperation we created a fish market, selling to the passing public directly from our boats. "Lady, how about this succulent cod—caught only last night?" The market was a shock success and yet we soon recoiled from it because none of us were merchants at heart. Soon it became obvious that the Western Ocean Fishing Company could not withstand the financial winds which beset it. So the *Fred Holmes* and the *Mike* were sold to new dreamers, and one by one we drifted into other ways.

☼

IN HARBOR

As Danish harbors go, this is a fine one, but the entrance between the breakwaters allows the general message of the outside weather to be delivered with regular certainty. Now a responsive rhythm has been established, the surging waters inside repeating the state of the sea outside. Almost exactly. Which is something to be wary about. If we are held here many more days, then obviously the minor effort of walking to the breakwater for a hopeful look at "conditions" is going to become more exaggerated with each examination. So that after a time we won't bother to leave the Black Watch *because we can stand on her deck and observe the situation inside and judge that it is still too rough outside. Then certainly after a few more days it will be too much trouble to go up on deck, since an estimate can be made by the gentle rise and descent of our bunks. Many people conduct their lives on this principle, unwinding until there is no force at all remaining in their springs and then it is too late.*

And in that way we may die right here in the harbor of Rønne, Island of Bornholm, Denmark.

These sometimes challenging encounters with basic reality are perhaps the most wonderful thing about sailing the seas in small boats or even small ships. For the oceans are exactly like anyone's life, at times tranquil and easy, and at other times turbulent, and exasperating and occasionally frightening. You can tell almost exactly which degree of security the master of a small craft has reached by observing the behavior of his vessel and her appearance. You can judge the influence of his wife upon his existence. It is not necessary to actually see the man to be convinced that he is a fool or a hero, bold or sly, old or young for his age. It is all to be seen in how he accepts the ever-varying invitations of the sea.

There are times when the provocations of the sea are uncomfortably direct and we are obliged to select and draw our own character for the day. Do we choose to be so old, or so young, so timid or so rash? The sea leaves it to us to live with ourselves for that day. Please, God, let the wind go down tonight so that the decision to sail or not to sail will be taken out of my hands!

☼

III

THE *ALBATROS*

☼

. . . REJUVENATED FOR HIGH SOCIETY

☼

NINE

THE San Francisco waterfront abounds in salty characters many of whom have an easy command of nautical terminology, a vast knowledge of all that pertains to ships and the sea, and practically no experience beyond the end of the dock. They are the Captain "Popeye" mariners who cling to every shipyard and port in the world like so many barnacles. They can and *will* tell how wrong you are doing whatever you are doing, and when you finally learn not to listen they simply stand about shaking their heads and predicting disaster.

And then there are a handful of true salts who spit to windward with ease and are otherwise inclined to keep their mouths shut. In San Francisco one of these men was Holcomb.

He was a dark, spare man with great heavy-fingered hands which he could employ most dexterously to any marine project. It was wondrous to watch him tie a rose knot, a Matthew Walker, a double diamond, or watch him sew a clew-iron in a sail, or fashion a spar with an adze. His face seemed sculptured with the same tool, chiseled sharply without a single compromise, and his eyes were such a deep brown as to be nearly black. His smile revealed two gleaming rows of remarkably long teeth which appeared overwhite against the musky color and heavy texture of his skin. His aquiline nose and black hair suggested he might be an Arabian pirate, yet in truth he was the most kindly and patient of men.

There was also something of the eternal little boy about Holcomb. In contrast to European custom most Americans who consider themselves true sailors and have the sea time to prove it would not be caught dead in any headgear which might even vaguely suggest the nautical. Yachting caps are for Sunday sailors and the permanently wharfbound. While Holcomb would have been flayed alive before he would suffer one of the modern shiny "fifty mission" caps on his head, he was always underneath a nautical specimen he must have resurrected from the slop chest of a California clipper. On Holcomb it looked right somehow and the waterfront would have been appalled to see him without it.

Although he held a master's license Holcomb was mostly self-educated. In his opinion no authors had written anything worth while since Hawthorne and James Fenimore Cooper. Sitting in the after cabin of his *Sea Runner,* a lovely little schooner he had built from keel to truck, Holcomb was fond of reading aloud from his favorites. His voice rose to a firm baritone as he sounded out passages from *The Marble Faun* or *The Pioneers,* and once rolling, he was as difficult to stop as a Baptist preacher.

Holcomb was also somewhat of a marine architect and it was

he who drew the original rough plans for converting the schooner *Albatros* into a hermaphrodite brig, or brigantine. She would cross four yards on her foremast and become the last true and active vessel of her type still actively sailing the seas.

Moore Shipyard in Oakland drew the formal plans, and their experts were obliged into great research to match maritime history with modern engineering coefficients. They could have saved themselves the trouble; for standing in their own yard was boss rigger Dickerhoff, who had forgotten more about ships and the sea than all the engineers' slide rules could tell them.

Dickerhoff was formidable. As befitted a former mate in sail, his nose was smashed and his jaw resembled the stern of a tug. A part of his right knee was gone as a result of a sailing-ship accident, yet his limp was barely perceptible. Although he was of ordinary height, somehow the proportion of his powerful neck and the defiant way he carried his head made him appear much taller. His eyes matched the Pacific gray seas where he had so long sailed, and he was not one to smile as a mere pleasantry.

Dickerhoff was royalty and he knew it, for he was recognized as master of a fast-vanishing art. He was a rigger extraordinary and all about him ordinary men became obsequious when he spoke. When he cared to expound, there came from his thin lips all the wisdom of a hard sailing generation at sea—the rumble of his voice was as the sound of a squall on the horizon, and his opinions, condemnations, and ordinary declarations were so spiced with colorful invective that all the seas of the world seemed to join in sluicing his tongue. Dickerhoff was of a gale off Cape Flattery, of the smoldering sun in the Bay of Panama. He was Stockholm tar and beeswax, sour-smelling marlin, coal oil, and manila rope. He was pride in his skill, disdain for the shoddy, and intolerance of sloth. He was the secret humility of up-through-the-hawse, and he was prayers when the wrath of God descended on his poor little vessel.

I could never quite be sure if Dickerhoff was simply a throwback or an actual reincarnation of a once renowned bucko mate.

Even Dickerhoff's normal regalia marked him as a man of distinction. There was his cap, which he rarely removed. It was not a nautical cap like Holcomb's and it would simply have been a cap had not Dickerhoff's somewhat less than delicate face seemed to support it. The peak was set precisely level with his eyebrows and served as an eave underneath which he stood and regarded the follies of others without compassion.

He wore overalls which always appeared to have been freshly laundered and heavy black high shoes as befitted a saltwater man. At work Dickerhoff was a walking rigging loft, and the heavy leather belt which seemed a part of his body supported the highly personalized tools of his craft. His long knife with marlined handle was sheathed and hung rigger-fashion nearly all the way astern of him. Next to the knife was his palm-sized sharpening stone worn with thousands of honings in his own spittle. His rigger's spike, so polished from use it appeared of sterling silver, hung conveniently on his right. On his left was a walrus tusk filled with beeswax.

So arrayed, Dickerhoff faced his daily shipyard realm, which had now been disrupted by the arrival of the *Albatros*. One hundred and eighteen days out of Holland, it was said! What a sorry record for any master to enter in her log. Yet she doesn't look like a cow, so it must be the crew to blame.

For a long time we stood together and regarded her as coldly as sailing men can view a basically beautiful vessel. At last Dickerhoff grunted, which I thought was more encouraging than no sound at all.

"Her foremast will have to be yanked," he said as if referring to the removal of a small flagstaff from its socket. "Then we'll see."

We'll see? I knew the foremast weighed well over two tons,

which is a fair-sized steel pipe to be dangling around just to have a look.

Soon I became numb to the repeated shocks of big shipyard events. Like it or not, I had found a new career. "Yanking" the foremast had been like pulling the keystone on a Roman arch and watching the whole forum tumble down.

Word of our project passed swiftly along the waterfront and experts appeared from everywhere. If the histories of all the square-rigged sailors who arrived on the scene were to be believed, then vessels during the twilight of commercial sailing were heavily overmanned.

The proper place for a galley in a brigantine was on deck, not below, European fashion; and if we were to work braces and sheets handily, then the boats must be stowed elsewhere than the deck. The *Albatros* still wore steel stanchions and wire about her afterdeck, but no graceful brigantine should be allowed to appear in such a dowdy rig.

So it was that one of the true genius shipwrights left alive joined Dickerhoff and Holcomb in re-creating a symbol of their youth. Pasquinucci the Magnificent! There was no other light in which to regard this paragon from Leghorn, Italy, who positively bounced with enthusiasm and energy though he was long past sixty.

Pasquinucci was very nearly a caricature of an explosive, vibrant northern Italian. I often wondered if he had learned his English from a stage comedian imitating an Italian. There was the inevitable shoulder shrug, the head cocked to one side, and the hands extended palms upward. In sympathy with the traditional gestures Pasquinucci's mobile face displayed a wondrous variety of masks ranging within seconds from uproarious comedy to stark tragedy.

There are shipwrights and there are carpenters and the difference between the two may be measured in light-years. Pasquinucci was unique even among the fast thinning ranks of shipwrights. As with his father before him, the shipyards of Leghorn had been his total formal education and the rhythmic sounds of calking hammer and adze were his infant lullabies. Somehow that early exposure to the building of ships must have marked Pasquinucci as great musicians are often influenced by their childhood environment. Certainly Pasquinucci's remarkable ability to measure distance, angle, and curve entirely by eye was not a skill that could simply be learned. The old-timers along the wharves knew of Pasquinucci's gift, yet it was difficult to believe in until actually observed. Time after time I watched Pasquinucci regard a location in the *Albatros* where woodwork was required, cocking his head from side to side, sometimes biting on his lower lip in thought. The pose would last for half a minute or so, then he would hurry away to his shop on his stocky legs. Soon he would return with the needed wood piece which miraculously would fit exactly in place. Perhaps Pasquinucci had a tape measure, but if so I never actually witnessed him use it to determine the dimensions of *anything*. Yet only rarely was it necessary for him to shave ⅓₂ of an inch or so to more perfectly complete a detail. Indeed, if Pasquinucci said a rail or a plank or a beam was 8 feet 2 inches long it was well to believe him, and if your own tape had just told you it was 8 feet 4 inches, then you'd better go back and remeasure. I was never quite sure Pasquinucci could read a blueprint, although he was a tender man and very considerate of others' feelings, so that if pressed he would assume his most solemn expression and pretend to study a plan. After a time I realized that he was looking through the paper and beyond to the angle, curve, and dimension his heart and genius declared must create the ultimate masterpiece. On certain occasions, standing beside Pasquinucci, I became lost in awe.

Once Pasquinucci was convinced that my plans did not call

for the usual chromium horns, wall to wall carpeting, and clever refreshment bars with nautical motif on the afterdeck, and all those revolting gadgets and bulbous lines which have transformed the average modern small vessel into a highrise of ugly elegance, he set to work with tumultuous energy. Day after day his thick hands flew signals of alternate despair and joy, and his blue eyes were always alive with inspiration. He seemed to be everywhere at once about the ship, howling his woes when one of his own ideas fell short of perfection, shouting in triumph when at last a length of wood pleased him in grain, form, and fit.

Thus did Pasquinucci alter the once cluttered and ill-planned main deck of the *Albatros* into a nautical masterpiece. Now instead of rusting wire and metal stanchions any apprentice plumber could have made in a few hours, a wooden taffrail of honest beauty swept a symmetrical line about the afterdeck. It rose from the cap-rail just abeam the mainmast, and with just the right amount of tumble-home seemed to flow in such a sensuous line that the rather ordinary quarters and stern of the *Albatros* became beautiful. I thought of changing her name to *Cinderella.*

Next, Pasquinucci seized upon the problem of our two ship's boats which must be handy for emergencies and yet not interfere with our work in the waist. Since he had accomplished the complex curves of the taffrail without troubling to measure anything, the boat gallows was as child's play. They were strong and practical yet Pasquinucci contrived to give them an aesthetic quality. For instead of erecting a square structure which would merely support two heavy boats in the eye-offending style of most old whalers, he gave the uprights the same tumble-home as the taffrail. The thwartship members were arced with the same camber as the deck and as a consequence the boats when secured appeared a part of the ship herself.

Then Pasquinucci applied himself to the new galley which

would be on deck just abaft the foremast. Deckhouses whatever their use are of two varieties—those sheds which are knocked together any old way and those which only the Pasquinuccis of this world know how to create. Any deckhouse is a hazard, because few can withstand the incredible power of an individual storm sea which may plunge upon a vessel in just the wrong way. The number of sea cooks who have been lost along with their entire domain is out of all proportion to the total complement of sailing ships' crews. In simpler times a fair number may have been thrown overboard along with their menus, but *good* sea cooks like Rogerts, who had chosen to remain with the *Albatros* rather than return to his native Holland, must be carefully protected. All this Pasquinucci knew as he labored about the new cookhouse. And again what might normally have been a humble structure became a thing of beauty. Instead of appearing a foreign structure simply dropped aboard like a box of cargo with structural lines in argument with every other part of the *Albatros,* the new cookhouse seemed to have grown out of the deck and at once it became an integral part of the ship. The four sides each followed the corresponding line of deck and hull. There were heavy half-doors for ventilation and portholes forward so that the interior became the most comfortable shelter on the ship.

Finally Pasquinucci built the fife rail which became his own pride. Here he could become the artist with every tradition on his side. All was of oak and the stanchions were beautifully turned and set to complement all vertical lines from the deck to waist height. Fife, monkey rail, port and starboard pinrails were all joined in one, and each was rounded with exactly the right curvature so a line under strain could run or be caught and stopped against a pin. Every functional part of the assembly was true, and smiles were everywhere about the *Albatros'* deck.

The same air of well-being did not prevail below, for I had

turned loose in the engine room a "genius" so highly recommended that I rarely went down to see his supposed rejuvenation of the African Queen. He was a big banana-fingered man who said little and thereby managed to cause an aura of wisdom to drift about him, and he was called "Teeny."

His natural composure was greatly enhanced by a certain turn-of-the-century resemblance to President McKinley. There were the same bushy eyebrows projecting over his rhododendron nose and a considerable paunch to balance his rather massive head. There was an honest accumulation of grime under his fingernails, and he had a way of staring off into the distance when asked a question as if the answer must wait his long deliberation.

There was a waterfront legend that Teeny knew things about engines even God could not comprehend. After swallowing several difficult times over his price I told him to proceed and do all that was necessary to the beast in its dungeon. And all the while the great Teeny was fumbling about in the engine room I kept reminding myself that "you get what you pay for." Occasionally, fearful the great man might become lonesome, I would slip below and try to cheer him with a few resounding ho-ho's or whatever jollity I thought might appeal to his quaint and somewhat ponderous sense of humor.

Ordinary ribald jokes concerned with sex failed to spark his interest, but the activities of anyone's bowels, mythical, actual, or allegorical, caused him to reel with laughter. During the first few days Teeny worked with remarkable zeal and soon every moving part of the African Queen was separated from the main body. The valves were in the engine room, the pistons were scattered about the dock, the rings somewhere, the water pumps were in Teeny's own house, and the main bearings were taken away to be remachined. The valve springs, push rods, and rocker arms vanished and when I inquired as to their whereabouts Teeny replied that he didn't rightly know.

Having rendered the ship's main engine unreparable by anyone but himself, the great man now proceeded in his own slow march time. At my added expense he hired an assistant who would supposedly help him reassemble the hundreds of odd pieces of metal which his early enthusiasm had distributed all along the waterfront. The assistant was a young man who smoked incessantly and spent the major part of his daily working time searching for tools he repeatedly dropped in the bilge. Teeny had now promoted himself to a supervisory capacity which allowed him much more time with his cronies, who had formed their own dock committee.

While Pasquinucci moved quickly and surely, Teeny and his dropsy-plagued assistant proceeded at an elephantine pace and I began to wonder if he would ever put our humpty-dumpty together again.

My growing uneasiness with Teeny and his assistant was soon lost in a confusion of other problems peculiar to re-creating a square-rigger in the space age. There was the matter of her four yards. The forecourse yard must be 42 feet long and have a center diameter of 14 inches.

Such a spar could be laminated, which was prohibitively expensive, or the original piece could be nature's own child. The omnipresent shipyard sages said all four spars must be fashioned from full trees which after shaving square must measure no less than 18 by 18 inches! The lumber dealers laughed at me and said they could not remember when they had seen such sticks of wood.

It was Dickerhoff who grunted like a wounded bear and said he would be goddamned if the world hadn't come to a pretty pass when a man couldn't buy a few mucking little pieces of wood for a jackass vessel no bigger than a rowboat. And he would do something about it.

Thus did the Hamilton brothers enter my life. They were both lean and spare and old and drank milk and were so much alike it was difficult to tell one from the other. Long ago they had fashioned spars for the sailing vessels of San Francisco Bay, but now with engines the master of what little commercial sea trade had survived the trucking industry, they made only flag poles. Which somehow they physically resembled. Even this business was dying and they claimed they were dying anyway and therefore didn't give a damn what happened to the flag-pole business or a nation of people who thought it was naïve and old-fashioned to hoist their national colors.

Like Dickerhoff and Holcomb the Hamilton brothers were anachronisms, which was probably why they became charged with energy when asked to work as they had half a century ago. The brother who had lost the more fingers at his craft spit into the sawdust and said he still had a few friends left in the world and he would find the wood.

A yard is not simply a hunk of wood rigged athwart the masts from which some optimistic sailor has hung some canvas. Not only must it be rounded off from the square timber, but it must taper gradually and according to a set pattern from the center toward each end. Then each yard, from the forecourse which is the lowest and largest, must be cut to the same design and successively smaller; so that the topgallant, which is the highest yard, will be of approximately one quarter the length and heft of its lowest shipmate. Moreover the yard ends and centers must be cut to accommodate the numerous metal fittings by which they are worked and hung. This is not a job for amateurs.

The Hamilton brothers owned the only wood lathe on the West Coast capable of turning timbers of such weight and length. When I first saw all four timbers stretched along the floor of the Hamilton loft, I was appalled, and when I watched 50 feet spinning like a candy-cane on the great lathe and saw the lesser-fingered brother resolutely apply a 3-foot-long chisel which bucked and jumped and sent off fountains of chips, I wondered at the daring of men engaged in the less spectacular pursuits. A diamond cutter risks not his life but his reputation when required to split a stone so precious he could not conceivably in his lifetime earn its worth. Yet he raises his hammer and hits, surely and smartly, catching his breath perhaps at the instant of impact, but outwardly as calm as a high-wire artist, a professional racing driver, or an astronaut. Now the Hamilton brothers move slowly along the length of that enormous whirling timber, pressing their chisels according as much to instinct as design, knowing full well that if they err they can never replace the wood they have removed.

Watching them I am ashamed of my own ineptness.

Daily I moved from one scene of activity to another, a man hopelessly caught up in his own devotions.

The ultimate failure which had been the inevitable outcome of our commercial fishing venture was as nothing compared to various forebodings which occasionally arrived to haunt me. Now I missed LaFrenier's unquenchable optimism, but he was happily employed at a safe distance inland and I had vowed not to tempt him. Once in his lifetime every man has at least the opportunity to commit a supreme folly and I had little doubt this was mine. Yet I knew it was now impossible to retreat. I must spin down in my own whirlpool trying to stay out of the vortex as long as possible.

In all of the junk shops and marine warehouses of San Francisco Bay we were able to find only one clew-iron and it belonged to the *Balclutha*, a former Alaska packer being restored by the Maritime Museum. So new ones had to be forged, along with iron hanks which I had always favored over clips for the smooth running of sails on a stay. And the hardware necessary to the four yards came to more than a truckload.

In his Sausalito loft Holcomb bent over his sewing machine

or sat on his bench engulfed by so much flax and canvas he seemed to sprout from it like a rock at half tide. It was always cold in his loft and his coughing worried me, but even on the most bitter days I found him sewing away. He was determined to finish a job he could view with pride and at the same time save me money by making the new square sails from the *Albatros*' spares. Holcomb's dark eyes would glisten with enthusiasm when he displayed how he had replaced a boltrope here, double strengthened a clew here, or cut the roach of the forecourse at a height to match my own, so that from the wheel I might see ahead. Through his eyes I could see the crumpled wavelets of canvas and flax about us set and pulling before the trades and the moments of my folly became glorious. I could not see that death was also in his eyes and that he wanted his work to survive him.

In the main shipyard Dickerhoff bossed a squad of riggers splicing, reeving, bending, and welding and riveting, in preparation for the day when the much altered foremast would be stepped.

In the secondary yard Teeny and his hapless assistant took more and more bits and pieces out of the engine room without putting anything back.

☼

TEN

If the ship be on the starboard Tack, close hauled, her Head North, of course the Wind at E.N.E., the Water tolerably smooth, and it be thought necessary to put about, and stand on the larboard Tack, everything being ready before: the first Precaution is (as indeed it should be at all times in steering by the Wind), to have her so suited with Sail as nearly to steer herself, with little assistance from the Rudder; by which management her way will be more powerful through the Water; she will be brought to the wind with a small Helm . . . and probably not have any Stern-way through the whole Rotation . . .

These gospel words thunder from the chapter entitled "Tacking Expeditiously" which is included in a mighty and durable work known as *The Young Sea Officer's Sheet Anchor.* It is a splendid book of nautical wisdom by one Darcy Lever, Esq., who desired to make life easier for ". . . the young Gentlemen of the Royal Navy, the Honourable East India Company . . . [who] . . . sometimes feel a diffidence in soliciting information; either from a fear of exposing their ignorance, or from an idea that such a request may be treated with ridicule."

In short it was intended to be a reference consulted in privacy, which I found it convenient to do. This jewel of maritime literature describes the intricacies of square-rigged sailing in rolling phrases to rival Gibbon. Reading it transports you back to 1819, the year its second edition was published, and as far as I could discover it is the only lucid treatment of the subject since that date. It saved me from making too many mistakes on the day the *Albatros* made her debut under square rig.

For at last the moment of truth had come and my grandest folly about to be exposed. Here was a ship of approximately 100 tons apparently ready in all respects for sea, and there just beyond the sheltering estuary a fine fresh wind was scuffling across San Francisco Bay. It was a Saturday and hence a union-proclaimed day of rest for Dickerhoff, who had grunted more ominously than usual on the night before and said he guessed he had done all he could do. I did not care to question him further as to the exact meaning of such a finality. Of course Dickerhoff knew very well that the Captain of this vessel had never commanded a square-rigger in his life, which may have been why, not wishing to witness disaster, he chose to stay home on this day.

To gain experience in a square rig of any size you must either be a foreign cadet (Japanese, Norwegian, Danish, Swedish, Spanish, Chilean, Portuguese, or German), or serve in the U.S. Coast Guard's *Eagle.* So I had to depend heavily on Lever's instructive companionship and upon Holcomb, whose nature being somewhat more tender than Dickerhoff's, caressed his dolphin-striker jaw and allowed as how there were enough menaces to navigation in the bay without turning me loose in a rig which at least *looked* complicated. To serve as crew I had assembled a heterogeneous group of people who believed that as I had managed to captain the *Albatros* all the way from Rotterdam without calamity, certainly an afternoon in the Bay should be a lark. I did not bother telling them how little I knew during a sort of rehearsal just before leaving the dock. It was easier demonstrating what I did know. I lectured slowly and with many repetitions, since I was aware that as soon as my supply of book learning was exhausted we would be obliged to sail.

Holcomb seated himself on the taffrail and watched me with a sort of bemused tolerance throughout the performance. I was aware that he shook his head in dismay several times and rolled one cigarette after another, possibly to keep his hands occupied so he wouldn't surrender to impulse and clamp them over my mouth.

I began by saying we could forget the mainsail, which remained exactly as it had been when the *Albatros* was a schooner and still functioned in the same way. Even those who sailed very small boats understood it. But now on the foremast . . .

I pointed out the four yards beginning at the highest, which was the topgallant, being careful in my newly acquired snobbery to pronounce it *t'*gallant. Captain Ahab might have been proud of me, but out of the corner of my eye I noticed a slight twitching about Holcomb's mouth as I explained that the t'gallant yard slid up and down a metal track which had been welded to the forward side of the mast in the German style.

Below the t'gallant was the upper topsail yard, which also slid on a metal track when being hoisted or lowered. Below it was the lower topsail yard, which was fixed in place vertically. The lowest and obviously the largest was the forecourse yard, which was also fixed.

When this brief tour was concluded I suggested that my audience should now climb aloft and have a look for themselves. "And don't be crawling through the lubber hole," I said with a swagger. I was pleased to see Holcomb's eyebrows rise and his dark eyes express both surprise and approval. Between the fore-course yard and the lower tops'l yard there was now a small platform welded to the mast. It was called the foretop and in olden times used not only for handling sail aloft, but as a perch for riflemen in battle. There was a hole cut through the decking of this platform on both sides of the mast through which were passed the yard halyards, buntlines, clew lines and sheets. It was also barely large enough for a man to squeeze through, if climbing to heights turned his blood to milk. The alternative was to use the futtock shrouds, which angled outward from the main shrouds to the perimeter of the foretop and thus obliged the sailor to climb about 45 degrees past the vertical. There was really nothing to it. To neophytes it just *looked* awful. I could not remember how far back in my lifetime I had read that anyone who crawled through a lubber hole was a farmer.

I took my hearties aloft and they were impressed with my movements because they did not know how many hours I had been playing monkey in this very jungle, or of a peculiar quirk in my nature which allowed me to be quite at ease at heights up to 100 feet. Perversely, anything above that altitude, such as the view from a high building, made my blood congeal. Sailing boats of the more modern design have long abandoned ratlines as a means of climbing aloft to the upper rigging. In fact it is out of fashion for sailors to go aloft at all and many boats would never be sold if the owner had to contemplate ever lifting his feet off the solid deck. With the great basic simplicity of modern sailing rigs, plus inherent material strengths, there is, in fact, little need for going aloft. The majority of repairs and maintenance can be done in some quiet harbor or shipyard, and whoever does the work is hoisted to his task in a bos'n's chair. This is all very fine until something parts or snarls at sea and then the fun begins. Every poor sailor who must then ride a chair aloft may do his own calculations as to the amount of "whip" created by a 60-foot stick swinging through an arc of 60 degrees while he clings to the end of it. At night it is unadulterated hell for those on deck trying to ease the strain on their comrade aloft, who is nearly helpless to accomplish anything but the most simple tasks. And for all concerned the whole operation can be exceedingly dangerous.

I have always been more comfortable in a vessel offering some permanent means of going aloft. Particularly for cruising, the added windage of shrouds and ratlines is canceled out by an added dividend in navigation. There is nothing quite so reassuring as a quick trip up the ratlines to spy an island or reef from which the deck would be invisible over the horizon, or to pick up a distant buoy, or navigate a difficult channel. The area visible to a sailor whose viewpoint is 10 feet above the water is a mere 3½ miles! Radar has improved the situation for those who can afford it, but radar cannot show the navigator a shoal or a rock awash.

There was certainly no lack of ratlines on the *Albatros*. The shrouds of both masts were wormed, parceled and served, and they were all used frequently at sea.

Climbing the lower foreshrouds was like walking up a giant staircase. The rigging was set up bar taut and the ratlines themselves were of solid oak so that even the most doubtful of our new crew felt secure. But once they had reached the foretop they found a change. To continue upward they must depend on "Lord Nelsons," which are simply hemp rope seized in ladder formation to the wire shrouds. Being of tender foot padding I had always detested Lord Nelsons, claiming they were for baboons; yet both Dickerhoff and Holcomb had said the *Albatros* would appear too heavy aloft if we used oak battens all the way, and they were right.

I was at least well qualified to demonstrate the proper way to climb any rigging regardless of its make-up, with the feet lightly on the ratlines and a firm handgrip on the shrouds themselves. "Then some wild night when you are up here and a ratline breaks . . . you'll still be here."

I also knew how to demonstrate how easy it is to go out on a yard and work—easy, that is, once you know how. I was aware that a new hand's first encounter with a yard is soured by a tremendous psychological block rooted in a natural human reluctance to leave the security of a tree's trunk for the end of a branch extending outward a considerable distance over nothing. It is also a fact that the footropes on a square yard are totally deceiving, it being inconceivable to the uninitiated that they could provide solid support.

I knew there was no use trying to tell them so . . . so just *go*!

The same people who would soon be swinging from mast to ratline as easily as stepping out their front doors now crept inch by inch toward their destination. There were a great many "after you's," and nervous laughter, and much time and effort lost fiddling with the arm beckets, which eventually became such a nuisance we cut them away.

The footrope of a yard is far more than a wobbly string hanging beneath a spar. To accommodate the average sailor it must be hung at 3 feet 6 inches below the yard; if lower, the sailor's weight is thrown out of balance, the footrope has excessive swing fore and aft, and about all anyone can do is hang on to the yard and curse; if too short, the sailor cannot adjust his body to the yard and maintain his fore-and-aft position unless he is a midget. The strange thing about footropes is that the right length *looks* much too short and feels so until you learn to trust your precious body in a rather ludicrous position.

It may be stated with some certainty that during a sailor's first trip out on a yardarm 99 percent of his energy is consumed in hanging on and the remaining 1 percent in looking about and wondering, What the hell am I doing up here? Yet in a surprisingly short time he stops trying to squeeze juice out of everything his hands, toes, and teeth can reach, he calms down and may soon become something other than decorative. He may even begin to enjoy his perch. Using his belly as a pad against the yard itself, he will venture ever larger rotations about its axis, so that when he leans far forward to reach down for a fistful of sail his feet swing up behind him on the footrope, then swing back again as he straightens and heaves up with both hands.

Good shipmates working together along a yard develop a rhythm so that their gyrations are synchronized, but we were a long way from such class and the mere task of letting go a few gaskets caused so much commotion along the yard the shouting sounded like a protest march. By the time we had reached the t'gallant yard and gone through the business of setting, clewing up, and securing all four square sails, most of the confusion had evaporated. Everyone agreed it was great for the waistline. I saw no reason to douse their enthusiasm with remarks about our ship's present position in flat, calm water and still moored firmly to the dock.

In the early afternoon we cast off and proceeded toward San Francisco Bay under the impetus of the supposedly resurrected African Queen. Enroute down the estuary we set the mainsail and rather smartly too, I thought, considering that the majority of the hands were new to the ship. While still in the protected waters we made for the yards and with only a minimum of delay cast off the gaskets on all four square sails.

By the time we had returned to the deck we were feeling the first surge of the Bay and I thought darkly that on this little shakedown voyage we could do with a bit less wind. But I looked at Holcomb perched like an owl on the taffrail and saw no hint of warning in his deep black eyes. Rather, knowing him so well, I thought there was approval in the smile which compressed his lips. He bent into the shelter of his pea-coat collar to roll a cigarette and suddenly I felt very alone; which I later realized was exactly how he wanted me to feel. Murmuring a review of Lever's historic instructions, I ordered the helmsman (who was a girl) to fall off before the wind. We would begin by setting the forecourse.

It took ages. And by the time we had the lower and upper tops'ls set, and the t'gallant, and were heaving up the foretopm'st-stay'l and then the inner jib, and finally the outer jib, I saw to my astonishment that we had almost run out of Bay. And if I had entertained any doubts about the speed of the *Albatros* under such conditions I could now forget them. The afternoon breeze had piped up to at least 20 knots and we were skating along at very close to 10.

We braced the yards around as hard as we could and then "feathered" them slightly, that is with the forecourse set hard against the shrouds and each yard above it spoked a trifle more into the wind. Thus the chance of being taken aback was greatly reduced since the helmsman had only to watch the t'gallant and hold a barely perceptible shiver in its leech. We were pointing as close to the wind as we could possibly go, and if the shiver increased it was only necessary to fall off a half-point or so.

So far all was well and Holcomb had not said a word. Nor had he moved from his perch, which was on the lee taffrail. I wondered if accident or tradition had caused him to settle there, since by historic custom the windward side of any quarter-deck was held the private domain of the Captain—phony or not.

Still panting from my exertions, I went to my mentor and

said with as much pride as if I had designed and built the *Albatros*, "She goes right along doesn't she?"

"She do."

Then I saw that Holcomb was not entirely with me. He was looking ahead to the horizon and his eyes remained fixed there as if directing mine toward the same target. And suddenly I realized that he was not only looking ahead, but thinking ahead, which in my excitement and preoccupation in this shakedown I had neglected to do.

Although we had managed to skirt the western shoals of the Bay and still hold the wind, I now saw how the distance between the *Albatros* and the long Richmond bridge was diminishing with alarming rapidity.

We did not have a speed log aboard, so I hailed the fast power cruiser which had been watching the show from just off our port quarter.

"How fast are we going?"

Her skipper removed the cigar from his mouth and glanced at the array of instruments before him.

"Twelve knots!" he shouted.

I obviously had very little time to comply with Mr. Lever's solemn dictum and have ". . . everything being ready before."

Moving closer to Holcomb for comfort, I said, "We'll have to come about in a few minutes."

"True. Unless you are awful mad at that bridge."

I had never seen a square-rigger coming about, hence I had been dreading this moment for months. It is one thing to read of a maneuver and have it all fixed in your own mind and quite something else to have all the right bodies in the right place doing the right thing at the right time. A fore-and-aft-rigged vessel missing stays or caught in irons during the labor of passing from one tack to another can be embarrassing enough, but somehow I had whelped the notion that a square-rigger badly handled might result in an actual calamity. At least I knew more than the crew. I had read a book.

Our rate of closure with the bridge was now augmented by the swift tide south of its approaches. If we should miss stays and be caught aback it was very obvious the combination of tide and wind would carry us right against the bridge before we could fall away and get organized again. In my nervousness I sent a man below to stand by the African Queen.

At last all was in readiness with the crew spotted about the ship according to Holcomb's soft-spoken suggestions. Two men were forward to cast off and then belay the headsail sheets. They would also cast off the forecourse tacks and belay the opposite one when we had passed through the eye of the wind. There were four men in the waist, two on each side to cast off the lee yard braces and heave in on their opposites. We had deliberately refrained from setting the mid and main stays'l for which conservatism I was now very grateful.

There were no winches on the *Albatros* except for the ancient contraption employed to raise her anchors. The mainsheet was hauled on a threefold purchase, so that with wind of any strength sheeting in the main became all two strong men could manage. This afternoon, with only Holcomb and myself available for the task, my apprehension was such I fancied I could do it alone. For here was the bridge, all concrete and steel and hardly a cable's length away. Still Holcomb failed to send me any signal that the time had come.

We sheeted in the main as taut as we were able, which caused the girl on the helm to complain she was almost hard over and running out of strength. I told her to swallow a silence pill and she said something about the difference between sailors and gentlemen. I didn't care. The bridge was right there on the end of the *Albatros'* jibboom, about to be speared just as the police boat had been in far off Maassluis, Holland.

I wanted to close my eyes.

When I was certain it was too late Holcomb said quietly, "Perhaps you might care to bring her to now."

"Helm down!" I yelled. The girl let the spokes fly and gradually the bow swung around toward the wind. The headsails began to thunder and I called for their sheets to run free. We slacked the mainsheet as the deck became level. All of this was easy—standard procedure for any fore-and-aft rig, but now under square rig we were about to take on some very special education.

The *Albatros* had lost nearly all her way and I feared we were surely in irons.

Then I saw that a marvelous thing was happening and from that moment became a confirmed devotee of the square rig. For instead of doddering around on the opposite tack like a schooner or ketch, gradually losing turning momentum until you sometimes wondered if the old bucket would get around at all, the turning speed of the *Albatros* was rapidly increasing. The square sails, all of them now aback, were shoving her bow around as if a powerful tug were at work beneath her weather bow.

Holcomb was watching the t'gallant, then his eyes followed the mast down to the course. "Whenever you're ready," Holcomb said to me and nodded toward the men in the waist. They had been standing like actors waiting for a cue, the yard braces in their hands with only a single turn around the pins.

"Midships!" I called to the helm.

Then cupping my hands, I yelled toward the waist, *"Let go and haul!"*

The ancient cry of the square-rigger maneuvering.

I felt self-conscious using it, an altar boy presuming to say the mass. I wanted to reach for my cocked hat, peg leg, and spyglass, and I could not put down a sense of great pride, because there were the yards swinging around of themselves and the men in the waist speeding them and checking their progress with the lee and weather braces, and one by one the square sails were filling, the t'gallant first, then the upper tops'l with a glorious boom, then the lower tops'l, and when the big course rose up against the forestay until the tacks were boused down and it became as curvaceous and full as the ass of a sultana; and when I saw that all of the square sails were pulling with a power that seemed to actually live, I wanted to cry out my exhilaration. Instead I managed a casual air so that the legendary coolness of square-rigger masters, whether truth or fiction, would not be desecrated by me.

Rigged as a schooner with the typical European depth of hull forward, the *Albatros* had been a slob to bring about and had sometimes barely made it. Now she was a new creature, vigorous and alive. I looked aft and could barely believe the apparent area consumed in our maneuver. We had come about in very little more than our own length this first time and I wondered at the feats we might accomplish once we had some continuous practice. And I realized suddenly that we were shamefully overmanned. British coasters of similar size and rig had often been sailed by two men and a boy.

During the next hour we remained within the upper reaches of the Bay and came about half a dozen times with varying degrees of finesse. There were other maneuvers I wanted to try, particularly heaving-to, but the evening fog was already oozing through the Golden Gate and my crew of assorted businessmen, students, and yachtsmen had to report back to their real world of wives, study, and landlocked tribulations. Most of them would never sail in a square-rigger again.

Our finale for the day was performed where we had begun, just off the mouth of the estuary, and neatly canceled out the strutting conceit with which we had been infected. The time had come to douse our square sails, and we discovered almost at once how desperately we needed actual experience. I blessed Holcomb for recommending we keep ample searoom, for without it our general bungling might have brought about any one or several of the serious misfortunes which had long haunted me. As it was, the process of dousing and furling only four square sails, none of which was large enough for a Cape Horner to blow his snoot in, took us one hour and a half. From a distance the exhibition must have caused old sailors to weep in mortification and it was a miracle someone was not hurt or gear damaged. With the evening had come a hard, no-nonsense wind sweeping between the city wharves and Treasure Island and those on the yards found life vastly different than they had expected. The booming, recalcitrant sails were only partly to blame for our mass ineptness and confusion as we discovered one of the inherent *dis*advantages of the true square rig. The ulcer of exasperation quickly spread over the entire area of the foremast because it originated at the fife rail where all the sheets, buntlines, downhauls, clew lines, and tacks terminated. All of the lines were new, and well soaked with spray taken aboard during the afternoon. Now they were stiff, swollen, and ran through even the best fair-leads with a reluctance that was maddening. Although we had been at considerable pains to make up each line carefully and place it on the pin marked with its name, somehow there had been a mix-up and when we heaved on a downhaul we would find we were hanging on a buntline, or when we wanted to free a sheet and let it run, a buntline aloft would let go instead and the resulting explosion of sail would nearly shake the men off the yard. The more we sought to unravel the situation the worse we seemed to make it. It was as if all the crew had become apprentices to a nautical sorcerer, and I certainly became Captain Confusion. The t'gallant yard would only come halfway down, the port lower tops'l sheet was jammed taut somewhere in the maze aloft and, defying any gravitational possibility, the starboard clew garnet on the course had somehow wrapped itself around the end of the yard.

In his grandest manner Holcomb left the despair to me and I in turn passed it on to a certain McDowall, whose nature was such that he could deal with such matters without losing aplomb. It was he who eventually made order out of the spilled spaghetti of lines which dribbled about the foredeck.

McDowall was a marvelously complex man and we had been fishmates for a season in the bone-racking *Mike*. He was very tall and very strong, blond, blue-eyed, and soft of voice. He often affected the manner of a simpleton, even occasionally allowing his jaw to fall slack while he pondered a problem. "Humph!" he would say as if the simplest matter was past his comprehension. Yet only hasty strangers fell for McDowall's private amusement. While he hemmed and hawed and scratched his head and confessed his utter bewilderment with whatever challenge was at hand, those who knew McDowall were not deceived. We knew he was an expert carpenter, a wizard plumber, a born mechanic, and among other things a first-class baker. It was fascinating to watch McDowall in the *Mike*'s galley, his great arms writhing like a pair of boa constrictors as he kneaded dough, or his powerful hands employed more tenderly when he plucked a straw from the deck broom and tested a cake.

When at last we made the calm of Oakland's estuary and all was once more shipshape and Bristol fashion about the ship, I called McDowall aft. Knowing he must be unwary and fatigued from his labors, I struck him between the eyes with an invitation I hoped he could not resist.

I asked him if he would care to serve as First Mate on a voyage to the South Seas.

He kicked a few invisible pebbles across the deck, scratched his head thoughtfully, and claimed he didn't rightly know just where the South Seas might be. So to please him, I solemnly explained where they were.

"Humph," he said when I had done gesturing toward the western horizon. "A body just might have a hankerin' to try it."

☼

IN HARBOR

The Danish sun is visible this morning. It has neglected the island of Bornholm for so long that we risk blindness in rejoicing at its reappearance.

It is not a mellow sun, rather it is like a polished brass plate resting on a Danish mantel, and people should be blinking at it through the windows of an oak-paneled room while they drink mead and smoke clay pipes.

Our room is the Black Watch, *which remains comfortable confinement as long as we do not remind ourselves that a sailing vessel is the world's most expensive way to travel third class.*

I think we may be going a little crazy. We are beginning to laugh at very little things which are not especially funny . . . and laughing too long. I have seen this sort of thing happen before and do not like the way it reminds me of the ever so brittle barrier separating the sane from the insane. This shocking revelation may be evident any time or place there are too many persons per square foot, which is inevitably true of small craft long delayed in port. Now my own laughter has a way of becoming falsetto.

Our salute to the sun is a mere formality, since it slithers behind some conveniently placed clouds after less than a minute, shyly, as if frightened at such adoration and we sense that it does not dare come out again. So I take my dog Felix, help him over the neighbor's sewer pipe, which is the only surface he has been unable to negotiate in all his life, and we start off toward the outskirts of Rønne where we will go for a land sail. We did not invent this sport; all little boys and some little girls are good at it, but thanks to our special climatic environment we have been able to attempt some otherwise impossible maneuvers. Felix is handicapped because he has no coat except his natural one, but he is much lighter than I am and when he leaps in the air this wind transports him horizontally as much as a yard. He is absolutely delighted with the game. By opening my coat and spreading my arms wide, I can also perform some fancy aerobatics particularly if I run against the wind. Felix can land-sail indefinitely while I am soon out of breath, and this morning I quit on the brow of a cliff which is to the south of Rønne harbor and overlooks the open Baltic.

The cliff is about 100 feet high and from that lofty position I can see a good way. The sea looks like my Aunt Moselle's embroidered tablecloth because everywhere it is more white than any other color and the threaded interlaced design is extremely complicated. But I am weary of comparing it with Aunt Moselle's handiwork. Hola! There is no hope in the panorama before me nor is there a boat or a ship of any kind in sight. It is so empty and depressing that I find it distracting to form various sizes of holes with my lips and by turning my head at right angles to the wind, endeavor to play a tune. Is it proof of my approaching insanity that I consider my performance virtuoso? Felix does this all the time although I think he is simply aerating his lungs or letting the wind flap his tongue. Now he is watching me contort my mouth in this strange fashion and his expression again reminds me to be grateful of my every breath. Some deep instinct compels all dogs to tell their friends how happy they are to be alive, so how can I dare be less aware? To hell with this Baltic gale. At sea it might unnerve me, but here in the safety of the land it presents a precious opportunity to review certain days of butterflies and ravens far away in the mighty Pacific.

☼

IV

THE *ALBATROS*

☼

. . . HER DAYS OF OCEANIC BUTTERFLIES
AND RAVENS

☼

ELEVEN

THE Pacific is not like any other ocean, regardless of its salt content or liquid mass. The Pacific is too big for ordinary minds to comprehend and too feminine for many men to understand. To some its enormity is more depressing than inspiring and its utterly female behavior can become very trying. There are really too many Pacifics and it is a shame the vastness is not divided up into distinctly named oceans for easier reference. At some time in its history an attempt was made to identify and separate the areas, but it was only a three-quarter try and the resulting nomenclature was a North Pacific, a South Pacific, and a Western Pacific. Somehow the possibility of an Eastern Pacific was ignored.

The Pacific is as feminine as the Atlantic is masculine, and the temperaments of both oceans seem to have penetrated to the marrow of the peoples inhabiting their islands, so that there is only a basic anthropological resemblance between Icelanders and Tahitians, or Azorians and Gilbertese—they are all recognizable as human beings.

Even the coloration of those great oceans seems to have gender. The Pacific is inclined to gayer hues although the pastel days seem dull indeed compared to the extravaganzas presented each dawn and twilight. We know that it is mainly the sky that colors whatever body of water lies beneath it and this is usually true unless we are observing clear shallows. But what of the depths, far beyond the shoals, where bottom character cannot influence the mass any more than can the band of man's junk and excrement which crusts our shores? There too in the wastes of the great oceans the color schemes remain faithful to gender.

The deepwater man's euphoric sense of removal begins when he passes into these vast regions of purity and endures most heartily until once again the poisons of sea and atmosphere merge into a shore line. Then he knows that his troubles will begin.

We sailed west through the Golden Gate on a glittering August noon. Holcomb and Dickerhoff and Pasquinucci and many others, including a coterie of local conquests that Rogerts the cook had made during his seven-month stay in port, bade us farewell from the shore. The wind and tide were fair, we dropped the guano-streaked Farallon Islands over the horizon just at twilight and the process of removal began among our ship's people. There was Gratiot, a dedicated surgeon who had so overworked himself he resembled a cadaver, and Yates, who had sailed in the *Albatros* from Rotterdam. There was the redoubtable Peter Dawson, who had become as much a fixture of the *Albatros* as her keel. There was Johnson, an ex-submariner, and McCullough, who had agreed to share duty in the engineering department. There was Atcheson an ex-frogman and the two now-experienced girl voyagers, Post and Henderson, who had sailed in the *Albatros* from Curaçao to San Francisco. Both could hand, reef, and steer. There was Hall, a total stranger who had applied for a berth with such perseverance I could not in the end refuse, and McDowall's wife, whose Alice-in-Wonderland manner was belied by her astonishing strength. There was son George, on leave from the Maritime Academy, who intended a career of the sea.

We were too many and the quarters below were anything but spacious, yet by the second morning the other world of the ocean took over and reasonable contentment prevailed. I was also a citizen in this deep-sea civilization although as captain not nearly so carefree as the others.

The sailing-ship route from San Francisco to Honolulu is over 2,000 miles and may be sailed by a timorous old lady in a well-found bathtub. Particularly in summer the weather is benign and the principal hazard is ennui. Therefore it is wise to have a good cook along, above all, a cook with imagination, for there are no available restaurants to relieve the martyrdom of monotony, and in easy weather ship morale is directly related to the belly. Let the cook be athletic, for even in an easy sea his task must be accomplished with one hand for the saucepan and one for himself. Let the cook be of angelic nature and of great humor lest the barbs which inevitably spring from smart-tongued clients after many days at sea cause him artistic distress and lead to menus of tapioca pudding, porridge and kale. Let the cook have a fetish for personal hygiene, since there is nothing quite like universal bowel complaint in a world of one head and a population of several; and let the cook most of all have a deep sense of service so that he will not feel abused when required to rise long before the sun and his shipmates to prepare breakfast. With such a paragon in the galley we can all sail to heaven.

Rogerts, who had been with us since Rotterdam, was imperfect and magnificent. We devoured his cakes on sight and the *bami* he had learned to cook in Indonesia was always memorable. If his fingernails were not always surgically clean, and if occasionally he wiped a plate with the same gray rag he used to swab the galley deck, it was of little consequence against his feasts. Their excellence never varied, though at times he often slid wildly from one side of his galley to the other in his bare feet, balancing pots and pans against the gyrations of the sea. Nor did the monumental hangovers he acquired in every port ever mar his eggs soufflé.

When we were almost 1,000 miles from any land I went for a row in our jolly boat which was 9 feet long. There was not a breath of wind and the Pacific was like a great sheet of highly polished metal. I rowed around and around photographing the *Albatros* against the gigantic cumulus clouds as one would a new bride, and then trying for artistic variety by posing her reflected in the mirror of the ocean. She presented a spectacular if discouraging picture of a sailing ship becalmed. Every rag she possessed was set in anticipation of wind that had failed to arrive and from my near-sea-level point of view she looked enormous.

Watching her now, caressing the water only occasionally with the oars to hold the jolly boat in position, I fell into a pool of maudlin sentimentality and nearly drowned before I was able to emerge. Yes, I was still in love, more so than I had been at first sight in Rotterdam. Yet how could a supposedly sensible man honestly profess love for an inanimate thing of steel and wood and plant fiber? I knew that in history other men had also lost themselves to individual ships, many choosing to share the death of their beloved rather than accept certain rescue, and I had doubted if the hoary tradition about captains going down with their ships had anything to do with it. No—I thought it must be something else and if I could understand it I might discover the secret of love itself. I thought of those friends who had fallen hopelessly in love with women of widely regarded beauty, charm, and glamour, although to me they were overscented hags of no use whatsoever. They disdained work of any kind and I had long suspected even their bedroom activities must always be a compromise between passion and caution lest some wisp of hair be disarranged. Yet they managed to keep their victims happy and content in their masochism long after their original beauty had decayed. How then, I had often wondered, could this be except that the man was in love and all men loved with their hearts and not with their minds.

My love was now a deteriorating anachronism with a broken engine, yet from just the right distance my eyes erased the rust forming along her hull plates and the here and there patches in her sails, and my eyes gave to her certain beauty marks which were either not there at all, or which others were unlikely to observe. This I knew was the processing of love for either a woman or a ship and I had willingly contributed to my own bewitchment ever since my very first siren, which I had christened the *Liberty*. In the once-upon-a-time she had been a cement-mixing trough with wooden sides and a tin bottom turned up at both ends. But in my young mariner's eye she was a craft of stunning beauty, and with the help of two friends I rigged a mast and for a sail one of us found a bed sheet which he claimed his mother did not want. We launched the *Liberty* in Lake St. Clair, which is some 4 miles in length and about the same in breadth. The wind was fair and we ran splendidly before it, shouting our joy at the *Liberty*'s speed. But as the shore retreated, the size of the waves quickly increased and the *Liberty* began to fill with their slop. The opposite shore was still far away when we realized our rejoicing must cease and bailing begin. We did our utmost, but then and there I learned certain elements of marine architecture and have never changed my mind. Give me a boat with a rudder large enough to hold her true before wind and wave and give me a keel of enough depth and weight to keep her right side up. The *Liberty* had neither attribute and when we were approximately in the middle of Lake St. Clair she capsized before an ordinary puff of the summer wind. We were a long way from any shore.

The wooden sides of the *Liberty* kept her afloat and we had sense enough to remain with her instead of trying to swim for dry land. We yelled our lungs out, together and separately, and now so far away in time and geography I can still hear our dreadful wailing of the word all people reach for when despair approaches—Help! . . . Help!

After a time we became too tired to yell so we fell quiet and it was then that a speedboat appeared only a few yards away. They hauled us aboard and while we stood shivering told us they had not heard our calling, but had only chanced along. There was not another boat to be seen anywhere on the lake.

As we sped away from the disaster of my first command, I watched the sunlit waves sloshing across her tin bottom and I wept.

At the time, I was eleven; the others were nine and seven—going-on-a-half. Now paddling around the *Albatros* I could still hear our thin little voices contesting the seas and the wind.

There had been many other sirens since that ill-starred summer but none to compare with the *Albatros*. The only one who had proved totally incomparable was the little *Restless*. She had foundered in San Francisco Bay only a short time before I became her owner and her bilges were still plugged with mud and slime. The *Restless* was not *quite* as rotten as the *Raccoon* had been, but then, at the time I bought her she was a mere seventy-six years of age. Her first service had been as a dispatch boat for the lighthouses around San Francisco Bay and she had all the classic lines of her era. She was 30 feet in length, extraordinarily graceful of line, and sat on the water like a little swan. Originally she had been propelled by a weak naptha engine. She was very slim of beam and her underbody flow was a gently undulating pattern. As a consequence, she moved if you sneezed. I thought she might suit a steam engine better than any conceivable modern power plant and soon a tall stack sprouted behind her curved pilothouse. I knew nothing of steam power except that I liked both its comparative silence and its talent for hooting melodiously if you pulled a lanyard. I bought a 10-horsepower steam engine, a boiler, and some coal.

Fortunately, before I blew up the *Restless*, she was overwhelmed with steam aficionados, who are not unlike the early Christians in total dedication. They are a sect rather than a group and they believe so utterly in steam power they will go to endless trouble to demonstrate its virtues.

Cruising about San Francisco Bay in a steamboat is a delightful experience if you don't mind a maximum speed of 5 knots, soot on decks and passengers, and have a faithful shipmate stoking the fire with wood or coal below and making very certain the boiler has enough water to avoid overpressure yet not so much that the pressure falls. Because if it is allowed to fall you wait until it comes back up again no matter what your plan. It is something like making a good cappuccino.

It is all very well to claim steam power is simplicity itself, but a properly seaworthy little steamboat requires much love, constant attention, mechanical knowledge of considerable degree, a private machine shop, and special skill in working metals. I had only love for the *Restless* but was only a passable stoker. I soon discovered that I was diplomatically guided toward other tasks by the aficionados who were ever present aboard. Somehow they sensed when I planned a day's outing and without formal notice all would be in readiness when I arrived.

"G' day, Cap! Had steam up for over an hour. Everything's percolating and we're ready to toot."

So I would step aboard with clean hands and leave with clean hands and I could sniff at the strange, tangy odor of oil mixed with steam and coal dust which is the sovereign narcotic of steam buffs, and I could steer where I pleased and blow the whistle if it took the wistfulness from my face. But that was all I could do without creating uneasiness among the aficionados. They knew well enough that the heart of the *Restless,* the true action, was in the engine room, which had no space for mere observers. Subtly, without evil intent, the *Restless* was being pirated from beneath my very feet. I knew it and was helpless to stop it. Eventually I sold her to a band of steam people. It was merely a gesture since they had taken her over anyway.

Now, rowing around the *Albatros*, I stood up in the jolly boat to try for a different photographic angle and saw that on the opposite side some of our crew had decided the *Albatros*' nearly stationary position provided an ideal opportunity for a mid-ocean swim. Peevishly I told them to climb back aboard. There had been no sharks in Lake St. Clair where the *Liberty* had sunk, but this was ocean. It might be very well, I thought, for skin-divers to punch certain sharks in the nose (or so they claimed), but no one as yet could tell a fat shark from a hungry one until it was too late. I remembered the limerick:

> There was a young lady from Guam,
> Who said, "The Pacific's so calm,
> I'll swim for a lark . . ."
> She met a large shark . . .
> Let us all sing the ninety-third psalm.

I saw the swimmers clambering back aboard like scolded children and I knew they were resentful because it was wretchedly hot and there was little to do except chip away at the scrofulous rust which forever cursed the *Albatros* like every steel vessel, or they could try to sleep, which was difficult in the heat, or sit about the deck and listen to the continuous and nerve-racking squeaks, rattles, moans and sighs which are the irritating cacophony of any sailing vessel becalmed.

When the swimmers had disappeared, I looked again through the view finder of my camera and had a haunting sensation that I was photographing another *Marie Celeste*. Since there was no awning over the foredeck, it was naturally deserted and no one was required aft at the helm. The shadows were deep beneath the awning we had stretched amidships, and in the view finder there was no sign of life.

There was, I hoped, more activity in the engine room, where despite oven temperatures Johnson and McCullough were striving to remedy our assorted heritages from the talentless Teeny. There was no separate fault to find with Teeny's work on the African Queen and her consort machinery—*all* of it was bad and some of the things we found were nearly incredible. We kept a special envelope filled with a random selection of the things we found in the crankcase of the African Queen. Eventually, when we finally sent it off to Teeny with a copy of his bill for "complete and major overhaul," the envelope included several oil-soaked cigarette butts, solidified carbon clinkers of handy nugget size, a length of copper wire, two washers that fit nothing whatsoever, and a fractured cotter pin. It was obvious Teeny had not even bothered to change the oil and it was a tribute to the African Queen that she had run even for a time in spite of him. Teeny had also supposedly overhauled the main shaft bearing, which had developed a tendency to overheat even at reduced speeds. After the second fire alarm caused by a smoke-filled ship we found that if we poured heavy oil into the bearing box every change of watch it would stay reasonably cool. The task was additionally aggravating because whoever poured the oil had to lie on his belly with his chin between the bottom step of the companionway ladder and the deck. He held a flashlight clenched between his teeth while he reached out at arm's length and held the oil spigot over the gear box. The necessary physical contortions to complete the task and the slippery mess when inevitably some oil was spilled caused Teeny's name to be mentioned colorfully.

I paddled around the *Albatros* for nearly an hour photographing as if my subject were a bride posed before Niagara Falls. And I tried to convince myself that this unnatural devotion to her every weary rivet was merely an infatuation and that soon a younger siren of less extravagant needs would come along and I would be able to walk away from her without so much as a backward glance. How unreal, I thought ruefully, for a man to invest nearly all the worldly wealth he has been able to acquire in a haggard rust-bucket which no one else would ever want. It was like having drunk too lustily and awakening to the vague memory of having met a stranger during the night's carousing and discovering her in bed beside you the next morning. There she was, revealed as a rather tarnished beauty old enough to have accumulated an abundance of personal problems for which there would never be any solution. Yet one could flee from a rumpled bed and become a monk. Here in the Pacific there was no escape.

"You old bitch!" I whispered. "Your butt is covered with barnacles and your bosom sags with weed. Your limbs are scarred with wear and your hair is dyed with rust. You are demanding and expensive and uncomfortable to live with . . ."

Suddenly, as if my rebellion could have been heard, I switched with chameleon ease from scorn to finding excuses or cures for all of her imperfections. And in moments I was so re-enchanted

I allowed the jolly boat to drift under her counter where I sat in the shade bemused at my facile self-deception. This absurd relationship between a man and his vessel would be better called a fetish than love, yet what in the end was the difference?

Later when I had cooled and quieted my doubts I rowed into the sunlight again and passed along the *Albatros*' hull until I was abeam of her lifeboats. I had been wanting to look up at them from this low angle and try to visualize how, if the *Albatros* lay hard over to one side or the other, we would ever succeed in launching the higher boat. The prospect had concerned me ever since the redesign had taken the boats off the deck and placed them up on gallows. I knew only too well how unforgiving the sea could be; consequently there was nothing carefree about the way the *Albatros* was inspected from keel to truck by the officer of each watch. His findings were recorded in the logbook as seriously as if we carried a thousand passengers. Fire drill was held twice a week and it was repeated until everyone aboard knew his exact station and action. Lifeboat drill had been carefully worked out according to the personalities and skills of our ship's people. Each lifeboat was equipped to support the entire ship's company for a long time if necessary; there was fresh water and nourishing food in sealed tanks, navigational and medical equipment, plus mast, sails, rudder, and oars for each boat to reach the nearest land. I had often sailed the lifeboats simply for the pleasure of it. In spite of their heaviness they sailed well and while it would hardly be a pleasure cruise I would not hesitate to cross half an ocean in one.

If all had not been made as safe as possible I could not have slept until it was. But I knew very well we would have a terrible time launching both boats unless the *Albatros* happened to be on an even keel. All we could do was to persist in the hard work of our lifeboat drills. The first day out of San Francisco it had taken us thirty minutes to have a boat slung out and ready for launching. By the second day we had cut the time down to ten minutes. We were still trying to achieve five minutes, which seemed about the minimum possible. I knew only too well that in a real emergency unforeseen hindrances would certainly increase the time and only hoped our adrenalin glands would create enough zeal to balance things out.

Before every sailing I had called all of those aboard aft regardless whether they were veterans or not. The speech which I had delivered so often it was nearly memorized was waspish and old-maidish as I could make it.

"There is nothing that belongs to this ship which cannot be replaced, but we cannot go to a marine store and buy new fingers, arms, or heads, so never forget the invisible power of the block and tackle or the heft of swinging gear. They can make a terrible mess of you. There is one great danger which is part of going to sea in small craft. Be sure you are on very intimate terms with God before you fall overboard, because the next voice you'll hear after you can't yell any more will probably be His. Even if we know you are gone the chances of our stopping, launching a boat, finding your precious little head bobbing around between ocean waves, and picking you up successfully are about one hundred to one in the daytime and one thousand to one at night."

Perhaps my statistics were somewhat pessimistic, and it was true that in recent years a few miraculous rescues had been made of people who had fallen overboard from small craft. But those few were the real favorites of God. We had smoke buoys, light buoys, and a thorough drilling on how to organize and keep track of a departed crew member in the water, and yet I had a minimum of confidence in finding anything without a powerful assist from luck. If I had any secret fears about the *Albatros* it was to hear the dreadful clanging of the alarm bell followed by "Man overboard!"

I rowed along to the sun-baked side of the *Albatros* listening to the lackadaisical chinking of rust hammers from the bow. As I passed parallel to the waist awning I heard someone in the shadows plucking at a guitar. It would be Durst, who was also off watch, and he would be lying in the beautifully worked hammock which he had made for himself, with his guitar across his bare chest. Although I could not see over the bulwarks I knew that Henderson, who was also fond of hammocks, would be swinging gently in her own nearby, because I heard her sing a few bars to accompany Durst's melancholy chords in her frail but always true voice. And I thought how fortunate we were to have Durst as Second Mate. He was very spare, quiet and intelligent and like all the others on board, except Rogerts the cook, was paid in food and grog and fresh air; but in every sense he was a professional seaman. Although he had just been graduated from the California Maritime Academy, his maritime education was far more extensive than any school could ever offer. When I first observed his navigational work I thought unhappily that he might be cheating, which is easy enough to do with a celestial fix. When there is nothing to see for hundreds of miles about, it is very tempting to ease your lines of position the mere width of a pencil point closer and thus display a more accurate fix—on paper. Durst had no need of such humbug. His near-perfect fixes were the genuine result of skill and utter devotion to the art. I had never before or since seen such work on a plotting sheet and my own rather carelessly drawn fixes were becoming embarrassing. And as if this young Second Mate were not enough competition McDowall had become remarkably proficient, although he was very shy about displaying his work in public.

Now I could hear someone pounding metal in the engine room, and looking aft I saw McDowall's head appear above the taffrail. He searched the horizon a moment as if expecting to see a distant ship and then pretended to discover me only a few yards away. In two strokes of the oars I was directly beneath him.

"Good day," he said as if we were in foreign vessels met for a mid-ocean gam. He shone with perspiration and he stuck out his tongue and panted in imitation of a dog who had run a long way. Then he said, "They're predicting a victory in the engine room. If they actually get the Queen started can I get under way?"

I asked him if he would mind waiting for me to get aboard.

"Not unless you put more water in the grog. Otherwise," he said, sweeping the horizon with a careless gesture, "the nearest land is that way."

"How about putting a little less grog in the Mate?"

The inference was deliberate because throughout this steaming day McDowall had been suffering from a certain lack of respect for the concoction now stored below in two 50-gallon casks. I had no longer been able to afford catering to individual tastes during the traditional Bardinet hour and had caused a certain refreshment to be created, the formula for which we dared not divulge lest it frighten the timid. It was intended to be used sparingly so it would last the voyage, and those who had ridiculed its powers were learning one by one. Fortunately McDowall's thirst for grog was not as powerful as his thirst for knowledge. It often seemed that his mind was equipped with a miraculous device which always placed one fact on top of the other in orderly array and after a brief ceremony (while he "humphed" to measure) it selected the logical combination of all related facts and placed them at their owner's disposal. Thus it took McDowall only a week to become a competent celestial navigator although he had never seen the related books of tables or held a sextant to his eye before. Watching his performance as he was introduced to the sun and the stars and the moon was like presenting a friend to a friend of a friend and standing back to see them become immediate mellow company.

McDowall would spread his long legs to brace himself against the roll of the *Albatros* and regard his sextant as if it might explode. Then he would "humph" a time or two and say, "Now which end does a body look through?" He knew perfectly well how to bring the sextant to his eye, but his preliminary playing of the eternal dunce somehow served to cleanse his mind of extraneous matters and he could proceed to the subsequent problem on iron rails. If it were a star he proposed to shoot he would inspect the evening sky as if he were surprised to see it really overhead and he would say, "How can a body tell which one is which? Can't I just take a scatter shot of several stars and sort of average them out?"

Having taught celestial navigation to people whose graduation time varied from two weeks to never, I marveled at McDowall's ability to comprehend the heavens after such hasty schooling and then reduce their information to a small criss-cross of lines on paper indicating the ship's position. I remembered with a certain smarting how laborious and bumbling my own early attempts had been and wondered at the mammoth difference in the receptive capacities of men.

Not long after the African Queen's resurrection we came into the trade winds and this time they lived up to their name. We bowled along in fine style with the wind steadily behind our left ears and the nights warm enough for the determined hammock sleepers to take their rest on deck. There was considerable fancy work done about the quarter-deck with Turk's heads below the compass, French hitching on the telegraph pedestal; and Post made a new bell rope which might have graced a smart clipper. The sea routine of day and night was now so well established it was difficult to recall when there had been other customs and habits. All of our ship's people were in superb health and Gratiot, the former cadaver, lost a year for every day that passed. His services were required only once, when a heavy hatch cover slammed down on Rogerts and made an ugly gash in his scalp. After the stitching was done the Dutchman merely shrugged his shoulders and went whistling back to his galley.

On the twenty-first dawn we were speeding down Molokai channel before a fine fresh trade and by noon we were partly redeeming our slow passage by making 12 knots across the spectacular stage which extends seaward from the city of Honolulu.

"Is this what you call the South Seas?" McDowall asked as Waikiki beach slid by only a mile or so inshore.

"You might say it's the entrance," I answered.

McDowall stared at the building-studded beach and at the backdrop of hills beyond with their patchworks of houses spreading up to the clouds. I knew McDowall had at least passed through Honolulu during the Second War, but he was in many ways a strange man and if he wished to pretend he had never seen it before I was too concerned with our tardy moment of triumph to either chide or challenge him. For now in the time of thrilling noon light every sail on our ship was hauling magnificently, all of our pennants and flags were snapping in the wind, and friendly explosions of sea glistened over the weather rail to refresh us. Our ship was stout, our people all well, and one more long voyage was history in our log. In my pagan way I whispered a prayer of gratitude. Then I saw that McDowall was still staring at the face of Honolulu.

"Looks like some kind of a skin disease," he said quietly, "and it's spreading."

☼

TWELVE

McDowall's scathing opinion of Honolulu was not voiced from any sense of superiority or even lack of appreciation. He was simply anticipating the shock which at first astounds and then numbs all sailors who return from their world to what has become the world of other men. Whatever their nationality and wherever sailors may sail, the Rip Van Winkle story becomes their own.

All of the extended passages I have ever made in any of the sirens, whether for commerce or pleasure, ended with the identical pantomime and the cast included every soul on board. A day or so before reaching port there would be a great primping and grooming of shore clothes and the body was lavished with attention. A very few minutes after the vessel was secured to the wharf an assembly of total strangers appeared momentarily on deck and then disappeared in the direction of the local settlement as fast as they could go. Perhaps two days would pass, although the interval was greatly influenced by the size of the port and the complexity of the sailor's tie with the land. Sooner or later they would come dribbling back to the ship, weary and vaguely troubled, although their activities ashore might have been most innocent. Most were strangely thoughtful and subdued as if their excursion to the landsman's world had revealed something they feared to question yet could not understand, and soon enough the entire complement would be back on board nestling comfortably into the routine environment they knew. Most could not be persuaded to go beyond the length of the wharf again and they lived in a state of suspended animation until the vessel sailed once more. At the next port the entire return to the womb performance was repeated, which eventually convinced me that the average sailor's shoreside binge was a very ephemeral affair.

We stayed in Honolulu only long enough to part with some of our crew, renew our stores, and be tattooed.

Teeny's workmanship could not be undone despite our best efforts, for he was a genius in his way, a master bungler quite incapable of petty neglects, and as a consequence what he had wrought in the engine room was fundamental rather than superficial. Putting things mechanically to rights in the *Albatros* would mean starting all over again and I could afford neither the expense nor the delay. I had been obliged to take all blame upon myself since I had left the rosette-nosed Teeny so much on his own. It seemed best to pretend the machinery was simply not there.

On the morning of our sailing the wind was just right for executing a plan which I had kept to myself lest some more prudent person succeed in discouraging me. Although my square-rig confidence had firmed, it was still far from ready to withstand any reasonable argument and the faithful *Young Sea Officer's Sheet Anchor* had little to offer on what I intended.

Depending on the era, there were three ways for a sailing ship to get away from a wharf. Her crew could be put in boats and with considerable oar-bending, tow her into the position where she would have enough sea room to make sail. When steam tugs came along the manual labor was replaced, although most skippers held a share in the vessel and objected so violently to tow charges they would attempt anything but a certain grounding to avoid them.

It would not have cost very much to have the *Albatros* towed away from our wharf, but somehow the dependence rankled and our crew was as puzzled as the crowd on the wharf when I asked McDowall to single up our lines and then set the upper and lower tops'ls. His "humph" was a question mark, but he said nothing more and went about his business while I gathered the balance of our crew and set the main. Meanwhile, I kept a wary eye on the American flag which flew from the Honolulu clock tower. It indicated a steady wind, not too strong and not too light, but if it changed direction as little as 20 degrees I knew we were in for great trouble and humiliation.

All men fancy being called daring, but none like to be labeled foolhardy. However, I had spent enough time studying our situation to convince myself that with a little luck we could accomplish a tour de force which might leave the old salts cheering.

We were secured alongside one of the regular steamship wharves which formed a long finger extending from shore toward the middle harbor of Honolulu. The next finger wharf was nearly parallel to our own and less than two ship lengths distant, and the middle harbor, where there was a turning basin, opened about five ship lengths from our position. Beyond the turning basin there was a channel which led southeast for perhaps a half a mile and then turned almost 50 degrees toward the southwest and thence held straight between breakwaters to the open Pacific. Our wharf pointed to the west and the wind was east, which I found an irresistible combination. I was about to try the third way of parting company with the land.

I asked Durst to reeve a long hawser from a piling at the end of the wharf and pass it through the hawse forward so it could be hauled upon and keep the ship parallel to the wharf. Then we cast off all our other lines and to the pleasurable excitement of all concerned we began to make sternway and a wonderful silence prevailed. There was no traffic behind us in the stream so I refrained from blowing any whistles and because of the quiet the soft farewells from both ship and wharf seemed especially touching and personal.

We gathered sternway rapidly while from above a squadron of sea gulls advised and criticized. We slid past the end of the wharf and a man in a hula shirt lifted the eye of our hawser from the last cleat and let it splash in the water. More than a ship length away on the afterdeck we heard his soft "aloha" and knew we were entirely free of the land. Somewhere beyond the end of the wharf a citizen was angrily pounding out his frustration on an auto horn, and somewhere beyond the horn a jackhammer chattered against stone. Suddenly both noises ceased and there was only the muffled resonance of the breeze. It was so quiet I spoke in whispers to Post, who was at the helm, and I told her this was the kind of a sailing in which I took an inner delight.

My contentment was short-lived, because even with the rudder hard over to port our stern was swinging toward a maneuvering dolphin which seemed to be equipped with a powerful magnet. We were drawn inexorably toward the ugly stack of upright timbers and I had time to think, Well . . . well, you clever fellow. Due to a slight underestimation of the current you are about to hang your ship on the only possible hazard available to you in this great harbor and when she snags on that dolphin she'll spin around and aim for the shallows and be well aground before you can do anything about it. And there you will be for days or maybe a month until the next high tide and all of the Honolulu harbor including the sea gulls will be laughing their heads off at your clumsiness. Ho, ho! He was too cheap to hire a tow!

The crew saved my face. As our quarter closed with the dolphin they rushed to the taffrail and fended us off so that only the stern of the jolly boat actually came in contact with the dolphin. It suffered a few abrasions as we swept on past and picked up some smears of tar, but suffered nothing more. We were entirely free.

At last we had gathered enough speed for some rudder control and the rest of our theatrics led to a consummate victory. As we left the shelter of the wharf the strength of the breeze increased as I had hoped and we had wind aplenty to force our bow around when we reached mid-channel. We swung the yards full to the opposite tack and as we gathered forward way, sheeted in the main. When the channel turned abruptly for the sea we wore ship smartly, and moments later were picking up speed for the true South Seas. We had set t'gallant and course before we were far from the breakwater and followed by setting the main and mid stays'ls.

We were very proud. No one along the Honolulu waterfront had seen such entertainment since the early years of the century.

For more than a week after we sailed from Honolulu the wind held fair and as a consequence our return to the peculiar tranquility of the marine world was accomplished to the melody of many low-key noises. Our senses were lulled by the consistent soft whirring of the wind about our ears, the liquid thumps of the water as our bow plunged into backs of countless waves, the almost inaudible hiss of the sea creaming along the hull plates, and before mealtimes the incongruous rattling of pots from the galley. For our eyes there were the garish dawnings and all through the day the wild monuments of cloud to be admired, and beneath them a sparkling carpet of blue marble, perpetually dancing and veined with white. At night there were the stars to reach out for; and it seemed they could be fondled with the hand as well as admired with the brain, for there are few places in all the oceans where the heavens are so astoundingly clear as between the Hawaiian Islands and the equator.

These nights the stars became more than aids to the navigation of our vessel—they were like escorts to our passage from normal life as lived by our fellow men toward a mystic existence where the sum of time might be said to have ceased. What occurred even the day before was almost impossible to recall because it was probably the same as today. Hence we had no sense of accumulated time even though all of our daily life was so strictly regulated by time. Aging goes almost unnoticed when people see each other several times a day and our whole world, town and country, consisting of thirteen individuals, seemed to be walking proof of relativity. How many years, I wondered, could we sail on before one of us inquired of another, "Have you noticed how so-and-so is slowing down?" or perhaps, "She *has* to be older than that!"

A part of our suspension was due to the regular ship's routine which changed so little from day to day, and a part to the sameness of the weather and ocean which comprised the total of our view beyond a maximum of 100 feet. Not only did this combination melt one day into another so that immediate history was lost, it promoted the inconsequential to very high rank.

We were hardly aware how little things had begun to please or offend, or how this new world-life had enclosed us in its beautifully protective cocoon. Our ship was small in fact, but to our eyes in good weather she was huge, simply because we could not get away far enough to truly judge her size. Likewise our selves grew beyond actual dimension and I often found disappointment in not being quite able to reach a block or a cleat or a pin when I had been sure I could. I was strangely chagrined to discover a familiar part of my vessel an unattainable few inches beyond arm's length and for a while sat back like a spectator, watching the expansion of my physical ego in so small a world being cruelly shrunk to reality by the unchanging dimensions of our ship.

Correspondingly all our ills and pleasures became magnified. We were disgruntled if we were not relieved from watch exactly on time, although of pressing appointments elsewhere we had none. We were annoyed to the point of fury when an object somewhere in the *Albatros* went adrift and banged a repetition of her rolling action over and over again. We were pleased when the ship's speed increased from 6 knots to 6½ knots and when we found the chronometer to be only two seconds slow instead of three. We were enchanted when a true albatross came to call upon his namesake and gave a breath-taking flying exhibition across, over, and between the fluid hills and dales surrounding us. We were delighted to catch three *mahi-mahis* and eat a part of them raw as sashimi.

So we continued for nearly nine days which could as well have been a thousand days, since the sensation of having entered upon some variety of eternal life was inescapable. Even our destination was still problematical. I had chosen Tahiti not out of any particular desire to go there, but because it is extremely difficult to maintain an aura of responsibility without a statement of your intentions. The real world simply will not cooperate with captains who admit, "Well, I'm not just sure where we *are* going, but hopefully we'll wind up somewhere." My hope was that Tahiti would only serve as the gateway to more interesting places.

Our euphoria nearly disappeared as soon as we came into the

doldrums, although the haunting sense of crossing from one life to another became even more pronounced. For us the doldrums, which are that frustrating band of calms lying to the north of the equator, became our purgatory. With the African Queen so feeble, it was necessary for us to follow the time-honored sailing ship route between the Hawaiian Islands and Polynesia. Thus we were obliged to make as much easting as we possibly could before crossing through the doldrums, and hopefully picking up the southeast trades a few days south of the line.

Sailors who have greatly sinned may expect to mildew permanently in the doldrums, although perhaps when their souls are covered with verdigris they may be promoted to ordinary hell. It does not do anything all the time in the doldrums—it is not even calm all the time. The wind may blow just long enough for a sailor to raise his hopes as well as his sails, and *then* it falls calm.

It will stop raining just long enough to trick you into removing your foul-weather gear and then some giant in the overcast retches a torrential downpour as if this opportunity had been long awaited.

The doldrums are the only place I have seen large and very sloppy waves created without a vestige of wind. The waves come from all directions, meet long enough to slap each other in the face, and run off to spread their miserable confusion elsewhere. En route they attack any small vessel in such a way that all of her usual stability is ruined and living conditions aboard become vile. The motion is so eccentric you wonder what ever happened to your sea legs. The gear of a sailing ship struggling through the doldrums takes awful punishment because there is not enough time between the periods of calm and the treasured puffs of wind to make sail and then douse it again. If you are ever to depart the doldrums then you must carry sail all the time and watch it chew itself to pieces most of the time. There were occasions when I wanted to weep for our poor *Albatros* and particularly her gear aloft, which grunted and snapped and cried out in all the manifestations of a vessel's agony against continuous and unusual strains. Since Rotterdam I had lacked true appreciation of flax sails because they seemed bound to stretch along the miter, but now I was deeply impressed with their durability under the most sadistic stress and wear.

Ever since the *Henrietta* I had been unable to regard any well-made sail with proper respect. For in that little Caribbean sloop I was shipmates with a sail so unique that it dominated life aboard. Bigelow, who would later serve as First Mate in the *Albatros,* had joined me in the *Henrietta* and had brought along his identical twin brother, whom for convenience I thought of as Bigelow number two. Both men were expert sailors and both were nearly hypnotized by the *Henrietta*'s unforgettable mainsail.

It was shaped like the ass of a hippopotamus and was approximately the same color. It was riven with holes. The clew was tied to the boom with a piece of twine and the foot was made fast in the same careless fashion. The luff was very loosely held to the mast by a frayed lacing of thin sisal, and the head was hoisted by a length of the same stuff. The mast was supported by two rusty wire shrouds on either side which were led to deadeyes served by lanyards of withered and quite unidentifiable rope. When under way in the *Henrietta,* particularly when the Caribbean breeze became a fresh wind, we stared at this assembly in wonder, and in the absolute certainty that any moment it must all come tumbling down.

The *Henrietta* was a sloop of 38 feet overall and of orthodox design for small trading in the Caribbean. She was built by eye in the West Indian tradition with strict economy being uppermost in the minds of both builder and owner. I chartered her because she was the only boat in the harbor of Antigua which showed a trace of new paint. She was owned and sailed by a giant blue-black man with one of the world's most engaging smiles. His name was Coagli and when I told him of my intention to cruise the Antilles and that I would pay him as if he were transporting cargo, he urged me to hire a yacht from one of the several available at English Harbor. But I had ever been a poor sybarite and at length persuaded him that although my intentions might be eccentric they were at least legal. The *Henrietta*'s mainsail was wrapped around the boom sausage fashion, and later I wondered if I would have gone through with our bargain had it been entirely visible.

It was the *Henrietta*'s mainsail combined with the presence of the twin Bigelows that nearly transformed me into a teetotaler.

As so often happens in the Caribbean the northerly winds turned chill and not one of us had brought any warm gear. Goose bumps peckled Coagli's mighty bare arms as he grinned and sang and leaned for hours against the mast. The staccato snapping of his shirttail in the wind was our anemometer and when the tempo quickened, whoever had the helm would automatically ease the sheet or come up a trifle into the wind. We made St. Kitts and Saba and in time came to anchor off Barbuda, which is an islet situated north and east of the principal Antilles.

We were by now deeply impressed by our shipmate Coagli. He was a sailor's sailor. When the winds had fallen so that ordinarily we would have been becalmed we had seen him take up a wooden dipper and throw salt water at his pitiful mainsail until the whole of it was soaked. To our amazement the effect upon our speed was immediately noticeable. If we had been nearly stationary in the water we would begin to move and if we had been merely lazing along with a whispering of water at the stem, then we would pick up a full half-knot or so and sometimes more without the slightest increase in wind. This condition would prevail as long as Coagli continued to toss water. When the sail dried, the *Henrietta* became lethargic again.

"The sail be thirsty," Coagli would announce and resume his water tossing. As if this eerie performance were not enough to make us question the laws of aerodynamics, Coagli would sometimes speak to the sail as if it were a living thing. He did not utter either well-formed or connected words but rather chanted sounds and syllables which he himself made no pretense of comprehending. All he knew, and all we could observe, was that his incantations worked. The sail and then the *Henrietta* responded exactly as if by voice commands he was controlling the power of an invisible sea serpent harnessed to our hull.

The more we studied the sail the worse it appeared. It had been stretched without mercy, several inches of the leech flapped uselessly no matter how we trimmed it, and the great bulbous area which presumably was the principal driving force of the sail was so low in relation to the remainder that it often plopped into the sea and collapsed. There was absolutely no scientific reason why the *Henrietta* should move in anything less than a gale, much less go dancing along like a racer in hot pursuit. Coagli had no explanation, but his inner pride became apparent when he said, "She jes go, that's all, she jes go! and go!"

All of the *Henrietta*'s ballast was inside and consisted of burlap sacks filled with sand and laid in the single hold. During the day if the wind made up and the cold spray doused us so that life aboard the *Henrietta* was as uncomfortable as Coagli had promised it would be, I would abandon masochism when my trick at the helm was done and slip down to the cargo hold. The sandbags were damp and hard from moisture and only a thin bar of twilight came through the hatch coaming, but at least there was no wind. Here in company with a multitude of sand fleas we slept. Here also I found the gloomy atmosphere conducive to specialized thinking. Why should the *Henrietta* sail so sweetly when Coagli was at the helm and become so listless when either of the Bigelows or myself took charge? I had supposed that after the first day we would get on to her, for certainly a man who could sail one vessel could with some familiarization sail any other—but it wasn't working out that way. My arms ached from heaving on the hardwood tiller and there had been times during this day's no-nonsense blow when I thought I should lose her altogether. The Bigelows, one after the other, were likewise sorely tried, and it was not until Coagli's turn that the *Henrietta* was tamed.

Coagli's innate sense of decency kept him from pointing out how remarkable was the change, but as I watched him leaning back and effortlessly mixing adjustments of tiller and sheet I listened ever more carefully to his calypso monologue with the mainsail. And in time I realized that he spoke in a rhythmic beat, a gush of syllables alternating with a silence as his tremendous chest swelled with air. Then he would exhale a singsong of syllables again and slap his bare feet against the deck while at the same time adjusting the mainsheet and matching it with minor movements of the tiller. Was it my imagination that suggested these actions corresponded with the heaving of the seas? Was there some mysterious accord between this blue-black genius and the ocean which enabled him to abide so much better with it and the wind than we could?

Because the *Henrietta* was totally dependent on her ability to sail, I had envisioned dreary delays waiting in some isolated port for more wind or less wind. I had therefore taken the precaution of stowing a modest-sized keg of rum alongside our water barrels and in the evenings when all was secure, I drew upon it. The rum was not of medal-winning caliber, but the color was pleasing and the bouquet not objectionable. In body it could not compare with Bardinet, but it did have a certain integrity. Unfortunately my appreciation of it was a lonely affair, since both Bigelows were Quakers *and* members of Alcoholics Anonymous. Coagli would accept a dollup in his glass which he seemed to use as a mouthwash. He would take a sip, roll it about his mouth, and when he thought I was not watching, spit it into the sea. I finally realized that his huge and sensitive heart had simply instructed him to keep me company.

I was brooding about our relative sailing abilities as we lay at anchor off Barbuda. There were fish frying over our charcoal brazier and in my hand, nearly finished, was my recond rum of the evening. I sat beside the keg trying to concentrate on the West Indian sunset which emblazoned the sky behind the Bigelow brothers, yet the business of the mainsail would not leave my mind. The Bigelows were equally perplexed. Bigelow number one said, "Coagli, are you sure you haven't an engine hidden below that only works when you take the helm?"

Coagli simply laughed and in his embarrassment spent some time readjusting the fire beneath the fish.

Bigelow number one said, "Eventually we will find out that Coagli has a trained dolphin who lives aft of the rudder and gives a shove when the boss says go."

"There are people who are one with the sea," Bigelow number two stated in his firm way. "They are part fish and part oceanic bird and our friend is a little of both."

"We think and he feels," Bigelow number one said.

The rum was souring in my throat. Could it be that all of this time I had missed some sensual connection with the sea? I had thought myself in complete harmony with it always, whether it chose to exalt or humble me.

Suddenly a possible answer came to me, for the Bigelow twins were talking together as they often did in a way that phased out any other present company. At such times so alike was their tone, phrasing, and pronunciation it was quite impossible to tell when one fell silent and the other spoke. I closed my eyes and listened. Every audible factor of their speech was identical, and listening I realized they were thinking as one; they were a man talking to himself. I opened my eyes and saw them still side by side in silhouette against the sun. And each of their movements was identical. They moved as one.

The rum, I thought, has brought me single vision instead of a double and I must not touch it again lest the Bigelows melt away entirely. And then I thought, Here were two mature and stalwart men, each in himself an accomplished personality and yet they were as alike as waves of the ocean.

I remembered then how rich the sea was in unexplainable things and how the ancients had accepted them readily and decorated their charts with wonders they could not hope to comprehend. Never before had I questioned the phenomenon of the Bigelows yet I realized now that it could not have been purely a matter of genetics. A kindred power enabled Coagli, who knew nothing whatever of coefficients, metracentric heights, or centers of effort, to sail his contradictory little sloop in a style far better than we could ever hope to achieve.

Suddenly I thought, A pox on this inferior rum! It had led me to inquiry instead of acceptance and thus stood me into the danger of losing my sailorman's peace.

In the *Henrietta* I learned that there are certain things of the sea we must accept . . . as is.

Compared to the Atlantic the Pacific is an empty ocean, a still primeval waste heaving undisturbed just as it did millions of years ago. It is no effort at all to turn your back on your own vessel and with the empty Pacific for a stage visualize the ghost of Bligh's *Bounty*, or an ancient Polynesian sailing raft sliding along the horizon, or perhaps a clumsy, stinking New Bedford whaler hove to for flensing. I was thus bemused one afternoon when my ghost took on texture, erected itself upside down in a mirage for a moment, and then rapidly became more distinct. I put down an urge to call out a resounding "Sail ho!" lest my shipmates wonder if the doldrums had unnerved me. A certain reserve and definite deck decorum were expected of a proper captain, so it was better to say of the first ship we had seen in over 2,000 miles, "Well, well. It seems we have company. . . ."

In minutes nearly all of our ship's people had gathered along the taffrail to watch the passing of another world inhabited by creatures like ourselves. The urge was irresistible, not only because of natural curiosity, but because after so many days when the total perimeter of a man's vision has been only a great expanse of emptiness, his eyes become lonely for the relief of objects. Let a chip of wood pass and invariably all heads aboard will follow it until its disappearance behind the ultimate wave. We are like rovers in a desert who will deviate from course at the excuse offered by a fragment of pottery, a strip of leather, or an old tin can. Why is it there? Who left it? Could it be of any use? These are only reasons to satisfy the mind—the needful pleasure of inspection may be seen in the eyes. Thus in mid-Atlantic during a gale did we nearly broach to because the helmsman decided to have a closer look at something he saw floating in the water. It proved to be a dead pig and speculation went on for days as to how it came to be there.

Now our own eyes watched hungrily as the stranger took form and soon we could hear the faint heartbeat of her engine. I saw that she was a fisherman. For a moment I became heavy with nostalgia for the *Mike* and the *Fred Holmes* and then I saw that she was a Japanese fisherman—a tuna long-liner, the very villain responsible for the demise of the Western Ocean Fishing Company.

We were nearly abreast when our ship's company began a spontaneous series of greetings. They waved and called out and some climbed into the lower rigging for a better view of the first new faces they had seen in a long time. They were rejoicing in the reassurance they were not the only human beings left in the world and in the temporary removal of the time capsule in which we had lived so long.

The Japanese were likewise demonstrative and it struck me that while they were easy to identify, if only because no other Orientals fished so extensively or in such fine vessels, they could not know if we were American, German, Portuguese, French, Poles, Russians, or British, and yet they were not shaking their fists at us. They were smiling and waving and they did not ask our creed or passport numbers before so declaring themselves. Well then, what a silliness we could not repeat this brief meeting on a grander scale and make the sight of *any* other human beings an opportunity for boisterous salutation. But only dreamers who refused to learn from history thought of such naïvetés.

My own hand was slow in rising because of dissapointment in discovering their flag, but before they had entirely passed I managed to crush the prejudices born of the Second War which had been long salted with the economic resentments of a commercial fisherman, and finally I was waving like the others.

We passed each other in seconds and I saw that one of the officers on the bridge was trying to take our picture and wave at the same time. Then in minutes they were far astern and once more only a speck on the face of the Pacific. I had not been able to shout any greeting, but now in my thoughts I wished them fair winds and a good catch. For they were, like us, so alone in the world.

Then they were gone.

At last, twenty-five days out of Honolulu, on a hot, steaming morning we moored stern to the shore at Papeete. Mistaking us for rich American tourists, the islanders made us welcome in their flower-scented way. But Papeete is no different from any other port in the world although it certainly ranks with Panama for airless heat. Papeete is the same as the rest of the world for those who come down to meet the ships, those who so often become the only friends a sailor makes in port. There are a few who are kind and genuine—and there are many more alert to the first sign of a foreign hull on the horizon so that they can cheat and exploit her sailors in every conceivable fashion. So it has been since the beginning of maritime history and so it will be as long as ships ply the seas.

There is an unwritten law against speaking ill of the South Sea Islands or even thinking of their people in worldly terms. And this is a very good thing. Legends of the South Seas have been fostered one upon the other and nourished by a multitude of dreamers until they have become the truth, and reality is an uninvited specter to be seen through.

The *Albatros*' principal cargo was dreams. A few were fulfilled in Papeete and many more were not. It was not written in the legend that Rogerts should suffer a vicious motor-bike accident in Papeete which only confined him to the hospital for a month, although it certainly would have killed an ordinary man. Hall seemed to have realized a dream, for he was not afraid to leave the womb of the ship or the waterfront. He walked off alone to disappear for days in the rain forests clutching the mountains behind the town. And perhaps Durst and Atcheson found something deeply satisfying in their giggling, sarong-clad friends who spoke not a word of their language, for when the time came to sail from Papeete, both men were difficult to remove.

It was in Papeete that Peter Dawson perfected his incredible communication method which was to serve him, and unfortunately only him, in ports ranging from the Tuamotus to the fiords of Norway. None of us could manage his technique of passing through the language barrier, not even those of us who spoke at least some French.

Peter Dawson simply ignored the fact that one language

might differ from another, and thus became the perfect sailor at large to the world. He did not speak one word of any language except his native New Yorkese, nor did he *hear* any language other than his own. He never raised his voice in a stupid effort to promote understanding, which is the shame of so many American tourists. He simply addressed every native of whatever land he visited as if they had been brought up in the same family together. He never bothered to slow his speech or enunciate any more clearly than his normal style.

He might say to a shopkeeper, "I'm looking for some hexagon nuts . . . three-quarter-inch, and I was hoping you'd have a few." Now the shopkeeper, who was Eurasian and had never seen Peter Dawson before in his life and who knew not a word of English, would reply in French, not a word of which Dawson would comprehend. Yet by some magic international telegraphy, communication had now been established and sympathetic understanding launched on its way. The shopkeeper might reply in the most idiomatic Tahitian French that he did not have any such hexagon nuts but knew of a friend who kept a supply. Little knowing what events lay before him the shopkeeper would transport Dawson to his friend, who also lacked any knowledge of the English language. Eventually the purchase of the necessary hexagons would be accomplished and with an ordinary customer the transaction might have ended there. But now Dawson would invite the pair of merchants back to the ship to see where the precious nuts fitted. Already under Dawson's spell, they would close up their shops, and babbling like magpies the three of them would escort two hexagonal three-quarter-inch nuts to the *Albatros*. When their tour of the ship was done one of them would feel obliged to invite Dawson to his home for luncheon, where in a matter of minutes the guest would have established sufficient rapport with the wife and children to be treated as one of the family. The chain of events was now forged and the links were never-ending. By early evening Dawson and his cronies could be seen testing the rum in the most active bistro and by then they would have been joined by a fourth or fifth friend who was also fluent in Dawson's special Esperanto. Within a few days, compelled by one need or another, Dawson would have repeated the pattern several times and his roster of friends multiplied with each new excursion.

I soon learned that wherever in the world we might be, if something was needed for the ship it was best to send our sailor-at-large.

On a sultry afternoon with the ship reeking of rum, coconuts, frangipani, and sweat, we sailed for the Tuamotu islands, which lie to the northeast of Tahiti. They are only a minute splatter of coral reefs emerging from a gigantic cobalt sea and they are so nearly alike it is extremely difficult for a stranger to tell one from the other. They are low and flat, fringed with wiry brush and coconut palms, white beaches, and land crabs.

Thus, approaching the Tuamotus for the first time from any direction must be attempted with the utmost prudence and most certainly in daylight. It was not for nothing that these islands were once called the "Dangerous Archipelago," and wrecks of the unwary are strewn all over the area. The golden age of sea exploration brought a brilliant parade of master navigators to the Tuamotus. Cook came and Bougainville, Bligh in his time, Kotzebue, and Bellingshausen. Whereas the same men accomplished remarkable feats of navigational accuracy in other parts of the Pacific, they all seemed to become bewildered once arrived in the clutches of the Tuamotus. Lesser navigators compounded the confusion by making charts with errors of as much as 4 degrees in longitude, reporting islands which did not exist, and totally ignoring many which eventually proved to be very solid. There are currents passing among the Tuamotus with flow rates as high as 4 knots, uncharted reefs only a few feet beneath the surface of the sea, hardly *any* aids to navigation, and innumerable cauliflower heads of coral spotted in inconvenient places. To guard you against these assorted hazards there are charts and pilot books to be had for a price, all of which announce with disarming frankness that they are not to be trusted. There are no recent charts available to the ordinary sailor and we considered ourselves fortunate to obtain one dated 1870, "revised" from explorations carried out in H.M.S. *Blossom* in 1790.

The circlet configuration of their islands has placed the sea within a few yards of the Tuamotuans all of their lives whether they like it or not. They cannot conceive of life without their sea. As infants they were bathed in it, as children they splashed in it, and as adults they clean and refresh themselves in it. There is the sea . . . everywhere. What else *is* there? This sprinkle of sand between my toes, that frond which decorates my hat, that rat which scutters under my house are things of the ordinary world, but they are nothing. Is not the sea so much larger than anything?

The people of the Tuamotus are permanently serving as crews on their little coral ships, and like all sailors they are never entirely able to escape the sea. It is there, all-powerful and reassuring, their true god, whom they have temporarily forsaken for a vague and sometimes incomprehensible spirit now residing in the white plaster church which they built in the shade of the palms only a generation ago. Once gathered inside this church with the breeze whirring softly through the paneless windows, they declare without intention their easily recognized master. Their voices give them away when they commence a hymn that begins like no other hymn in the rest of the world. It begins with a sort of humming, a tentative reaching for a suggestion of vastness, then the singers develop a soulful moaning which rapidly approaches the listener and finally crashes among the wooden pews.

And at last, if strict attention is paid to the melody, a few notes of "Safe in the Arms of Jesus" may be recognized. But only a few. The rest is the sea in all its moods, the surf, the storms, the currents, the life in the deep, the soft breezes, sunlight, and the stars of the night. As if their voices were not enough hosanna, now the entire congregation begins to sway rhythmically back and forth in a striking duplication of the ocean's ebb and flow. Beyond the paneless windows, framed between palm trees, there it lies, its great thundering metronome beating time for the singers. Who would dare to think of life without the sea?

☼

THIRTEEN

We left the amiable Tuamotus and sailed even farther northeastward to fetch the dark and frowning islands of the Marquesas.

The Marquesas rise boldly from the sea and are covered with such heavy vegetation they offer a forbidding face to all sailors. Not so long ago they were inhabited by some of the most fierce people in the South Seas, and even now the geographical features of the islands suggest an atmosphere of hostility. The mountain peaks extend high enough to create perpetual cloud about their general area, and when the sun finds a hole in the overcast its heat is fetid and cloying and immediate escape from it seems imperative.

There is a topographical magnificence about the Marquesas not to be found in any other South Sea Island group although the pitiful survivors of her once great people are now so few the islands barely qualify as inhabited. Their spirits appear to be quite as dead as their ancient gods and the air which clings to their suffocated mountains. Virgin's Bay is a gash in the flank of Fatu Hiva Island. We entered it one blazing morning and discovered such beauty we nearly ran aground before I could look away from it and give the signal to drop anchor. All of our ship's people were awed by the gigantic formations which enclosed the *Albatros* upon a crystal-green pool of water. The Bay is a cul-de-sac formed by cliffs and hills of imposing stature and at the end of it, fringing a white beach, lies a thatched village. Beyond the village there rises a series of ridges and pinnacles of fantastic shapes and beyond them brood the higher mountains.

We were still running out chain when the first of a host of outriggers set out from the village, and anticipation aboard was such that the normal chores required in putting our ship to rest were carried out halfheartedly.

The same anchor winch which had originally dismayed McDaniel in Rotterdam was still on our foredeck. It was a huge assembly of gears, shafts, drums, clutches, brakes and cranks invented by some long-forgotten Dutch mechanician of very dubious talent. I knew very well it was regarded as a man-killer by all who were obliged to sweat over its inadequacies and often, in sympathy, took my turn at cranking its miserably underpowered gears. And always I promised myself that as soon as I could afford further improvements about the *Albatros* the accursed anchor winch would be the first item thrown over the side. Because of its deficiencies we had fallen into the dangerous practice of letting out just enough anchor chain and not a foot more. We could only think of how it would all have to be wound in again and in hot weather. If we were about to anchor in fairly deep water I could hear agonized groans from the anchor watch all the way aft to the quarter-deck. Thus, on this morning we did drop our starboard anchor in a mere 3 fathoms and let go only a single shackle of chain.

Soon the outriggers were upon us and immediately engaged in transporting most of the crew to the land. I was as curious as the others, but there was something about Virgin's Bay which made me uneasy. Henderson, who was notably independent-minded for a young lady, decided to stay with me as did Atcheson, who said that one island was beginning to look too much like the last and he was inclined to skip a few. We enjoyed an hour or so of that strange peace which descends upon any vessel suddenly abandoned by all but her stand-by watch; then as the wind gusts became more powerful I became very glad of the others' company.

I was in the charthouse engaged in the eternal guessing game of pre-voyage planning. The chart of the Pacific was spread beneath my hands. Soon we would sail away from the Marquesas bound north again for Honolulu, where the *Albatros* would be laid up again. I was dispirited, for however great his original passions, man cannot long abide an expensive and troublesome mistress. No wonder my thoughts turned to the little *Thetis,* whom I had so adored. She was so understanding.

The *Thetis* proved to be about as charming a vessel as any man ever loved and I was a fool to have sold her. I should have kept her until the day I die and even after that my descendants should keep her in a bottle. For she was the only siren of them all who was utterly without fault.

The *Thetis* was only 28 feet long, which gave her the status of a bird feather upon the open oceans. She was the only maiden I had ever possessed who could honestly lay claim to the class of yacht. Perhaps as some unkind gossips said, she was too plain of line, and it was true that she lacked sheer; yet somehow this lover of sheer found her lack of it a part of her special appeal. She drew 5 feet of water, which is very much for so small a craft, but both her draft and the design of her underbody gave her a remarkable stability without crankiness. She rode the big Pacific swells like a brave little petrel and though we never challenged a gale together, there was rarely a time when it was not possible to slip below to her tiny cabin and sleep or eat a meal in comparative comfort. In smooth water she sailed so smartly and maneuvered so easily in tight quarters that I often forgot she had an engine beneath her cockpit deck. I used it so seldom the starting battery finally expired and I never found it necessary to replace it until that disgraceful day when in a sudden fit of cowardice I decided that a man without more money than he needed should not own a boat.

At sea in the usual chop created by a smart breeze, the *Thetis* would sail herself for hours. A few minutes were required to adjust her sheets and off she would go holding course as if guided by the finest autopilot.

She was rigged as a yawl with a club jib, and was thus a one-man show. It was my quiet joy to tack for hours through an assembled fleet, or between and around coastal rocks so the seals could admire her dexterity. A mere half-turn of her dainty wheel and she would start saucily into the wind and then perhaps another quarter-turn would bring her through the eye of the wind and quickly to the other tack. Coming about or jibbing was effortless. All of her parts were perfectly balanced, which is a great deal more than can be said for many staggeringly expensive sailing craft. Her designer was unknown, which is a tragedy because if I could discover that genius I would this day beg him to create another.

The *Thetis* was built by her original owner in his back yard. He was obviously a superb craftsman and every detail of the

Thetis' woodwork reflected loving care. It seemed as if he deliberately postponed completing his memorial, for the building of this little treasure took him eight years. Then he died.

In the little *Thetis* you were one with the sea. By simply reaching out with your hand you could often touch it. You breathed it whether you wanted to or not, you felt it and heard it every instant of the voyage.

One day, dancing along before a fresh breeze, we were ambushed by a flying squadron of porpoises. They swept in upon both sides of the *Thetis*' bow and began their usual overtures for admiration and applause. They were big porpoises, some I thought to be a third the size of the *Thetis*, and they chose to surface so near that even above the sound of the wind and waves I could easily hear their breathing. There is some stingy entrepreneur in the deep who always curtails a porpoise show just as it really begins and I waited with reluctance for the usual signal which must translate, "Come now, my great hams, you give too much for nothing. Come away! Life cannot be all play."

I clapped my hands repeatedly and bravoed, and waited for the inevitable fast exit which would leave us alone again. It was just before noon when the troupe joined us and to my amazement their performance continued until nearly four in the afternoon. Perhaps the acrobatic ballets to be seen off the coast of Guatemala were more spectacular, but never had I observed a porpoise show of such duration. Only the supernumeraries departed for urgent business elsewhere. I began to recognize the stars one from the other and gave them names. There were Harlequin and Nijinsky and Dame Margot and a rather shy substar whom I dubbed Evangeline. When at last they departed I became almost unbearably lonely and brooded upon the reason they had stayed so long with me. And I decided that unlike other huge and fast vessels before which they were required to play command performances, they had regarded the little *Thetis* as one of themselves and were trying to persuade her to join their company. All of their cavortings were intended then as invitations—"See how this is done? Now you try it."

In little boats like the *Thetis* such thoughts are possible and the dreams of ordinary men can become realities. In little vessels there is joy. In large vessels there is travail and perplexity.

And so I was yearning for the *Thetis* on that gusty day when the *Albatros* lay at anchor in a place known as Virgin's Bay.

Had the two of us been alone I could have tied the *Thetis* to a coconut tree like a little lamb and we could have slumbered together all afternoon. Yet now, here was the *Albatros* surging uneasily at her anchors and seeming to present no end of problems. For the first time I dared to wonder who was owning whom. I had now to remind myself that the African Queen was so undependable we could barely trust it for in-port maneuvering much less to make the easting we must have before setting a final westerly course toward the Hawaiian Islands. If we took too much easting then we would needlessly prolong the voyage, and if we took too little then a few days of freak weather or winds could throw us *west* of the Hawaiian group, which would be a pretty pickle indeed. To fetch Honolulu after such a calamity would require us to sail nearly to the latitude of Japan before we could again bear away for the islands with the wind anywhere near our backs.

There were no agents or port captains to plan these matters for the *Albatros*. We were very much alone in a world that had no time for the problems of sailing ships. Very well, then the challenge was all the more stimulating. How many days to Hilo? To Honolulu? To Molokai? Twenty-five . . . thirty? Water? Stores? When once again in the doldrums should we whiplash the African Queen and risk its total collapse or conserve its fading strength for those last few miles where, as had so many sailing ships before, we might lay becalmed for days?

My guides for reflecting on these matters were the same old wind and current charts which were something like opium and about as reliable. How promising the little wind arrows! How comforting the low percentage of gales and the absence of fog! From past experience with these same elaborately plotted charts, which must have cost our government a great deal of money, I would not have been surprised to observe heavy fog in the Caribbean and snow squalls in the Indian Ocean. Yet there was no denying their powers of enchantment. Your spirits fly across a wind and current chart, scudding before the carefully plotted trade winds, sped on by the blue arrows indicating faithful currents. You become lost in such charts even though you may know how they lie of the heavens.

I was still spellbound with the wind and current tables when eventually we sailed from Virgin's Bay. We had endured no end of anchoring troubles while in its confines and I was relieved to be out of it. Had it not been for the aid of Henderson and Atcheson we might well have been blown on the beach by the gusts which tumbled down off the spectacular cliffs. To avoid a disastrous stranding in Virgin's Bay the three of us had spent hours resetting our first anchor, then dropping a second anchor and finally letting run all the scope of chain in both lockers. Scenic beauty being a relative quantity, I should happily have traded some of the Virgin Bay scenery for a dark and muddy bottom.*

Now once again we were bound to sea and all of the mutual busyness of post-sailing had begun. Since sea-watch routine had not yet taken over, everyone was awake and we seemed a great

* *Albatros*' near sister ship, the famous *Yankee,* was lost in the Cook Islands under very similar circumstances during 1965.

many on deck at the same time. From now on so many people would not again be visible except for the Bardinet hour each day. Sometimes a person would decide to sleep through it or be otherwise engaged and so it was possible that a person in one of our three watches might not see a friend in another watch for two or three days. Then, of course, the standard greeting was "Excuse me, but haven't we met before?"

☼

FOURTEEN

IT takes a few days to discard the softness of the land and sleep comes only in patches until the body is once more accustomed to the rhythm of the sea. Then too there is an inner excitement that partly originates in a renewed sense of freedom nearly impossible to achieve on land. At last! My responsibilities are clearly defined. They are just this and no more, you see. I rise at this time and tend to my physical needs. Then I do this or that for a specified number of hours and if I have trouble with this or that, there is always a higher authority to whom I can appeal for help. And he will solve my trouble because he must. All the while I am surrounded by stark beauty and a strong suggestion that while my time on this planet may be limited I am for the moment a person of some importance. There are no strangers in my world, not even any strange faces. I know every one of my fellow citizens well and it is my privilege to love or detest them. When my watch is done, then I again may tend my body and even my mind if it pleases me, and when both are weary I may sleep as in my tomb. These are benefits which quite balance out whatever it was that held me to the land.

The hour of Bardinet was over and soon afterward I shot the first of the evening stars.

There is a sense of mystique inherent in celestial navigation, and the view through the telescopic sight of a sextant can be as profound as the eye of the beholder makes it. There, I have plucked Capella from the still deserted heavens and by a mere movement of my hand contrive to slide it downward through an arc of a trillion billion miles until it bounces upon the sea. There, Capella, a mighty sun thousands of times larger than our own, remains my personal captive held in suspension against my personal oceanic domain. When it glitters exactly upon the horizon I can move it up or down by only hinting at my fingers and thus resolve a line of our position on this mediocre speck in the universe we exalt with the title Earth. I have only to regard the great Capella with care, making sure that it is perched just so, and forget that distances to such places are best expressed in parsecs only one of which equals 19.2 million million miles.

In the divided mirror of my sextant I can see on one side a pale evening sky and a few little nimbus clouds touched with the last vaporous brown of the descended sun. In the adjoining mirror I have Capella awaiting my pleasure. It appears to float uncertainly until I bring it to rest upon the horizon. Having done so I may now take the precise time of my observation from the chronometer ticking away in the charthouse, which is 11 seconds slow according to the domineering father of all clocks located in Greenwich, England, on the other side of the world.

My eye commanding my fingers has enabled me to capture Capella at the one instant in eternity when it glistened at exactly 27 degrees and 8 minutes above my personal horizon. It can never ever happen again and I will now write down this fact which no other human being has hitherto been able to record honestly, nor can it ever be recorded again.

Having learned all I can from Capella I must now have further celestial opinion concerning our situation, and I must hurry, for the horizon is melting into the darkening sky. There is Canopus just revealed by the coming night and I will cross the line of it with that of Capella. Greetings, Canopus! May I ask our whereabouts?

Once again the reply is recorded in perpetuity—31 degrees and 18 minutes at an instant in Greenwich time when the people of that rather dull London suburb are drinking breakfast tea.

The advice gathered from one star is useful, but inconclusive and even the lines of position created by only two stars must still be viewed with suspicion. They might be like two witnesses to a crime who may by pure coincidence tell the same story. So at least one more testimonial is required and I turn to the planet Jupiter, which has just appeared from behind a cloud. Hail, mighty Jupiter! Is this puny creature here or there? I must propitiate my human ego which insists I am needed somewhere in the future, and hence to complete the present journey I must know where I am now.

The telescope of my sextant is not powerful enough to reveal the moons of Jupiter, but knowing they are faithfully circling about their master planet like obedient concubines gives me great satisfaction, for with a twist of my fingers I can bring the entire court down until it is poised just on top of the black waves.

There. Jupiter has been caught at 38 degrees and 12 minutes, and I have my third witness. It is practically impossible that number three may also be guilty of coincidental testimony, so the summation of what all the trio has to say must be the truth. I can stop now if I please with confidence, but there is Durst on the foredeck patiently and accurately shooting five stars for a pin-point fix and since I am the Captain I cannot seem less desirous of the absolute. So with the last of the horizon light I humble Pollux to the wave tops and then Fomalhaut.

The charthouse is hot and stuffy. I must keep the after door closed lest the glare of the worklight blind Post, who is at the helm, and Dawson, who is responsible for the lookout. Durst and his watchmates will relieve us at midnight and to pass time he will then plot his own observations, but now mine are the only record of our position in the Pacific. Actually the small criss-cross design I have drawn on the chart represents a simple arithmetical synopsis of the stars' information. The small triangle in the center is history telling us not where we are, but where we were some thirty minutes ago when I made the actual observation. I am very pleased with tonight's fix, the five lines having intersected one another like spokes of a wheel, and I have not had to cheat even a little to make such a pretty display. There have been too many times in my voyaging when because of careless work at least one of my lines bisected the interior of the Gobi desert.

I can now adjust history by reading the dial of our "log," which we trail over the stern as deep-sea men have done for generations. The dial is actuated by a long line at the end of which is a brass spinner with vanes so designed that it will twirl with some degree of constancy in spite of variations in wind and wave. Sometimes a great fish may decide the spinner is a mouthful, which is infuriating because spinners are very expensive, and we wish that fish the world's worst bellyache. Usually, however, the log spins off thousands of miles without accident and when a fine breeze is blowing we delight in the whirring sound of the connecting line.

I open the charthouse door and call to Dawson. "What's the log?"

He moves against the stars and his flashlight finds the log's dial. His nasal New Yorkese cuts like a dagger through the tropic night. "Sixty-four and a half."

"Thank you."

"Don't mention it."

I close the door. Now I will move up the past until it stands with the present. When I took my tale from the stars the log stood at 61. Therefore in the intervening half-hour we have progressed 3½ nautical miles, which is satisfactory if not spectacular. I place a dot on the chart 3½ miles to the northeast of my criss-cross design. I draw a small circle around the dot and write the time beside it. There we are.

I study the distance we have come and what there is yet to go. We are well past halfway and we have come through the doldrums with a minimum of aggravation. We are making good speed and sometime tomorrow we should be able to come about on the opposite tack and make straight for the island of Molokai. Yet there is something nagging at my sense of well-being and I cannot explain it.

The strange uneasiness has been with me ever since our sailing from Virgin's Bay. Or did it begin with our anchoring troubles? I have spent long enough at sea to know very well how things go. At sea as in a man's life there is an inexorable balance of events ordained by some ultimate power. For hours of joy and content we must pay tribute with a certain number of suffer-and-dread hours. We had now sailed some 7,000 miles with only two very minor incidents. In addition to the anchoring difficulty in Virgin's Bay a native pilot had rammed us into a coral head in the channel at Maupiti, despite the fact that it was plainly visible below the clear water and he had plenty of room on both sides. By great good fortune we had struck it directly in line with the keel skeg and bounced right over the ugly formation without damage. The affair had done nothing to enhance my opinion of pilots in general, particularly since the day before I had managed to take our ship unscathed through the same channel without local assistance.

We had not even had any bad weather since sailing from San Francisco nearly half a year ago. There had been perhaps four days of squalls altogether and some heavy rains in the doldrums, but nothing more. So? When was the collector coming?

Here in the charthouse I can review the actual record simply by flipping through the pages of the logbook which is kept beside the chronometer. On this day we had some trouble with the gaff jaw of the main. Two of the bolts had fractured and the sail lashing had been partially cut. It had taken three hours to make repairs. Nothing. Here on this day a strap on the main boom preventer tackle had fractured. Replaced. Here were notes on several days of troubles with the galley stove leaking oil and going out. We were still messing with it and since it usually went out just before mealtimes, Rogerts' Dutch profanity could be heard all the way to the t'gallant yard. But the stove was merely frustrating and could not be considered an evil event. Here was mention of an electrical storm one day and on another day a notation that we had copra bugs aboard. A thorough disinfecting seemed to have solved the problem.

I close the logbook. The answer or amount of our penalty payment for such tranquility is not to be found in its pages.

A drop of sweat rolls off my chin and plops on the chart. I wipe it away as I have so many other droplets deposited by others of our crew. I will keep this chart long after I have ceased to sail the seas, for its surface is now a rich gravy of grease, graphite, sweat, salt spray and dirt, and in one corner a few faded brown splotches were formed when someone absorbed in navigating forgot he had cut his finger. There are places on the chart where the film of these things is so thick it is impossible to read the fine depth figures which are underneath, yet taken as a whole this much-abused record speaks most eloquently of our long voyage.

We are running nicely before a quartering wind so there is no need to brace myself as I regard the chart. Occasionally my pencil will roll a few hundred miles to the west in response to the motion of the ship, but then in a moment it will roll back past its original starting point and roll nearly as far to the east. My body is now so accustomed to instability that I must consciously note that we are rolling. It will be stability itself that will shock my legs and the inner canals of my ears when eventually we reach port and the deck becomes steady once again. Now only the movement of the pencil indicates we are at sea, although occasionally the long-necked chart light swings an inch or so, sweeping the chart with its own bright sun. Ever since our sailing from San Francisco Dawson has been fussing with red paper and red paint to relieve the glare of the chart light, but as with the persistent leak over my bunk, he has not conquered.

While I contemplate our position on the chart and what it means to our future strategy I am lulled by other sounds of the sea. The six portholes of the charthouse are all open and in the blackness beyond them I can hear the faint liquid hissing of the waves as we slip through them or roll into the backside of one. I am rather sorry about the lack of sound from our masts, which are of steel. If they were of wood, then we would have a constant and traditional melody of creaks, squeaks, and groans. Never mind. We are blessed with the strength and known integrity of steel.

Just behind me, surrounded by a wooden railing, is the companionway hatch which leads to our quarters below and the engine room. It is black down there and utterly quiet. Everyone below is asleep. Later I can be quite certain that Henderson, who is cursed with bouts of insomnia, will appear in the hatchway and ask the time. She is a small, wide-eyed girl of electric wit and a genuine love of the sea. I will tell her she has another hour or more before she is due on watch and she will say "Oh?" as if disappointed at the news. Then she will descend into the blackness again like a fallen angel commanded back to hell and I can never be quite sure if she has really appeared at all.

Beyond the chartroom door I can hear Peter Dawson talking with Post, but I cannot distinguish their words. I am suddenly lonely. Then why am I lingering in this Turkish bath of a charthouse when I could be on deck beneath the stars watching my proud little ship hustle through the night? I have established our position in the scheme of things and Durst with his own calculations will confirm it, and McDowall will advance and reconfirm it when he relieves Durst soon after dawn. We are indeed, if anything, overnavigated and the only possible hazard other than an unlikely collision with another vessel is a lozenge-shaped shoal indicated on the chart by a dotted line. A note in the center of the lozenge advises that the shoal was reported in 1938, which is a long time ago. It may be there and may be not, but we have given it such a wide berth we could not possibly sail into it now. Then what is the trouble within me and why have I lighted another cigarette immediately upon the last when I have sworn I will not smoke again for the duration of this watch? It has been a good day. We have made 161 miles since this same time yesterday. What then? Our sails? We are dependent on one suit and the outer jib has nearly gone to rot, but the rest of our canvas and flax is still in good condition and with remarkable caution they should all hold easily until Honolulu. Our drinking water is a bit cloudy and bears the essence of rusted steel, but it is not otherwise contaminated and there is still enough if we are delayed. All of our people are in fine health except Rogerts, who still suffers occasional headaches from his cycle accident, and Post, who bruised a rib between Takaroa and the Marquesas. But she is a skier of considerable repute and has formed the habit of shrugging off minor wounds.

I catch the pencil which has become annoying with its easy travels over the miles we work so hard to achieve, and place it in the holder just above the chart table. I switch out the light and stand in complete blindness for a moment. There is no solid reason for this silly apprehension. We are a stout ship and a stout crew now that we have spent so long together. None of us are paid and yet the atmosphere is as if we were. Duty is done and well, and that is the end of it. Every soul on board knows his job as well or better than most professionals and I believe we could sail to the end of the seas with such a company.

My vision returns enough to recognize the faint discs of starlight formed by the portholes. I move around the hatch rail to the door and open it. There is Post perched upon the wheelbox and beyond the black silhouette of her figure rises the giant constellation of Andromeda. Though she is surrounded by a billion light-years, only the yellow binnacle light casts a hint of illumination across her face. Occasionally her hand passes through the light as she moves the helm a spoke or two. Beside her, leaning against the wheel box and puffing on his pipe, is Dawson.

"Good fix?"

"Yes. We still have a long way to go."

I move to the lee taffrail and flip my cigarette in the sea.

"The wind seems to be picking up a bit." Dawson is indomitable. He always announces that the wind seems to be picking up even though it is diminishing, for his heart is so young and optimistic that he sees only good in all natural manifestations. Long ago he had the wisdom to bury his wraths and will now loose them on only two subjects—taxes and the New Haven Railroad, upon which it seems he has spent a good part of his life commuting.

I told Post she could bear away a few degrees to the east and try to pick up another half-knot or so of speed. Then we were silent and soon the loneliness left me.

After a time I looked aloft and watched the t'gallant sweep across the nebula of Orion and conceal it momentarily, then reveal it again in all its glory as we rolled the other way.

When my eyes were ready for the night I moved around the taffrail ostensibly to check the lashings of the jolly boat. Actually I wanted to watch our wake for a time, a solitary activity to which I had been long addicted and which I could not seem to share with others. In tropic seas the phosphorescent organisms bestirred by our passage through the water are so vivid we seem to be trailing a luminous gown. Staring down at the undulating column of light had always rewarded me with a sense of swift progress and well-being and the pyrotechnic display of twirling globules was as I should prefer the path of death to be, mysterious and inviting and awesomely beautiful.

After only a few moments watching our diaphanous wake bubbling and tumbling away into the night I lost my strange anxiety as easily as if I had dropped it into the pools of reflected stars. Hola! I had been too long at sea. I was beginning to fret about portents and nothings like a dithering old maid.

On the sixteenth day of our passage from the Marquesas toward the Hawaiian chain a new-born lizard was discovered in McCullough's bunk. We could not find the mother and the otherwise implacable McCullough was distraught with concern for his surprise guest. He claimed that he most certainly knew nothing of the creature's presence aboard or its missing parent and there was considerable raillery about his having sponsored an immaculate conception. Others saw the event as an omen of good luck and tried desperately to keep the little creature alive.

They were successful, but he was undeniably puny and later, because of his utter dependence on us, we had reason to reflect upon his fate.

"All is in apparent good order." That phrase has been recorded four times a day in the logbook by the officer making the ship inspection. It is the sort of monotonous notation we welcome and is not intended to cover petty matters such as the leak over my bunk, since it does not affect the safety of the ship. As it is for all sailors, my bunk is my home at sea and now I have a leak in the roof. I have tried to persuade myself this is meant to be, since the area occupied by my head is to the total area of the *Albatros* as a single star is to the universe, and yet there, right there above my left ear, is the *only* leak in the entire deck. The seas are eternal, but so are deck leaks, which have frustrated sailors for thousands of years because they are difficult to find and where the water comes through below may be far removed from the weak spot on deck. We have tried everything to find the leak and stop it and even Peter Dawson has withdrawn in defeat from the problem. So we have compromised.

Now I am watching the slow swinging of a coffee can which we have hung below the leak. I should be sleeping, but in another few minutes the can will be full of water again, and I must reach up, unhook the can, and pour its contents in a bucket placed beside my bunk. Then I can go back to sleep again for at least another hour. I have things fairly well timed and know that at the approximate rate of precipitation occurring when I came off watch, it will take about an hour for the can to be filled. If I should be too languid to reach out for it the inevitable spillage will chillingly remind me of my neglect. Sometimes, when there are seas swashing across the afterdeck in addition to rain, my protective time schedule becomes confused and my slumbers end abruptly. I have been using my foul-weather gear as a blanket ever since we passed through the doldrums, but it works away from my head after I am asleep and then there is my ear waiting like a cistern.

Although the leak has robbed me of many hours needed rest, I no longer curse it. Somehow I have grown rather proud of its ability to render me physically miserable. And I see in it another thing. During my hours of supposed relaxation it reminds me that even an emperor's crown may pinch his head. It never lets me forget that we are at sea.

As now, the coffee can appears to swing lazily from side to side when in reality the ship is swinging about *it.* That wretched tin can, already half full of water, marks the gradually increasing arc of our roll during the past three days. It will not be ignored, although so far I have done nothing about it except to caution McDowall and Durst to keep their eyes open—as if they had not the wit to do so on their own. Three days—or has it been four days? It commenced with an oceanic restlessness which had been with us for some time before any of us recognized its presence, and it had taken so long to multiply itself to its present status we could almost believe this was the natural way of things.

After the first two days I had reasoned that the fetch of the Pacific was so great the swell might come from a disturbance as far away as the roaring forties. And then I wondered if it really could be so. Yet there were no indications of local or even neighborhood phenomena which might cause such vast convolutions. The glass had been steady, even rising a little during my last watch.

The occasional rain squalls had been of short duration and the evenings had regularly promised that the next day would be a sailor's friend. And still the ponderous swell continued to increase. Perhaps an elephant had decided to go for a walk in the Bay of Bengal.

I have never seen the *Albatros* slipping through the water under such visually thrilling conditions. For nearly a week the wind had been just right, slightly abaft our beam, and varying between 10 and 15 knots. With such benign breezes our actual speed was hardly exciting and the heavy grass skirt the hull acquired during our layover in Papeete subtracted at least 1 knot per hour. But with such winds we could carry every sail the *Albatros* possessed including the main tops'l, which we had set only once since leaving San Francisco. Altogether we were carrying eleven sails day and night and such was the constancy of the wind we had not heard or seen so much as a flap out of any sail though we maintained a course as steady as a steamship. This was sailing in the grand manner with one dreamlike day melting into the next, the kind of sailing that writers who have never been to sea write about.

As if the orthodox wind was not enough, the sea itself remained extraordinarily smooth so that life aboard had been transformed. We had removed the fiddles from the dining table and no longer kept a wary eye on our soup. In anticipation of dry-land pleasures McDowall's wife had rigged a tennis ball arrangement of fish snubbers and line which enabled her to practice her strokes when off watch, and all of our people had soon found amusements which sheer weariness under normal sailing conditions had prevented them from enjoying. There were solemn chess matches and scrimshaw workers and water-color artists. There were cameras clicking everywhere as if we had never seen the *Albatros* before and had just embarked on a holiday cruise. Bathing facilities aboard the *Albatros* consisted of a hose on deck and now we gasped and shouted our discovery of water cool enough to be refreshing again. At night we wore sweaters and rejoiced in the relative crispness of the air.

My own deep pleasure had been to behold the *Albatros* come to life in a way I had never seen her before. I tried every vantage point and never became satiated with watching my love perform. When the swells came on I longed for some means to stand off a half-mile from her so I could appreciate the spectacle in its entirety. I stationed myself as far away as I could, on the very end of the jibboom, on the t'gallant yard, and on the very end of the main boom, which seemed a foolhardy place to be, since if I slipped or the broom dipped in the sea it would be a long time before the *Albatros* could be brought about to search for her master. Yet such was the smoothness of the ocean and the steadiness of the wind, my platform moved up and down only a few feet and the mainsail behind me was solid as a wall.

All of this was because the major movement of the sea was at first so subtle and when the might of the ocean began asserting itself it still remained submarine and the eye was not readily conscious of its immensity. It was necessary to stand away as I attempted to do and regard known proportions against the heaving background. Then I could appreciate why our decks seemed as steady as a liner's, for the *Albatros* was reduced to the size of a child's playboat. These same swells, I saw, could give a big ship a very bad time, while we, being ever so much shorter than the length of the swells, simply rode up and down without sensation of great movement. On the second day I experimented with my sextant and roughly calculated that we rose and fell upon the still unruffled sea, some 20 feet. On the third day I experimented again and found the sum of vertical difference to be closer to 30 feet. I did not believe it and kept the observation to myself. In my salt-water years I had heard more than enough of 30- and 40-foot waves, which always seemed to be observed by people for whom I had no nautical respect whatsoever.

Now lying in my bunk and watching the slow gyrations of the coffee can I wondered if the purely sensuous joy I had derived from watching my ship under such sailing conditions had not perhaps lulled me into abandoning a long-held suspicion of the elements. Some still alert fiber in my marine cabinet had caused me to write an order in the logbook to oil and grease all freeing ports, but I had not as yet made sure they worked easily. And that was all I had done about the swells. Every rag we had was still flying and we were carrying on as if out for a Sunday sail on some sheltered bay.

The tin can swung slowly back and forth and for a moment my thoughts returned to our fifth night out of the Marquesas, when we had witnessed an eclipse of the moon. We had all remarked on a strange phenomenon which accompanied the eclipse, because none of us had ever seen such a thing before nor did there seem to be any plausible explanation for it. We were nearly on the equator, far from any terrestrial dust and the night was perfectly clear. As a consequence we were able to observe a total eclipse throughout its entire cycle and under ideal conditions. What puzzled us was the color of the moon after it stood fully in shadow. For several moments it appeared blood-red.

Henderson was in charge of omens aboard. I must ask her if she could detect any connection between that night and our present swells.

There is a porthole alongside my bunk and by raising my head slightly I can see out of it. It is one of the few portholes in any ship in the world which does not leak; perhaps it dare not because it is under water half the time anyway. When the *Albatros* is on an even keel the porthole is about a foot above the waterline so that if we are on the port tack it is submerged continuously and if we are on the starboard tack it is alternately pointing at the sky or the surface of the sea. At night, when the view is entirely submarine, the phosphorescent bubbles, plankton and algae slip past so swiftly it is like riding full speed with Jules Verne. When the porthole points at the night sky and the stars are visible, the rolling movement imparts a similarly weird sensation of tremendous speed, an optical illusion which permits me to play at realizing an unrealizable ambition. I too can be an astronaut. It is not easy to close your eyes with this sort of thing going on a few inches away so I often wedge a book over the porthole to assure my peace.

It is late afternoon now and I have done with resting. I have been thinking about our sails ever since awakening, and reviewing certain things I had ready long ago about how the old clipper masters would carry sail until the masts blew away and be damned to the consequences. To command a small clipper with zest and style must have been a very fine thing, but I am sailing in a different world and can no more thumb my nose at consequences than I can become an astronaut. For one thing our masts are of steel and are not going to blow away no matter what; and the unpaid members of my crew are entitled to as safe a passage as we can make and I have no right to submit them to unusual dangers. Where should I draw the line then? They would be the first to protest if I doused sail every time a black cloud appeared on the horizon. And yet if we are caught with too much sail they will have to go aloft and do the dousing under conditions which might overtax their abilities—to say nothing of my own. It is hard to believe that the *Albatros* and I had never been together in a blow. From Holland to California to the South Seas, and now halfway back again in some 12,000 miles of sailing, we have never encountered a wind of more than force-6. In the great gales which swept northern Europe during 1936 the *Albatros* was reported to have survived 100-mile-an-hour winds. But she was serving as a pilot vessel then and easily rigged as a schooner and presumably her crew had spent their lifetimes at sea. How would the *Albatros* now behave in a blow such as LaFrenier and I had encountered in the little *Fred Holmes*?

The following day, which was our eighteenth out of Fatu Hiva, a real albatross chose to circle our *Albatros* for the better part of the afternoon. I was so utterly entranced with his aerodynamic efficiency and consummate skill that I nearly forgot how much help he had drawn from the elements. For he too had ideal conditions and took full advantage of the steady wind and nearly unruffled sea. In the best manner of soaring pilots he used the combination of wind and surface to provide him with lift, diving to pick up needed speed, then nearly stalling out when he was in maximum vertical lift. Not once in all the time he was with us did we see him make the slightest movement of his wings. They remained spread out and as fixed as any glider and he knew precisely how close he could skim the surface before natural lift would elevate him again. I cheered him, for he was making the great swells his servants and demanding they provide effortless flight. He would skim a crest at great speed then catch the rising air on the back lip of the swell and rise according to his fancy, then zoom for the surface again. Apparently he was not hunting or even interested in food for he ignored the chunks of bread we dropped over the side. It seemed to me that he was flying for the sheer joy of flight and in my envy I called him a crass exhibitionist.

It was not until the albatross at last departed that I appreciated our own flight over the ocean. Certainly our speed seemed to have increased. Yet how could it, since the wind remained the same as it had been for days? The log also denied there had been any change. Yet we seemed to be rushing along with the swells and all of us agreed their size was increasing.

There was nothing in the evening sky to concern us. There were a host of stars to fix our position at a mere 250 miles to the southeast of Diamond Head and the quick-falling night obliterated the mountain ranges of swells.

It was shortly after nine o'clock when Durst took over the watch from me. At midnight I knew he would be relieved by McDowall, and then I would be on deck again at five for the morning stars. As usual I spoke my gratitude for the day to the heavens and then went below, where I watched the gyrations of the tin coffee can while I waited for sleep. There was no water in it, because it had not rained in three days nor in such smooth seas had we taken so much as a dollop of water on deck.

The coffee can moved like a sluggish metronome and I thought for a time about the psalm singers of Takaroa, whose vitals provoked this same majestic rhythm among their pews. Here, in my little body-length cubicle, surrounded by petty treasures of books, a pistol I once carried when flying the mails and which I have not the slightest idea why I still keep near me, a bos'n's whistle hung from a fancywork chain which Bigelow made for me as a parting gift in Barbados, a worthless "sailor's" knife of American stainless steel which I keep forgetting to throw overboard, and a chunk of oak I am trying to carve into a chessman, here I have often pretended to escape the responsibilities of a small sailing-ship master in the supersonic age. Here I have sometimes been able to shed the frayed pea jacket of a nautical Rip Van Winkle and assume that the lovely dark mahogany with which my cabin is lined is the way ships are still built, and the fine brass lamps with gimbals formed of sea serpents are the normal light for every well-found ship. There is no chromium or formica or Fiberglas in this mellow, polished world; nor engines or electronics or any security save in oneself. Such dreams have lulled sailors since the beginning of time.

☼

FIFTEEN

SOMEONE is shaking my shoulder and I rise from slumber quickly for I have really been only half asleep. It is McDowall. Then it must be after midnight. His face glistens with moisture and he is wearing oilskins.

"Good morning . . ." How can it be morning? Except for McDowall's flashlight it is black in the cabin. "I was wondering if you'd like to come on deck and have a look at things. They have sort of . . . deteriorated."

"What time is it?"

"About two. The way things are going makes a body wonder—"

If McDowall is wondering then immediate attention should

be given to his perplexity because he is so dedicated to understatement.

"Sorry to wake you." Sorry? I am already out of my bunk and slipping into my dungarees. Now awake, I can feel the urgent heaving of our ship, a sort of grandiose bucking and twisting with a whip at the termination of each motion. It is difficult to stand. It is difficult to sit on the bench and pull on my boots. There is a general thundering sound everywhere and I can almost guess what it is like on deck.

"Durst is still on deck and so is his watch. She seems to be straining a bit and we thought you might like to get some sail off her."

"Has the wind shifted?"

"A body might say . . . some little bit."

Through the deck hatch above the center of the after cabin I hear a shout. It is Atcheson's voice. Then there is some pounding of feet on the deck followed by a heavy shuddering as if the *Albatros* had been picked up by a giant and shaken.

"I'd better get back up on deck." McDowall is gone and I call after him that I will join him at once. But it takes a long time to don foul-weather gear when the business of fighting for balance demands the major part of your energies. If a vessel is rolling regularly you can employ kinetic energy for such ordinary chores as slipping on a boot, but when there are sudden explosions of force, then the time required for the most simple function such as pulling on a sock seems intolerable.

On deck it is not nearly as bad as I had thought it would be. There is a hard feel to the wind and it has increased considerably, but it is not gusting. There are white wavelets skittering across the great swells, the sky is black, and there are occasional broad flashes of lightning across the whole northern horizon. A circle of anxious faces awaits me near the helm. They also know that our speed through the water is too fast. Everything is bar taut and the tremendous forces involved in driving our ship so fast are felt rather than seen. Thirteen . . . fourteen knots? Perhaps more. The sea hisses along our lee rail. We must hurry.

Now, too late, we must acknowledge the message borne on the swells. Four days and nights they have been announcing the impending arrival of a tempest and I, having behaved with carefree arrogance rather than humility, will now be retaught my manners. The same fierce tutor has chastised me before.

Johnson is at the helm and obviously has his hands full, for when the ship is caught up from astern by a larger than usual swell she charges on before it at what must be very close to maximum hull speed.

"Come a little more before the wind. Try ten degrees to starboard."

Few men can awaken with their courage instantly at hand and my own has always been laggard. I would like to retreat to my bunk and place a pillow over my head, but such thoughts are not permitted a master whose crew waits so confidently. The omnipotent you who will and can solve all things. *You* there, conceal your faint heart.

I am relieved to see that McDowall has already doused the main topsail. Now I ask him to douse the mid-stays'l and outer jib. His wife is with him, McCullough and Durst when they make their way forward.

My own watch are still asleep below. I will leave them there for the moment, partly because of a long-ingrained aversion to the "all hands" command. It is perhaps a carryover from flying, where to admit an emergency exists inevitably seems to double the trouble. Atcheson and Hall are waiting unassigned.

"Which one of you lucky fellows cares to join me on the t'gallant yard?" A worried man often hides behind nonchalance.

Now with the deck still canted 20 degrees and the solid martial drumming which seems to rule the night, I would as leave shoot off the t'gallant yard with a cannon and never leave the deck. I could order a paid hand aloft, but I can only invite these friends. Although both volunteered immediately, I chose Hall to climb with me, since Atcheson, I thought, better knew our rig at the fife rail and would do a faster job unraveling if anything went wrong.

We pause on the foretop and I call down to cast off the t'gallant yard halyard. There is a great thundering from aloft as the wind tears at the loose sail. We start our long climb for the sky.

We pass the lower tops'l yard and the upper tops'l yard. Both sails are ballooned forward into the darkness and the whole foremast trembles in response to their surging power. Far below I can see McDowall and Durst heaving on the jib downhauls.

We move upward from ratline to ratline, having to pause when the ship rolls past our vertical and leaves us clinging to the shrouds with nothing between the sea and our backs save hard wind. And it is the wind which now shocks me, although I know well enough how amazingly it compounds in strength for every foot above the surface of the sea. I also know that in the life of every ship there must come a day of trial and as we climb I wonder if this might be the time for the *Albatros*.

We catch our breaths at a place just above the upper tops'l yard where the shroud joins the mast. From here there is a detour into space to catch an after stay with one hand and swing into the topmost ladder of ratlines with the other hand. Thence, after a little more climbing, we will be high enough to make our way out on the t'gallant yard. Even in the darkness there would be nothing to it if the yard would only be still, but the mast is transmitting its nervous palsy to everything dependent on it. The shaking will not cease until we secure the sail itself.

The t'gallant now squirms restlessly across the bulging face of the upper tops'l. Below, Atcheson has heaved on the proper clew and buntlines for the t'gallant and it is now gathered in fat balloons known as whore's drawers.

We move outward along the t'gallant footropes and find the wind actually to our favor since it is of such force as to press us against the yard. Below, they have the outer jib captured and the vibration is easing. We bend our bellies over the yard and claw at the rampant sail.

We are panting with our exertions and must pause occasionally to regain our strength. We have the starboard side of the sail secured in gaskets and now we must make our way around the after side of the mast and complete the job on the port side. We are driven by anxiety, for the wind is hardening even more, not quickly as I remember it descending upon the little *Fred Holmes*, but gradually and very surely as if in preparation for a major attack. I am concerned because our defenses are not yet ready.

We are nearly done and must rest again. We are swinging through the wild night sky like monkeys on the tip branch of a great tree. The total arc of our swinging is some 50 feet, yet if we concentrate on fisting the sail just at arm's length then we are not really conscious of anything except its stubbornness and the wind.

During our brief respites I have surveyed all quadrants of the night and found little comfort in any direction. Every possible course we may choose ahead leads directly into a long flashing line of oceanic artillery and it is too late for turning back. Heave to? We cannot risk a full swing around against such swells and wind, for if we should be lucky enough to miss broaching-to at the start of the maneuver then it would be asking too much of luck to avoid being hit broadside by wind and swell in just the wrong way and rolled right over on our beam ends.

Hall, the man I hesitated to take aboard for the voyage because I believed him oversoft from office work and perhaps too gentle a man to serve in our crew, has once again proved how grievously I misjudged him. How far he has come from his gray flannel suit, discreet tie, and well-shined cordovan shoes. Now barefoot, he rides a thin wooden spar 70 feet above the surface of a black and roiling sea and his voice is exhilarated when he calls out to me. "What a wonderful way to finish off the voyage! I was hoping for something like this!"

Ah, Hall. I well know that heady elixir to be tasted when you are risking your own life, but I assure you it sours when others are involved. Then, my gentle friend with the daring of a lion, your audacity melts and you become an elderly pigeon cooing beneath the eaves.

On deck McDowall now has both the outer and inner jibs secured and is free to man the fife rail. So Durst and Atcheson join us on the upper tops'l yard and with two men working each side we soon have it in gaskets. There is a summons from the deck and I must leave them before we are quite finished.

Johnson is having trouble at the helm. "She almost gets away from me sometimes. I put her hard over and she barely responds."

Johnson is easygoing. He is a good helmsman yet now his eyes are worried.

"I'll ease off some mainsheet."

I am reluctant to do this, but we are caught in the classic dilemma of too much sail for the wind. I am the culprit who has allowed the basically sound design of my vessel to be violated so that now the mainsail is fighting with our normal means of steering for control. The mainsail should have been reefed yesterday afternoon. It can win this test with our rudder because it has a thousand times the area, and when a blast of wind hits its expanse then it is bound to take charge and swing our stern away from the body of the wind.

So far, by using full opposite rudder, Johnson has been able to halt these unnerving swerves toward broaching. Letting out the mainsheet should ease his task, yet that too has its perils. We will roll much more and as a consequence invite the end of the boom to dip into the seas. If the clew of the mainsail also submerges, then we will have a countering drag some 30 feet outboard of our hull. We might then be swung so far the other way we would jibe all standing and with such a wind the damage could be very serious.

I have ceased calling myself a heedless fool, thinking to better employ what time remains in redemption. The sight of Dawson bracing himself against the pilothouse door instantly lifts my morale. He is still rubbing sleep from his eyes and his voice is a croak. "What's going on?"

"We're going to catch it."

Dawson emerges from the doorway, glances up at the looming mainsail and then at the hissing sea. "Jesus . . . !" I ask him to ease the mainsheet while I take a strain on the boom preventer tackle.

I move cautiously down the inclined deck to the after pinrail where the hauling part of the preventer tackle is belayed. Here is a dark and noisy place, a cave of turbulence where the ship seems to be fighting the sea. As my fingers seek the hard and wet preventer line I cannot account for this being such a lonely place. A downdraft cascades off the lee side of the mainsail. Its force, redoubled by the shape of the sail, seems to press me into the deck. All around me there is an evil moaning in the shrouds, a low vibrato that strums a beat for the rushing seas. As I work, a wave crest leaps over the bulwark and buries me to the knees, then before it can run off, a second charges aboard and raises the level to my thighs. There is a moment's inexplicable calm, then the turmoil begins all over again. In my loneliness I make my first prayer for the dawn.

We ease the mainsheet as much as we dare—some 3 feet—then secure it again. I climb back up the deck and, facing aft, seize the binnacle for support. Johnson's eyes are still worried. He is braced against the wheelbox and in spite of the enormous leverage at his command is having a hard time achieving full rudder.

"Another hand to help you spin?"

"I could use one."

Dawson steps to the low side of the wheelbox and reaches for the spokes. I had never thought I would ever see two men required at the helm of the *Albatros*, but the need is obviously vital, for now they are able to make corrections more quickly.

We are like a rabbit pursued by hounds. For a moment we have found shelter, but it will not protect us long, so something must be done. You there with the cock-o-the-deck swagger, you the Captain who learned to sail square-riggers from a book, what now? Will you crawl down to your cabin and consult *The Young Sea Officer's Sheet Anchor*? Like any rabbit, what I would like to do is turn back the clock and start all over again. We would not be going so fast and we would not have a steering problem, because we would have everything off of her except the fore-topm'st-stays'l and the main in which we would have tucked a nice double reef. And we would heave to and squat like a fat dowager until the blow was over, and to pass the time we would take pictures of approaching waves to substantiate future lies. Now thanks to my procrastination it was much too late for heaving-to, so I had better think of something else. Of course this *might* be all the harder the wind was going to blow, in which case we should simply hang on and enjoy the sleigh ride.

"How is she steering now?"

"Better."

McDowall and the others are finished forward. They have secured everything except the fore-stays'l and the relatively small lower tops'l. It is one-hand-for-thyself-and-one-for-the-ship weather, so the work has taken them over an hour. Now they gather on the quarter-deck, each grasping some fixed piece of the ship. We all sway in a sort of demoniacal dance according to the motion of the *Albatros* and our tune is the moaning in the shrouds punctuated by drumhead thumps as seas pound against the hull.

"It's not really too bad."

"No. It's not."

Our voices are of children hoping in darkness.

"It's hot."

No reply. We are all, from our individual stations in our individual way, staring at the black, racing sea. For the moment only Johnson and Dawson at the helm have something to keep their hands busy and thus relieve their thoughts.

"If it gets any worse we'll stream some of those oil bags we've been carrying around for two years."

"Oil on troubled waters. . . ." Post had said it, but I would have thought it more in Henderson's style. Suddenly I realize Henderson is the only member of the *Albatros* crew not on the quarter-deck.

"Where is Henderson?"

No one knows. She has not been seen on deck, which is at least reassuring. I send Post off to make certain she is safely below.

Is that hint of light the first of the never-coming dawn? The flashing cannonade ahead has diminished and I try to convince myself that it is going to be just another hot and muggy day. I open my foul-weather jacket and turn toward the wind to cool my body. What can be taking Post so long below? How many minutes does it take to make sure a person is there or not there?

"If we pick up any more speed we'll break out those hawsers in the lazaret and stream them aft." It is something to say while waiting for news of Henderson. It is one of those ideas with two faces. True enough a vessel may be slowed considerably by dragging lengths of heavy rope astern and her tendency to remain straight before wind and wave instead of sashaying dangerously may be much improved, yet fleetness, if it can be controlled, is not to be forsaken in favor of sluggishness. For to slow a vessel of *Albatros*' modest freeboard overmuch before breaking seas would certainly invite a pooping, which is not at all as funny as the term. A sea overtaking the hobbled *Albatros* could, in a matter of seconds, wash her decks clean of houses, gear and people. Even if we were spared such a final catastrophe a series of boarding seas could soon cause dangerous flooding below.

"Are all hatches dogged and secured?"

"Aye, sir." McDowall reserves such quaint and such positive parlance for times of stress and he has also recognized our situation.

Come along now, Post! Bring us the word that Henderson did not come on deck and disappear but is quite safely below.

If it blows much harder or the steering becomes any more difficult I have one trick which I prefer to oil or dragging a tangle of lines. It is a heritage from my days of fore-and-aft sailing in schooners and can be done quickly. We can wait until the very last to employ it.

Post is in the pilothouse doorway. She waits for the deck to level momentarily, then makes a dash for the binnacle. She turns up the brim of her sou'wester but it is still so dark I cannot be sure of her expression.

"I have a message for you from Miss Henderson, who is in her bunk. If you need her she will come on deck instantly, but if not she says it is just as easy to drown down there as up here."

There is no price on the value of laughter amid danger. Suddenly the rumbling of the wind which has been our all-pervading sound for too long is relieved by our spontaneous appreciation of Henderson's aplomb. One of the dark figures surrounding the binnacle chuckles and supposes that Henderson is eating chocolates and reading a French novel in her bunk and another voice announces that the wind would not dare blow harder without Henderson's permission, and in a series of nonsensical comments on damn-the-torpedoes people and the blessing of haughty courage, we forsake the paralytic silence created by individual frights blooming in the same small arena. Henderson has taught us to dismiss dread as a mere nuisance and once again we are a crew each inspired by the other.

We wait. We listen and watch with all our senses, breathing deeply to maintain our new confidence although sometimes our very inhalations seem to be sucked away by the wind. I am able to discover a certain wry amusement in waiting attendance upon this dawn and some comfort in the assurance that the arrival of day can transform nocturnal despair into victory. I can hardly look away from the east. What is this about the speed of light? How can it take so long to arrive? Our speed will appear to diminish if we have light and that in itself will be welcome.

Dawson and Johnson have been relieved from their efforts at the helm. Now McDowall and Atcheson are taking their turn.

"Doing all right?"

"Yes. But I'm thinkin a body might have some trouble if she comes on to blow any more."

You are quite right, McDowall. But let us not admit even to each other that we are tight-rope walkers nearly arrived at the end of the rope. If we can avoid falling either way for just a little longer, then the lights will come on and we can see what we're doing and I think the band will play a triumphal march. Meanwhile, if you could take your eyes off the compass long enough to look beyond the starboard rail you would see that when we roll that way our main boom just skims through the water. Just a little bit now. A rooster tail of spume across every wave top. This is not a good thing. Yet we dare not haul the boom in more because then you could not steer and we dare not let it out more because certainly then it must smash heavily into every sea.

Why is it so warm? A hard thundering wind, unless originating in a typhoon, has no business being so warm. And this isn't typhoon country.

We have all found some place on the quarter-deck where we can be reasonably secure if we keep one arm wrapped around something solid. I have never waited for dawn with so many people before. I wish they would talk more to one another, because silence is the nursemaid to fear. Now I can make out their bundled shapes although not individual faces. They are huddled along the high side of the pilothouse and four of them are clinging to the port taffrail which is canted toward the sky. I have staked out my own claim of deck space and have found the iron balls on either side of the binnacle handy grips when I wish to swing around and change my field of worry from one direction to another.

We are all on deck now. Even Henderson could not abide the turmoil below. She is hanging on to the bell gallows which is fixed to the after hatch. She does not appear to be afraid but rather peeved. Suddenly I realize that I can actually see her expression! Here is light! Here is dawn! Yes, the mainsail has become a solid rather than a looming shadow against the night. Yes, there is now a difference between the sea and sky.

Just as I am ready to cheer, my spirits plunge back into darkness. There is the sound of an approaching jet aircraft followed by a thunderous explosion on our port quarter. I look up and grab the binnacle with both hands, for the Pacific ocean is coming aboard. I am astounded at the weight and force of the water. In a moment I am encased in it, then it draws quickly away and I look about to be sure everyone is still in his place. I try to count the figures about the quarter-deck. They are gasping, spewing salt water and invectives, and some are trying to laugh. The lee side of the deck is flooded to the height of the rail, but the water is running out the scuppers and freeing ports. So much for those nautical sages who had once told me freeing ports were utterly useless. Now I treasured each one of them, for we could ill afford any extra burden of water if we were to be boarded by more seas. We wait apprehensively for another wave to overwhelm us, but one after another snarls up to our transom and slips harmlessly on by.

Now I can see even those faces farthest from me and they are all of a kind in their weariness. The eyes of my friends are half closed, staring rather than looking at the sea and the sky, as if they are each in a private trance. I am aware that my own face is sagging, and while nothing has really changed except the intensity of light, a great lethargy has come over me. I want to lie down anywhere and close my eyes.

My standing-up sleep is terminated by a dull explosion forward followed by a flat sound of distant thundering.

"Fore-stays'l's blown!"

Dawson, who is on the high side of the deckhouse, starts forward. Durst and McCullough follow him to secure the tatters now flaying about the forestay. I am not surprised the fore-stays'l has gone at last. It had been much patched and its strength had withered all along the leech. What concerns me now is the effect its absence may have on our steering, for we had sheeted it taut amidships, thus employing it as a preventer against our bow coming around to windward and setting us up for a broaching.

I watch McDowall and Atcheson at the helm. They work fast and hard when more than one turn of the wheel is required yet they seem satisfied with their control.

"Any difference?"

"Negative."

Very well. The lower tops'l, our only square sail still flying, will do the job then.

It is light enough at last to take a chance at getting the mainsail down. If the attempt is successful, then we can run out the duration of this wind under the lower tops'l alone at just about the right speed. Steering should be easy and if we need more stability for comfort we need only set the mainst'ys'l and sheet it down hard. How quickly do our troubled thoughts move from desire to completion thereby softening the fact that running down the wind in this wild fashion will make dousing the main somewhat more than a routine task. Since we cannot come about in the normal fashion we must slack halyards and ease the main down little by little. We will need two men each for the throat and peak halyards, one to pay off and the other to make certain the coils will not slide across the deck or foul in the running. We should have a good man on the downhaul, and one for the after vang, which is a long line made fast to the end of the gaff. Also someone to slack the boom preventer tackle. And a lot of muscle on the mainsheet. We can set everything up beforehand with the mainsheet sweated in as far as we dare, the topping lifts hiked, and the lazy jacks taut.

What else? Every free hand to pounding down the canvas and hauling in the mainsheet. Then someone to pass gaskets. Altogether eleven people involved in dousing a single sail which in smooth waters I had accomplished alone. I will take the helm and Rogerts, who has a passion for steering matched only by his devotion to geneva gin, can bear me a hand.

Now that it is light I can foresee only one major difficulty and I will try to solve it by putting more beef on the throat downhaul. The mainsail is pressed so hard against the after shrouds that the after ends of the oak ratlines are clearly outlined along the surface of the sail from gaff to the boom. It is obvious the mainsail is not going to slide down as handily as we would like to have it. It is wet and stiff as metal. It is going to be like collapsing the façade of a fair-sized building with our bare hands.

In daylight our speed appears slower—12, perhaps 13 knots—but the low rumpled gray sky holds no promise of relief from the wind. We must get the main down and then Rogerts can produce something from his galley and those who have been on watch the longest can try to sleep. And I can cease worrying about broaching.

I am about to take McDowall's place at the helm when some genie, invisible beyond our steeply canted stern, opens an icebox door. I cannot believe what is happening nor can my comrades. Dawson, who has been around the sea longer than any of the rest of us, looks at me in wonder, his eyes bewildered. Both of us know that what has happened is meteorologically impossible, yet here it is. Ever since that long-ago time when I first came on deck the heat has been oppressive and the inside of my foul-weather gear is soaked with sweat. And all of the others had been the same with more moisture produced by their bodies than they acquired from the sea. Now, in the space of a minute or even less, when I have simply moved a few paces, the wind has turned bitter cold. I am astonished to see my breath in this latitude and all of us turn as if by command to look in the direction of this new wind which is so different from that we have known through the night.

We are stricken by this new and cruel wind. It is much heavier and immediately the *Albatros* responds to its power by seeming to flee before it. The whole ship vibrates with our speed. We heel far over until the taffrail is continuously buried in solid water. I had stood near it many times, caressing its varnished beauty, and I had said, "Well, one thing—the sea will never catch her here." Well, never had come.

A great wall of water plunges on deck filling the lower third to the height of a man's waist. At the same time the main boom is buried in the sea for nearly half its length, the whole foot of the sail scoops up tons of water, and a sickening convulsion is transmitted through the mast to the entire ship.

This new wind is not just a hard blow to test our skills and nerves. It is not going to diminish with the dawn, and unless we can do something about the main immediately we are in trouble. I loathe the word more than ever, because in this case it is a reflection of my carelessness.

We cannot douse the main in the careful fashion I had planned, for already our principal working deck space has been usurped by the sea.

We take a long roll to leeward and hang on to watch the taffrail vanish again and the ocean plunge aboard. It pounds down on a heavy teak deckbox and explodes it into several pieces as if a grenade has gone off inside. We are momentarily blinded in spray and I feel solid water clutching at my boots again. Then with a great shuddering the *Albatros* rolls back to windward like a harpooned whale and emerges from the sea.

My own view is first of McDowall's boots, then behind him I notice that a section of the deck grating surrounding the wheelbox is gone. In a trice the sea has taken it away, though it is perforated with two hundred square holes, weighs almost a hundred pounds, and was tightly wedged in a steel support.

I swing into McDowall's place at the helm and send him forward with orders as ancient as the gaff rig. "Scandalize the main."

With Atcheson to bear him a hand he makes his way slowly and carefully along the deck. They disappear around the deckhouse and I alternately mind the now vivid green sea for our steering, and the main gaff which should soon descend.

Dawson is at the helm with me. I am certain that if it were not for the wind I would hear him grunting with his exertions. Durst and Rogerts are manning the main vang. In ordinary sailing the vang helps to reduce the movement of the gaff aloft and when the sail is doused it helps to control the gaff's descent.

We roll into another great sea. Parts of the deckbox are washed forward to disappear beyond the deckhouse; then as we roll back, a bright orange life preserver floats across the quarter-deck as if looking for the box.

Still no movement about the peak halyard blocks, which are 80 feet above the deck. The paint on one block is badly chipped. We must get after that soon. Tacky blocks . . . tacky ship. Indeed! If we fail to bring the gaff down quickly, we may not have a ship. McDowall, what takes you so long?

It is extremely hazardous to attempt deck work in solid water and I will not ask any of our people to risk it. McDowall and Atcheson are well enough off because there is no need for them to venture below the mid-deck base of the mast. From there they can cast off the main peak halyard, which if it runs free will immediately drop the end of the long gaff and thus automatically reduce the area of the mainsail by nearly a third.

Come, McDowall! How long does it take to remove a coil of line from its pin and lay it on the deck ready to run? Never mind. I know. When you are sliding about and trying to work with your every movement hampered because of wind and sea, it takes forever.

The peak of the gaff is at last arcing down. Already I can feel an improvement in the helm.

The mainsail is becoming a crude triangle, black against the sky. The boom, now solely dependent on its wire lifts for support, bumps and skips angrily along the sea. Each collision seems certain to snap it off, but after a spasm of shaking there it is again.

A deluge of rain is dumped by the wind. It spews horizontally upon the backs of our foul-weather gear, making so much noise we can hear it rattling on one another. McDowall returns from the mainmast. He cups his hand to yell at my ear.

"A body could do with a little less noise!"

"Why didn't you let me sleep?" If McDowall must show his lack of concern, then so must I.

He chooses five hands and starts inching in the mainsheet. After a few feet he looks back at me, his eyes inquiring of the effect on our steering.

"Yes. Still all right."

Another few feet. The yellow jackets move in unison against the green sea as their owners heave on the line.

"Okay?"

"Try a little more."

We are winning. I can feel it in the helm. The end of the main boom is less than 6 feet outboard of the taffrail and we still have full steering control. Yet we must hurry it in far enough to douse the sail, because the wildly swinging gaff will soon saw a hole through it.

"Try some more. We almost have it."

A chant rises from the yellow jackets as they bend their backs to the mainsheet. They must sit down and haul because they cannot stand without grasping a fixed object. The mainsheet moves continuously, an inch or two at a time. The wind swoops down on their voices, collects and merges their tone to make a chorale of effort. "Ho! . . . Heave . . . Ho! . . . Ho! . . . Heave . . . Ho!"

I watch the end of the main boom creep in as a person watches a nightmare flow through his sleep. This eerie, flat half-light of dawn is populated entirely by people in yellow jackets and they do not make the sounds of my time. It seems inconceivable that I once commanded a machine that flew. That must be in some future time. The now is this dimly lit scene of reincarnation where voices sing and grunt at brutal manual labor.

"Hold fast! Belay!"

The main boom is in as far as we dare to bring it. We are

just at the point where the helm can dominate the steering, but we cannot relinquish any more of its power. Enough—just enough.

Our speed has slowed to 9 or 10 knots and our lee scuppers hold only knee-deep water. Only occasionally does a solid sea come charging aboard. We may go to work now dousing the main sail, hoping to save it for another day.

It took us over an hour of continuous labor to secure the main. And still, with only the lower tops'l set, we often slipped through the water at almost 7 knots. Yet concern had left us when we regained control, and what had been a tempest became merely a tough blow which we had simply to endure. Rogerts went off to his galley and was busy with his pots, although we still occasionally dipped the lee rail in the sea.

As if demonstrating the relativity of all trials, Post and Henderson and McDowall's wife were sloshing about the decks picking up the flotsam scattered everywhere by the boarding seas. There were innumerable pieces of the deckbox and most of the gear which it had contained. And from everywhere about the ship came an assortment of tools, buckets, clothes, wood, and some paintbrushes I had not seen for months. As the ship rolled, the entire mess swept grandly back and forth across the waist deck.

I supposed that my own face was as weary as McDowall's, but I could not believe it. There were great pouches under his eyes and his head was bent like a man who still waited a verdict. He kept flexing his big hands and rubbing at the stubble of his beard while he momentarily closed his eyes. He had been continuously alert and in motion since midnight, which in these conditions was a very long time. Durst had been on his feet even longer, and in spite of his youth now moved like an elderly man.

Most of our company were sprawled in grotesque yellow bundles about the quarter-deck—waiting for the next task. The drowsy exhaustion of a long and anxious night was upon them and I wondered what other possible endeavor could cause them to so spend themselves. Now that they had the time, I thought, they will take time to fear and that will be an utterly useless expenditure of their remaining energies. I wondered how I could assure them that everything was now all right and that after food and sleep by tomorrow or the next day this would only be a memory?

I called to Post and Henderson, who came to me, heads bent against the wind and rain. And I told them to fetch a jug of rum and cups for all. It was a time for breaking rules and the heavy overcast obliterated any hint of the sun's position. So for the first time on the voyage we were not going to wait until it descended below our yards.

Three days later, with some whimpering help from the African Queen, we stood into the Hawaiian port of Hilo. There we learned of the destruction wrought by the same storm which had so tried us. In its rampaging progress it had destroyed many dwellings along the northern coast of Oahu and crushed windows on the bridge of the 15,000-ton liner President Cleveland.

When at last the wind subsided I thought of the lizard. And though we searched the entire ship, he was never to be seen again. I wondered if during that dark and troublesome night he had lost faith in us and decided to abandon ship.

There had been moments when I could not entirely blame him.

☼

IN HARBOR

This morning things eased to half a gale, so we were encouraged to look beyond the breakwater. We could have saved ourselves the trouble. We were lured into optimism because the entrance channel to Rønne harbor is deep and thus a heavy plaything for the wind. From a distance it appeared to have lost its nastiness. But on either side of the channel there are shoals which extend a considerable way offshore and which are afroth. The shoals are marked by broomsticks after the Scandinavian way of marking minor channels and hazards and they give the whole business of navigation a sort of Hans Christian Andersen air. Yet the method is wonderfully efficient and since nearly all Scandinavian waters offer tortuous navigation it would be difficult to follow any other type of marker. The shafts of the brooms are painted maroon and the brushes are of black straw as preferred by witches. The maroon shaft may support one, two, or even three brooms and for necessary variety they may point either up or down so that many combinations are possible.

"Well enough. We've just fetched that two down and one up . . . now the next stick should have all three brooms pointing down."

All of this is precisely illustrated on the marvelous Scandinavian charts about which there is some civilized controversy. The Swedes say their charts are by far the best, the Danes say theirs are better, and the Norwegians insist theirs are the best of all. Foreign sailors are so impressed with their accuracy of detail and ease of use they can only cheer for all three productions. As if their technical qualities were not enough they have a picture-book character that makes them a delight to study—which does not at this time help us to escape from Rønne harbor. Our draft in the Black Watch *will not allow us to leave the entrance channel and if anything went wrong and we were forced onto the fuming shoals that would be the end of things.*

So we have returned to this vessel and set about the business of waiting again. It became easier about an hour ago when the wind piped up again like the preparatory tuning of an orchestra. Now it is screeching away at its monotonous symphony and we are congratulating ourselves on our common sense. This shows the considerable deterioration in our spirits since our first day of confinement to Rønne harbor. We know very well that only common things are accomplished when common sense prevails. Our handy excuse for this new hesitation is the fisherman who made port last night. In the best tradition of a dedicated dock committeeman I put on my foul-weather gear and stood in the lashing rain while he secured his vessel. Then I annoyed the exhausted man with questions until he decided to hide behind the language barrier. However he did advise that he had come from the Island of Gotland which is to the north of Bornholm so I thought him a very stalwart individual indeed. He also said that the wind would subside soon, which it did, and then blow like hell again, which it is now doing. It was September, he reminded me, and what could anyone expect? Since I certainly could not argue that September was the most pleasant time to be at sea and since he obviously hadn't the slightest interest in what I thought of September, our rapport came to a sudden end and I wandered off through the spume trying to reassure myself about the Ides of September. It had been in September that I lost the Uncle Sam *and it had been a long-ago September afternoon when as master-owner of the sloop* Raccoon *I had won further age by being bold rather than hesitant.*

☼

V

THE *ALBATROS*

. . . THE CHAINS OF POSSESSION . . . AND TRAGEDY

☼

SIXTEEN

THE *Albatros* laid up in Honolulu and her crew went their various ways. A year passed while she gathered weed, rust, and a living museum of vertebrate and invertebrate undersea life along her hull. And gradually I sensed that she was in command of my destinies, rather than the other way around. There were times when her monopoly of my thoughts and actions became intolerable, and so like all men discovering they are possessed, I sometimes reviled her. What could I do with this demanding bitch before I forgot the meaning of freedom?

A square-rigged vessel the size of the *Albatros* was not exactly a prime market commodity and brokers shook their heads when asked about sale prospects. Yet I could not afford to keep such a costly courtesan. I sought everywhere for a buyer and had not far to look for windy customers, since an endless parade of them found their way to dream for a while upon the *Albatros*' decks. They were each in his own way fascinating with their schemes and plots and devices intended to transfer ownership of the *Albatros* from my name to theirs in the nebulous future. I was offered all manner of partnerships, from running contraband to treasure-hunting expeditions, and they were all identical in one factor—a total lack of money. Yet no matter how wild-eyed the visitor or how crackpot his proposal, I forced myself to listen patiently, for I remembered how so short a time ago my own dream had barely survived.

At last I decided there were no customers for such a vessel in America and resolved to sail the *Albatros* back to Europe, where I hoped there might still be some appreciation of a fine sailing ship. I signed on a much smaller and more frugal crew in San Diego, and as so often happens in such affairs, a genuine buyer appeared on the dock even as we were casting off our lines. His name was Sheldon and he wanted a school ship. He was a fine sailor and a sincere man of purpose, although I flinched when he took a metal tape from his jacket and began measuring the anatomy of my still-beloved. It was as if another man had come to view a marvelous woman whose every attribute was known to me and every fault forgiven; and circumstances had forced me to part with her so that for a time she stood naked while vulgar eyes feasted upon her beauty. And then along had come a man who jangled his purse and announced, "I will have her, but I will change the diameter and deflection of her breasts, stretch her neck, add pink to her nipples, and fatten her pelvis."

I was very pleased that my *Albatros* was destined to be embraced in such capable arms, but I invented urgent errands ashore when the measuring became too intimate.

We agreed that ownership would transfer in Portugal half a year hence. And so I sailed her away to a final assignation.

Somehow the voyage eastbound for the Atlantic seemed like a personal defeat. An air of melancholy enwrapped the ship and at night when I set out alone for the routine inspection my roving flashlight beam seemed to have developed an uncanny knack for revealing the ghosts of my devotions. It would pause on the bitter end of a topping lift where one sultry morning while we were anchored off Hiva Oa I had placed a whipping and topped it with a monkey's fist.

When I stood in the waist and turned the light upward the beam would outline the foretop, and climbing to it I could only think of days when I had come here to read or dream, or the nights when I had come for solitude beneath the undulating stars. For here on the foretop it is always the heavens that move while the ship remains still.

These are different times in the *Albatros*. Now because of devotion it is possible to sweep the flashlight beam around the engine room without illuminating potential disaster. There, polished like a museum display, stands the African Queen. Hola! Although she still stinks outrageously, I know she will function perfectly on demand.

All of this will soon be gone; the figurehead of the cannibal girl I designed and which now adorns the bowsprit, the fancy ropework that Post has done on the bell harp, the star on a shield of red, white and blue which I carved for the binnacle, and the skin-smooth taffrail where I cannot place my hand without a secretive caress. All is for another man.

Sheldon came aboard in New York and resumed his measuring. And while he was at it I made all haste to escape for a final romp before his omnipresent rule revealed the sum of my remorse. What had I done? Where in all the world would I find another vessel to so capture my passions?

As soon as possible we sailed for London. We were passing up the East River when I spied a dilapidated wharf on the Brooklyn side and suddenly envisioned a scene I had nearly forgotten. There in the mauve light of a March morning lay a siren who had taught me that the mind is the greatest of all adventurers.

The *Margarite* was a former coasting schooner of some 250 tons burthen. As such she was considerably larger than the *Albatros* and had I possessed her entirely, she would certainly have been my heftiest vessel. In truth I "owned" only a very small part of her and never sailed in her.

Like any active member of the International Dock Committee, the wharves and estuaries of the nearest port were my obligatory patrol. It was my duty to know something of every vessel larger than a motorboat, even in a port as complex as New York; and had I lived in Boston, Philadelphia, New Orleans, Rangoon or Sydney, the brotherhood would have expected the same encyclopedic information. Only ocean liners and naval vessels were excluded from this regular vigil since, strangely, their movements are of little interest to dedicated committee members. The comings and goings of all other vessels must be carefully observed. What is that tug doing in the East River? She belongs in the Hudson. A freighter up from Yucatan. Bananas, no doubt. Well, well . . . laying at Fulton Street since morning and still has ice in his rigging. Has he unloaded his cod? A newly arrived yacht here in the Hudson basin—English by the boxlike cut of her stern, and when will they ever learn to design a boat to please the eye? Right—there's her red duster.

Such trivia crams the mind of any good committeeman and

he cannot acquire it unless he devotes a great deal of his spare time to patrol. It is a very cheap form of research which is undoubtedly why so many active members are somewhat less than wealthy. This was my circumstance when one day on patrol through the less frequented estuaries of Brooklyn I came upon the *Margarite* and stood too long admiring her in the chill afternoon.

I thought she had probably been employed in the coal trade to New England ports and also had probably brought lumber down from Maine, although she was smaller than the many schooners once so engaged. No matter. They were gone forever and here was an obviously genuine survivor, a vessel fit for a man, with an expanse of deck to accommodate his stride. Her mainmast was gone and there was only a stump of a foremast on which a hoisting boom had been rigged. Her jibboom had been sawed off by an extraordinarily clumsy carpenter and long threads of dry oakum protruded from most of her seams. But the basically fine lines of her transom were still apparent and a splendid taffrail extended nearly to her waist. She had once been painted a green which time and neglect had faded to a lime-yellow, and there were great splotches of bare wood, scrofulous undercoating, and bubbled areas of paint festooning her hull everywhere. She was such a colorful hag that I was as taken with her as I might have been with a dockside harlot who though long past her prime had contrived to keep her jollity.

Gazing upon her I wondered why I had not previously been aware of such a rare specimen and I nearly fell off the wharf trying to see her hailing port. The lettering was so faded I could not be sure, but I decided it must be Providence. Then perhaps she had been a Portuguese, since there was still spasmodic sail trade between that city and the Azores.

I was about to leave when I heard a heavy coughing in her

after cabin. After a moment a man stuck his head out of the hatch and spat accurately over the taffrail. He was bald of head and the soft whiteness of his dome contrasted remarkably with his crimson face and nose. He was wearing long underwear which I guessed might not have been removed for some time. His eyes found me, narrowed, and I became so uncomfortable under their careful scrutiny that I wanted to reach out and stuff him back down in his box. Then he called to me, "Chilly day. Right, mate?"

Now I had never in my life been called mate by a true sailing-ship man and the greeting so warmed me I forgot his penetrating eyes. Then he said that he would never learn to like March in New York and his deep voice boomed and reverberated through the wharf pilings like an enormous bullfrog croaking in the shadows. We drifted into a brief discussion of the refuse in the East River and how for some strange reason it did not offend the nostrils.

"Maybe it's just because it all stinks so horrible," he said with a patronizing wave toward Manhattan and its skyscrapers. Thus far I had refrained from inquiring the *Margarite*'s last port and her purpose in New York, for I was aware that unless you were a uniformed customs man or other official such questions were often answered with obscene suggestions as to what the nosy inquirer might do to himself.

"Like to come aboard?" the man asked.

I swung down to the deck before he could change his mind. He remained half submerged in the hatch while I strolled forward to the bow and then turned back toward the *Margarite*'s waist. All of this time the man said nothing, yet I was aware that he was watching me. Finally my tour brought me to a position just at the break of her poop and I had either to invade the quarter-deck, which seemed overbold without further invitation, or clamber back on shore.

I waited indecisively for some signal of further welcome from the man behind the cerise nose. But the only movement of his lips involved manipulating a toothpick from one side of his mouth to the other. I was close enough to him now to see that his nose as well as his jowls were flaked with filaments of purple, and a great red wen blossomed from the right side of his neck.

Suddenly his volcano voice rumbled again.

"Sailing man?" he asked.

The instant I decided upon my reply I sensed it would lead me into trouble. Instead of telling him that I had only sailed in small boats and had never made my living as a sailor, I implied that I was a professional by saying, "'Here and there." I should have realized that while I surveyed the decks of the *Margarite* another even more perceptive examination was being conducted by my new friend in the long underwear.

"Then come have a look below," he said, and like a blunt-ended iceberg his dome submerged within the hatch.

We sat in his cabin, which was decorated in a general motif of bare-breasted females advertising various petroleum products. He said that his name was Tilley and when I asked if he was owner as well as Captain of the *Margarite* he said that indeed he was. He offered me a glass of red wine from an amber jug which he kept handily in his bunk. "It's just Dago red and won't hurt you none. Rejuvenates the blood." He smiled. It was the first time he had smiled and his dentures gleaming against his jowls and nose made a drollish clown mask of his face. He took a draft of his own glass, and after a prolonged fit of coughing wiped at his watering eyes and in a voice that was anything but feeble murmured several times over that he was not well, not well at all, at all.

"What am I to do?" he inquired as if I actually might provide the answer. "I never wanted to go into steam and now it's too late. But *Margarite* and me have got to keep busy or we starve. Done very well we have too, thanks to our special knowledge. . . ."

I liked the way he referred to the *Margarite* as a living partner in his enterprise, whatever it was. I told myself that this man truly loved his nearly exhausted vessel.

"*Margarite* and me have been together thirty-one years now and that's a fair trick."

"When was the last time you sailed her?"

"Way back—oh, way back. The fall of nineteen twenty it was. Then we laid up in Providence for the winter and our troubles began. Haven't had a rag on her since because it don't make sense, like you know."

I could not avoid wondering if Captain Tilley had ever been in politics since his stentorian voice and expansive manner would have marvelously suited a legislator. And as he brought me into his professional confidence I experienced a warm feeling of participating in his problems, and such was the magic persuasion of his style that soon I had developed a powerful interest in the *Margarite*'s future well-being.

Waiting for Captain Tilley to further outline his views on all things maritime, I noticed that in addition to the suspenders which passed over his long underwear, a belt wide enough to belong on a saddle cinched his great belly. And for a moment I wondered if his voluminous pants concealed a peg leg, for it seemed to me that John Silver had certainly stepped from the pages of *Treasure Island*. The fleeting impression vanished when he began once more to complain of his health.

"It's been too much work for one man and it is gettin' worse as my verterbra gets the clicks." He removed the toothpick from his lips and pointed it at the back of his neck. Then he squirmed around in his chair, hunched his shoulders, and slowly twisted his head. And sure enough I did hear a clicking.

"Hear that?" He squirmed again. "Hear it?"

"Yes."

"That's what convinces me the time has come to take a partner in the *Margarite* . . . a man who understands the sea. I had in mind a younger man, like say yourself. There's a fortune to be made with the *Margarite* if we play it right."

We? Was this salt-encrusted veteran offering me a job? If so I was ready to sign on immediately. I now asked him what he had in mind.

"Salvage! You can't believe how much salvage there is on the eastern coast of the United States. Could keep us busy for years. And after I get too old—who knows?" He shrugged his shoulders as if daring me to forecast the future. "Maybe the *Margarite* would end up all yours." Again he took the toothpick in his fat fingers and wielded it like a baton.

"A young man who's smart goes into business with an older man, because all he needs to do is wait awhile and time gives him a present."

He started to laugh, but another spasm of coughing struck him and created such upheavings of his belly that I thought even his great belt would burst.

When at last he subsided he seized his chair between his legs and eased himself closer to me. Now his voice became carefully modulated and confidential. "You wouldn't believe it. In Flushing Bay alone I know a wreck that's got ten thousand dollars' worth of junk in it—metal and all. Just there for the hauling out and taking away. The old *Harvester*—there she sets high and dry just waiting for someone to come along and pull her to pieces. Best of all you're not wasting all your time runnin' to and fro, because there's a Jew right here in Brooklyn will buy every ounce you bring him."

Now instead of *we* it was *you*, which I took to be me. I was hopelessly lost. I could already see myself, bronzed and weary after a hard day's work at the donkey engine, leaning over the *Margarite*'s ample bulwark and sizing up the situation for the morrow. Even if we would not actually be sailing I would be serving in a true sailing ship. I wondered how little I could afford to accept in pay.

Captain Tilley soon clarified matters.

He well knew the value of silence preceding any statement of significance, so while my mind raced through certain personal arrangements I would have to make before going to sea in the *Margarite*, he waggled his toothpick at the skylight and his eyes took on a remote look as if he had removed himself from this crude cabin and would not return until beseeched.

At last he spoke and his voice rumbled straight up from his groin. "What I had in mind was to make someone like yourself with experience at sea a plank owner in the *Margarite*. Know what that is?"

Ashamed to betray my total ignorance, I said that I thought I understood.

"It means you don't have to work, which is a nice position to be in. They had plank owners in clipper ships and just about every other kind of ship what was built of wood. A plank owner just sets on his ass in his shoreside home and when his ship comes to port he's right there holding out his big mitt for a share of the voyage. And he's protected like no other investor ever is, because he actually owns a piece of the vessel and it can't be sold without his say-so or do anything else. Get the picture?"

My own voice was merely a disappointed whisper when I told him that I was in no position to finance a voyage even if it was only to Flushing Bay.

"Oh, but you don't have the picture at all. I am not speaking of a large sum. As the market goes today I'll be frank and say maybe *Margarite* wouldn't fetch more than ten thousand dollars

—just sold as is, understand? Now suppose you became a plank owner for one tenth—say put up one thousand dollars. It would all be legal and all with your name right on the ship's papers, spelled out right under *and owners*. So say this first trip up to the old *Harvester* brings in ten thousand dollars. There you are right there with your investment back and you still own one-tenth of the *Margarite*."

I told him I had no hope of sparing a thousand dollars.

"Well say five hundred then—go for a twentieth."

I said it was highly unlikely that I could find even five hundred. Instead I offered to work for him if he could pay me enough to squeak by until the first salvage job was done. He did not seem to hear me and I saw that his toothpick slid impatiently from one side of his mouth to the other.

Still looking up at the skylight he intoned, "Tell you what you do. Go home and think this over. Come back tomorrow and bring two hundred bucks with you. There's no great harm in starting out small and I'll put your name on the papers for one-twentieth anyway. You can make it up with your profit share of the first voyage. How's that?"

I never knew whether Captain Tilley had consulted the occult or was possessed of psychic powers himself, but he had named the exact amount less a few dollars in my savings account. Nor could I ever decide if he knew I would return the following day with a cashier's check for two hundred dollars, which he solemnly placed in a cigar box. Then he had such a frightening spasm of coughing that I wondered if we would actually be able to execute the next ceremony, which involved my signing the *Margarite*'s papers as a co-owner, with Tilley's initials beside my name. There were several lines for signatures, but I could not see if there were other co-owners, because Tilley's fat hand persistently covered the signing area and when the matter was done he slapped the paper shut with firm finality. I did at least note that the papers were the *Margarite*'s. She was described as engaged in the "coasting trade and mackerel fishery."

"I'll get some grub today and sail tomorrow," Captain Tilley said heartily.

"Are you going to work alone?"

"Oh always—always. I don't have business with the scum you get along the waterfront these days. When they're not eatin' they're drunk and when they're not drunk they're asleep."

The *Margarite*'s progress through the water was entirely dependent upon an ancient Bolander diesel situated deep in her bowels. The exhaust was a long tin pipe which looked like a howitzer and sounded much the same. For all its raucous farting the engine developed very little horsepower and I was as much impressed with Captain Tilley's ability to handle such a large vessel alone as I was with the salvage task before him. So I wished him a good voyage as gravely as if he were bound round Cape Horn and gave him a telephone number to call when "our" ship returned with her treasure. And I said that I would be watching the East River and would probably see him homeward bound.

Before I finally waved farewell I stood for some time on the wharf admiring the vessel which was now part mine. And my satisfaction was immense.

"I should be back in two weeks," Captain Tilley had said.

My impatience could not tolerate such a long time, so at the end of the first week I borrowed a pair of binoculars and took the subway and the bus to the shore of Flushing Bay. The few unwelcome doubts that had occasionally bubbled in my thoughts were at once dismissed, for sure enough there was my *Margarite* lashed alongside a derelict hulk and I could see her boom moving back and forth between what I knew must be the *Harvester* and the *Margarite*'s waist. And each time it moved there was some object dangling from the cable. From my position on shore the *Margarite*'s deckhouse blocked my view of the donkey engine so I could not see Captain Tilley, who I assumed was operating the winch. I was somewhat disturbed when my binoculars picked out a stranger, a much thinner man who reached out for the cable and raised his hand to signal. Well, well. Tilley had found another hand was necessary. It was quite all right by me if he could get the job done faster. I only regretted that the operation must be carried out so far from shore and in the middle of the swift tide and current gushing through Hell Gate. Even if I could find a rowboat it was no place for one, so I contented myself with watching through the binoculars for more than an hour.

Finally I turned back toward the real world and went away, and that was the last I ever saw of either the *Margarite* or Captain Tilley.

For years, on one occasion or another, I searched the eastern coast of the United States for my missing pirate and his ship. There were no storms between the time of my last sighting and the day that I discovered the *Margarite* was no longer in Flushing Bay, so there was no reason to suppose they might have met with disaster. Once, sailing near New London, I thought I had spotted the *Margarite*, so I took up an interception course for a better look. Alas, she proved to be a large dragger of vaguely similar form and color.

I continued to search for the *Margarite* and Captain Tilley, not out of vengeance but because I wanted to tell him that he had indeed shared the profits of his voyage. For to me the rusting debris he tore from the hulk in Flushing Bay was like gold lifted from the strong room of a galleon. A full month had passed before I was obliged to admit that Captain Tilley had absconded and during that time I had luxuriated in one of the most precious gifts one human can give to another. With a flourish of his toothpick Captain Tilley had caused me to be concerned with enterprise and adventure and enabled me to at least sniff the thrilling winds of discovery.

As the *Albatros* moved past the *Margarite's* old haunts en route to England, I wished again that I might find Captain Tilley so I could tell him how these things were, as always, worth far more than a bag of coins.

If we had been sailing for England via Sandy Hook instead of the East River I should have missed a momentary reunion with another of my most favored sirens. All the way from Brooklyn Bridge the river traffic had been heavy and to guide our way I stood on top the *Albatros*' deckhouse, calling down orders to Post at the wheel—"Five degrees port . . . five degrees starboard" —as required. And from this elevated station I could see a considerable distance. When we had passed the wharf which had revived the ghost of the *Margarite*, Welfare Island was coming abeam and then Hell Gate was at hand. Beyond it I could see just part of a factory roof, yet I knew it must be the same structure which had once sheltered a man named Dinwiddie.

Suddenly, as I looked down upon the swirling, sewer-brown waters of Hell Gate, it struck me that I suffered from the very same illness which had so infected my one-time friend Dinwiddie; for had he not also dearly coveted a possession which was in truth a disease of the mind and heart, and had I not watched it spread to petrify his spirit as surely as any terminal malignancy? Here I stood aboard "my" *Albatros*, inwardly seething at the thought that another man would soon own her, and yet such identical behavior had once caused me to hold Dinwiddie in contempt.

Dinwiddie was a slight, opinionated man with a sculptured beak of a nose which invariably supported a droplet of mucus in winter and of sweat in summer. From him, when my finances had barely recovered from adventuring with Captain Tilley, I bought the sloop *Uncle Sam.*

Dinwiddie variously claimed to be an Englishman, a New Zealander, or an Australian. He seemed to take on nationality to suit his story and mood of the moment. I always regarded him a true citizen of the world, since he was a living pilot book and his acquaintance with the international brothel situation was as detailed as Admiralty directions for making a difficult port. I respected him because his knowledge of all things nautical exceeded my own beyond all measure. He was an expert caulker, as he had certainly need to be in view of the *Uncle Sam*'s failing health; he was a rigger, a tier of rose knots, Matthew Walkers, Turk's heads, crowns, and bell ropes, and he was a passable sailmaker.

The box in which Dinwiddie dwelt was discreetly hidden in the ruins of an abandoned piano factory. They were actually two buildings, and Dinwiddie was located on the second floor of the building nearest the sea.

Dinwiddie called it the sea though in fact his view was of a muddy tidal flat, a patch of filthy water beneath the huge Edison power plant, and the western side of the prison dump-ground forming Riker's Island.

Here amid an industrial devastation of broken glass, twisted iron and sagging concrete, Dinwiddie had by a miracle of will and labor created a sort of shipyard. Here he contrived to haul out very small boats and make elementary repairs on them. The only thing Dinwiddie owned of any consequence was the *Uncle Sam,* and he loved her passionately. Then one day I saw her, became entranced, and resolved to take her from him.

The *Uncle Sam* was forty-two years old when I first chanced upon her. She was a true Maine-built Friendship sloop, a type which had made such a reputation during the early nineteen hundreds fishing in New England offshore waters that it had become internationally respected. Friendship sloops were reasonably fast, marvelously seaworthy, and especially graceful of appearance.

The *Uncle Sam* was 40 feet long and Dinwiddie claimed she was the largest Friendship sloop ever built. This was not true, although the average length was about 30 feet. The *Uncle Sam* was in every exterior sense traditional. Her hull was black and her spars were painted a yellowish ochre with white topping, and her topmast was varnished. Her jibboom was long for a boat of such length and it was stayed with chain. Her standing rigging was set up with deadeyes and lanyards. She was steered with a wheel instead of a tiller and there was often heated controversy among those who knew her whether this was traditional or not.

Dinwiddie accepted my admiration for his darling as obligatory and my hundred-dollar deposit as a simple blood offering from a capitalist. He shared my secret conviction that I would never be able to pay off the balance. Meanwhile, since I had paid something and possibly could be milked for a little more, I could play with the *Uncle Sam* all I pleased.

For over a year I saved Dinwiddie the trouble of maintaining his boat. I scraped and painted and scraped some more and one day in spite of Dinwiddie's protests I hauled out the ancient Dodge engine which he had installed in the cabin and dropped it in the mud. I did not want an engine of any kind. She would be a true Friendship sloop and her cabin, which had been the fishhold, would smell of Stockholm tar instead of grease and engine oil.

Dinwiddie could not stop my alterations. I had learned something from fat Captain Tilley and this contract stated that the *Uncle Sam* was all mine. I simply could not move her until she was all paid for. But month by month I had been paying Dinwiddie twenty dollars until now the balance stood at only eighty. In Dinwiddie's opinion the situation was getting out of hand.

One day he came to me, and with a mighty sniffling from his beak, told me to sit down.

"Take an equal strain on all parts," he began, "because I have terrible news for you. There is something I sort of forgot to tell you about *all* Friendship sloops," he said. "I should have done it a long time ago, but somehow it slipped my mind."

Dinwiddie had a very prominent Adam's apple which slid up and down with great rapidity during moments of high emotional stress. Now I saw that it was nearly dancing.

"All Friendship sloops were built on a here-today-gone-to-morrow basis," he said. "The wood was terrible green and that is why I guess there is more dry rot in this old hulk than most anything afloat!"

He fell ominously silent, seized my arm and hauled me down to the cabin. He pointed to the ceiling, which in a boat is not overhead but is that wood which is laid along the inside of the hull and over the frames. It serves as insulation as well as a finish for the interior. Before I could say anything Dinwiddie seized a heavy caulking iron and proceeded to pry away a section of the ceiling.

"I do not know how I could have done this to you!" he mourned as he reached into the opening he had made and brought out a fistful of black powdery muck which much resembled snuff.

"Look!" he said, thrusting it to my face. "Smell!"

I obeyed, although it was unnecessary. I had a vast amount to learn, but I knew dry rot when I saw it.

"Can you imagine? The whole boat is like this! All, *all* rotten . . . *rotten*!"

I told him I had known there was a bit here and there but certainly it was nothing serious.

"Nothing serious? My dear fellow, I certainly would not be able to sleep nights thinking of you at sea in such a rotten vessel.

Why, she'll come to pieces the minute you have enough wind to move her, which I might as well also admit, takes half a gale."

I was beginning to enjoy myself. Here was a man in torment of his own making. After exploiting his love without mercy he could not bear to see another abducting her.

"Now I have a sensible suggestion for you," he went on. "I know where there's a lovely little Nova Scotia schooner which can be had for only two thousand dollars if it's me makes the buy. To anybody else the price would be at least three. You forget about the *Uncle Sam* and let me get that schooner for you. She's a sweetheart."

I told him the *Uncle Sam* was just right for me even if she did have a few flaws.

"Nonsense. She's not worth scrapping."

I looked about the vessel which had now become a part of my life although we had never sailed an inch together. Working alone and sometimes with friends I had created a cabin which was marvelously warm in atmosphere, and all of the niceties a man could desire were waiting to be enjoyed. There were oil lamps which I had found in a salvage store, a coal stove for heat and dryness, and I had placed a barrel on deck and led copper piping from it so that there was running water below. I thought the head problem nicely solved within my very limited means and in a way that would insure against mechanical breakdowns: I had purchased a brand-new toilet seat and beneath it there was a new bucket which was moored in a wooden guard and which would always be kept half full of sea water. I had fitted up a galley with a counter for slicing, and a secondhand kerosene stove.

While he stood dribbling dry rot through his fingers I told Dinwiddie that if all went well I hoped to pay him off in another four months.

"Never mind, never mind. I'm not worrying. What worries me

is the thought of your going to sea in this bowl of mush. Why she's positively *punk*! It's a goddamned crying shame!"

"Will you give me my money back if she goes to the bottom?"

Dinwiddie was shocked. He looked at me as if I had offended him deeply. "I couldn't do that. You've had the use of her."

"Only here at the dock."

"I could have sold her several times for more than you're paying. You've had her tied up and now if you don't complete payment I'll have all the expense of putting an engine back in her."

"I thought you said she must be scrapped." I laughed and called him a bastard in a friendly way and broke out some of the cheap wine I kept on board in the grand manner of Captain Tilley, and I let him go on and on. We drank a great deal of the wine because Dinwiddie was in desperate need of consolation. His love lay with another man. Finally he staggered ashore, muttering something about taking green seas over his bow. Watching his perilous journey along the rickety dock, I knew he would never forgive me when I really kidnapped his *Uncle Sam*. At last the day came when I was able to pay Dinwiddie his due. He had no choice but to stand amid his ruins and wave us away.

He took it bravely, although he was frequently compelled to blow his beak in a red bandanna handkerchief. And his eyes were embarrassingly moist and his Adam's apple slid up and down at high speed when he said, "I wish you all the goddamned luck in the world. Please don't founder until you're out of sight."

Like all craft originally designed to earn their living, the *Uncle Sam* was no toy. Hence she was heavily sparred and all of her gear in keeping. Her main boom was a beast, so long it hung well over her counter, and her gaff was equally clumsy to handle. With her long topmast she was able to carry a great deal of sail for her size and at first I despaired of ever sailing her alone.

There was no winch for weighing the *Uncle Sam*'s heavy old-fashioned anchor, so I rigged an overlong handy-billy of two double blocks and a length of manila line. With such an amount of purchase I eventually managed to sail from any anchorage without assistance. I would set the mainsail and stays'l, then heave with all I had on the tackle. As the *Uncle Sam* began to sail toward her anchor I would move aft crab-fashion, maintaining a constant pressure on the line. By the time I was all the way aft and within reach of the wheel the anchor would be free of the bottom and we would be under way. Later, when there was time, I would rereeve the tackle and bring the anchor to deck. It was a most satisfying show and I finally became so smug in its performance that I ran hard aground in full view of many skeptical spectators one lovely Fourth of July. The *Uncle Sam* and her cocky master were suitably humiliated not 50 feet from where we had begun.

There was something about the *Uncle Sam* which made her popular in the way that a good-natured waitress in an all-night diner may sometimes become every customer's confidante though she may be neither beautiful nor buxom.

While my own affection was easily accountable, total strangers seemed instantly taken with her, and those who really knew the *Uncle Sam* regarded her as they might a favorite aunt. She was a natural beauty and utterly without pretension, which may have been why owners of the most fancy yachts persisted in leaving their splendors and lingering for hours about the *Uncle Sam*'s decks. Friends of the *Uncle Sam* volunteered their labor to keep her shining, painted, and generally spotless, although sometimes they were not even rewarded with a sail. Neighbors to her anchorage offered all manner of marine gear—free. ". . . Here's fifteen fathoms of good manila. You can't have the *Uncle Sam* hanging on that old string you've been using."

"Here's a jib which has a few years left in it. I was thinking it might do just fine for the *Uncle Sam*."

"About that rot. I'll come aboard this afternoon before I go to my own boat and bring some Cuprinol and we'll at least stop it before it gets worse."

I could never decide why the *Uncle Sam* had this peculiar facility for making friends.

Perhaps it was because everyone knew she was indeed so rotten that when sailing on the port tack, daylight could be seen through her topside seams. Perhaps it was because I was given some fancy trail boards from an old schooner which fitted exactly and much embellished her bows. Or because I carved a figurehead of Uncle Sam, fists clenched and beard thrust defiantly forward, which when gaily painted and viewed from a distance seemed as if it had always been there. Perhaps it was because she was sailed without an engine that others, in vicarious hazard, cheered our better maneuvers. Once, caught clumsily between tide and wind, we collided with a fancy power cruiser peacefully anchored where she had every right to be. The heavy *Uncle Sam* broke away unscathed, but there were ugly scratches along the hull of the cruiser. The owner would have been more than justified in at least cursing our lubberliness. Instead he shrugged his shoulders and said, "It's not too bad. I understand."

Lindstrom, a great and wonderful Finn who ran the shipyard in Connecticut and who was noted as much for his contempt of anyone who sailed for pleasure as he was for his high prices, became so taken with the *Uncle Sam* that he built a taffrail around her counter with his own hands. It was a structure of rare beauty and his only charge was for the lumber.

When I went away to war the entire nautical community took the *Uncle Sam*'s welfare to their hearts. At least fifteen persons involved themselves in her care in one way or another, but none of them could stay the final catastrophe.

The autumn hurricane season was at hand and I was as usual flying somewhere over the North Atlantic. When we landed at

Newfoundland I saw the newest hurricane on the weather map and my premonitions began. The storm was moving up the East Coast and would strike New York and Connecticut at any hour. The *Uncle Sam* was waiting out the war at anchor in a small Connecticut inlet which might or might not offer enough protection.

I fumed all that night in our barracks and fumed through the following morning while we waited for the aircraft we would fly down to New York. I haunted the weather office, but no detailed reports were available. The map only indicated that the hurricane had moved as predicted and, having reached Massachusetts, moved seaward.

Late that day I knew the worst. From the air I could see how trees were flattened all along the New England coast and the cove in which the *Uncle Sam* lay was almost directly on course in what had obviously been the path of the wind.

We came upon the cove in the late afternoon and I made one circle directly above. It was enough. There, with our wing tip pointing accusingly at the scene, lay my beloved *Uncle Sam*. She was far from her original position, half submerged, and lying on her side. The seas were still large and they were pounding her to pieces.

As the *Albatros* passed the piano factory I could not resist climbing into the rigging for a final look at Dinwiddie's private shipyard. Except for a few old power boats the area appeared deserted and there was no sign of life about the buildings. I wondered if Dinwiddie was dead and if he knew that his *Uncle Sam* was no more.

Dinwiddie's mud flat dissolved in haze and industrial smog. I remembered how little the *Uncle Sam* had cost and how very much had this splendid brigantine, the *Albatros*. And I hoped I would remember that at night there is no difference to the covetous between a diamond and a crumb of coal.

Once again the *Albatros* was upon the Atlantic, although this time our circumstances and environment were as different as our compass course.

We had a total of twelve souls aboard for the eastbound crossing and could manage to divide our strength over three watches because in addition to those serving on deck two very important replacements had signed the articles.

One was Hacker, which was pronounced "Hekka" and which was not the man's name at all. It was Yutaka Tamura. Hekka proved to be one of God's great natural gentlemen as well as a superb engineer. He was a Japanese, long resident of Honolulu, and he was known as "The Hacker" because of his skill at judo. Yet he was so shy and spoke so softly that we often asked him to repeat whatever it was he said. Hekka never used the stereotyped Japanese "ah-so's" but instead employed a series of low *hm-m-m-m*'s to punctuate his conversation. He had a way of increasing or decreasing the frequency of these *hm-m-m-m*'s according to the vitality of the subject matter so that you always knew his degree of interest or boredom.

If Hekka had a temper he left it ashore, for few men have so patiently endured frustration. Though he soon mastered the African Queen, her ills were those of extreme age and therefore fundamental. In spite of Hekka's ministrations she was still given to fevers, acute bronchial complaints, and occasional hemorrhages. She was in truth dying, but Hekka refused to recognize this and so he mixed special potions of graphite and kerosene to ease her pains and keep her from swallowing her valves. When Hekka slept it was our task to squirt three different kinds of lubricant into various parts of the African Queen's anatomy, and we marveled at how much better his concoctions affected her than the commercial varieties.

The other new crew man was Ptacnik, the cook, replacing Rogerts, who had long returned to his native Holland. I have never understood how Ptacnik slipped through my suspicions, because he was not even a professional cook. He was a professor of English literature who looked far more like a flamenco dancer. He was suave and quick of wit and his Mexican-Czech ancestry had created a remarkably facile face which could at times be quite handsome and again become as droll as a carnival mask. If he had any fault as a cook it was his custom of serving philosophic homilies along with his repasts.

Ptacnik learned to cook simply by loving the art, and the results proved his consistent devotion. He had never been out of sight of land in his life and yet, like Rogerts, he was never seasick. Thus he was that wonder of wonders, the ideal sea cook, and we all made a determined effort to master the Slavic pronunciation of his name. Our desire was to please him as he had us, and our admiration continued until the very end of the voyage.

Eastbound in the *Albatros*, our Atlantic passage was the opposite of our original crossing when we had so yearned for wind. It is in the contrary nature of the sea that when our mechanical power was useless, we would lack wind; and now that Hekka had the African Queen panting for action, we had wind to spare.

Our passage took eighteen days and included two gales. Force-6 and -7 winds were the rule rather than the exception. We also encountered considerable fog, and on the very last day somewhere off Ushant we inadvertently sailed through the combined operations of the NATO fleet. Suddenly the fog lifted just long enough to reveal an eerie assembly of great battleships entirely surrounding us and then it closed down once more. We had no choice but to continue upon our anachronistic way hoping the radar target of a square-rigger in their midst would not hopelessly confuse the observers.

There is often great pride to be found in little accomplishments and somehow this odd relation is often magnified when the deed is a revival of the past. And since the past did require more individual resourcefulness, perhaps there is a deep hunger within us which begs for satisfaction. Thus do men still climb mountains they could fly over as easily as moving from one chair to another, and Chichesters sail alone around the world without bothering about sightseeing. Thus do many herdsmen still ride tall in the saddle when a jeep could often do the job more efficiently, and so do archers still hunt with bow and arrow when they could use a more certain and deadly weapon. It was so with us when we persisted in sailing the *Albatros* from the mouth of the Thames almost to her moorings in the Pool of London.

The newspapers claimed the feat had not been accomplished in a square-rigger since Nelson's time, which I considered highly improbable, but a series of minor miracles did conspire to make this passage something of a triumph. The wonders joined hands in the early morning when we were off Gravesend and remained steadfast until the very last moments, when Tower Bridge lay close before us.

From Gravesend to Tower Bridge is some 20 miles and the span of the Thames between carries a heavy volume of commercial traffic of every variety. Near Greenwich and thence on to London itself the course of the river becomes tortuous, so that holding anything like a fixed course is impossible. At times a course change of 90 degrees or more becomes imperative, which ordinarily would make life difficult for a sailing vessel. Combine traffic, winds, and tides of considerable force, and you have the sort of situation which causes the most devoted of sailormen to vow they will saw off the masts and go into steam.

We prepared for this ordeal with nerves which were still raw from the discovery that by the grace of God we had somehow completed our Atlantic passage by passing around and *behind* Bishop's Rock light. There had been heavy fog and somehow we had neither heard its horn nor seen it.

During our passage up the Thames we were not even tried. At every turn of the river we anticipated dousing sail and starting the African Queen, but lo! whether the wind backed or veered, it did so in accordance with the course of the river. We had not once to beat against it, and the closest we came to labor was swinging the yards for an easy reach. We were at some pains to assure the Trinity House pilot who was our guide and who had never been in a sailing ship of any type before, that our lives were not always so well managed. "A piece of cake," he kept repeating as he watched the zero longitude marker at Greenwich slide past and soon afterward the glorious *Cutty Sark*. We thought the stalwarts who had once sailed in her might have lined her bulwarks this day and cheered us.

☼

SEVENTEEN

THERE is a unique softness about an English afternoon and in the early fall the high northerly latitude permits the light to remain long into the evening. It is the mellow light rendered so truly in the paintings of Turner and Constable and it creates an ambiance of tranquility and stolid confidence in man's place on earth.

It was in this luminous atmosphere with the lavender of evening just arrived that for the last time I observed the *Albatros* putting out to sea.

We had been outward bound for Portugal from Germany and had reached the English Channel when I received a radio message telling of the sudden death of my father. We had made at once for the nearest port, which was Cowes. Atcheson had taken over command, and now, still stunned by the loss of a man I had so loved and admired, I stood very much alone on a pier watching the anchor chain slithering through the hawse. The *Albatros* was nearly half a mile offshore yet I could see figures moving about her decks. It was as if I was observing them from another world, and since I knew them so well it was easy to recognize them as individuals. Hekka appeared from the after deckhouse for a moment and then vanished somewhere below. Post was in her usual place at the helm. Ptacnik came out of his galley and strolled aft to her. I was certain they would be discussing stores versus menus. Forward I could see Dawson's white-thatched head moving about the anchor winch and Cox was easily identified because of his size. With them was Lauritzen, a charming Dane who had joined us in Copenhagen. Gillette was hosing the Solent mud from the chain as it rose. That was all. They were going to be on the short-handed side if they encountered any rough weather, but Atcheson was a shrewd commander and would not be lured into trusting the Bay of Biscay.

The wind was light and in my direction, so I could hear the anchor winch. From such a distance its multiple parts did not clank together in their usual fashion, but tinkled, as if suiting their truly raucous character to my diminutive vision of the ship. How small she was, I thought, and yet how long she had been the boundaries of my world.

I tried to turn away. I would leave this scene and step into the nearby pub and have a gin or two until the ferry came to take me on the first leg of my journey back to the United States. But I could not turn away, because I knew this would be the last time I would see the *Albatros* as mine again. What sentimental foolishness! I condemned to hell the unknown romanticist who originated the ridiculous fancy that a man might fall in love with a thing. And what else was a vessel but a thing? Yet long before my time men ensnared by this same suspect fetish had lavished both affection and fortune on ships in which to sail the seas. So doughty and yet so amorous a man as Nelson referred to his great ungainly flagship *Victory* as his "little darling." Drake was nearly maudlin about his awkward, roly-poly little *Golden Hind*. There had been legions of sailors great and unknown who had been compelled to express their devotion in words or print and it seemed they became all the more eloquent when parted from their favorites. It was as if they lived.

Few men go about publicly proclaiming their wives as faithless whores, extravagant bitches, or foul-mouthed shrews, even when these things are true and when, in desperation, the man resolves he can no longer endure his marriage. And no more will a man speak ill of his vessel, though he may own but the smallest piece of her. Only *after* the inevitable parting might he concede that the craft which had held his affection was actually a bit on the lethargic side, or she might have a cranky way of bashing her occupants about, or was ravaged with disease, or had a mind of her own when maneuvering.

I was as guilty as any other sailor. Here I stood in a sentimental funk watching the *Albatros* as if she was the most perfect vessel ever created.

At the age of twelve I had felt the same way about the *Diver*, which was the second craft I had ever commanded and which I proposed to finance by raising Indian artifacts and perhaps even treasure from the bottom of a Minnesota lake. Now with memories of my father so vivid before me I wondered how he must have truly regarded the *Diver*, because it was he who had lent me the fifty dollars for her original charter, accepting as security my vow that I would stay out of mischief that summer and perform brilliantly in school the following semester. He lost on both counts.

The *Diver* was 16 feet in length and of open launch design.

Amidships there was a small one-cylinder engine which made a very satisfying racket when I could finally persuade it to function. The *Diver* leaked in an extraordinary number of places even for a lapstreak boat and I soon discovered she was a beast to row. Yet when the summer ended and I returned the boat to her rightful owner I did so in the manner of a benefactor. "This boat," I stated authoritatively, "can go just about anywhere in the whole world. You should have seen her in that storm last week. And, why I could row her clean across the lake without getting tired if I just wanted. Sure the engine needs some fixing, but once you get it started, mister, it just never wants to quit."

It had also been my indulgent father who had financed the little *Caroline* because he believed some further seafaring could only improve a young man. But he was suspicious of sailboats in Lake Michigan, and so the *Caroline* was strictly a motor cruiser. And still I came to love her.

They were hoisting the main on the *Albatros* now. What an esthetic mistake I had made in changing the cut of her main from gaff to Marconi. But the sail was of course much easier to handle and apparently we had suffered little loss in speed.

Go away, wench. I can very well get along without you.

There was the *Don Quixote* in Spain. We had sailed together in the Balearic Islands for a time and I had never known a clumsier vessel. She was 30 feet long and double-ended and her engine was a single-cylinder Bolander diesel of unknown vintage. From the first I regarded the engine as senile, but it was not only because of its age that I so rarely employed it. It was located in the small midships cabin and thus occupied the only shelter in the *Don Quixote*. Starting the engine was a nervous business which you commenced by lighting off a blowtorch and directing the flame upon the cylinder head for several minutes. The blow torch was kept on a shelf between the bilge frames, and beside it was a wine bottle filled with ether-alcohol. When you supposed the cylinder had reached easy combustion temperature you turned off the blowtorch, opened a cup valve on top the cylinder, and poured a jigger of the ether-alcohol therein. Assuming nothing had gone wrong, such as spilling too much of the highly explosive mixture in the bilge, you at once grasped the heavy flywheel in both hands and swung it with all your might. If the engine failed to fire after three spins of the flywheel you waited until your heartbeat and breathing subsided and started all over again with blowtorch and wine bottle.

The exhaust of *Don Quixote*'s engine was short, so it would not interfere with passage of the sail across deck and it was aimed straight up in the air. As a consequence it blew the most perfect smoke rings I have ever seen and sometimes I would start the engine in port just so visitors could admire the display.

Yet the principal reason I avoided starting the engine was the terrible vibration which accompanied its cruising power. The *Don Quixote* was steered with a tiller and the only possible place for the helmsman was to sit on a little deck at the extreme after end of the hull. Here the vibration was such that I often feared for my sacroiliac and the entire world became a blur. Conversation was discouraging because everyone whimpered. The violent shuddering imparted a plaintive vibrato to the voice and everyone aboard sounded as if he had just been cruelly beaten. For these reasons I normally chose the lesser of two evils and sailed the *Don Quixote*.

I had never been shipmates with a lateen sail and so I asked Xavier, who owned the *Don Quixote*, to instruct me in its time-honored ways. Xavier had left the sea, having found an easier way of life selling "Spanish" knickknacks to tourists. But he did know his craft and once he had convinced himself that I would not deliberately stand her into peril, he left his sister's ninth son, Oresté, as my crew and returned to his busy shop.

The ninth son was much too small for his job, yet his willingness and utter devotion to the vessel made it impossible to contemplate replacing him. He was very old, as the youth of Spain may sometimes be, and he told me that he had fourteen years of life on earth, which I knew was a lie because Xavier had said that he was not yet twelve. Except that he smoked the blackest, foulest-smelling cigarettes I had ever seen whenever his hands were momentarily idle, Oresté was a comfortable companion and possessed a rarity among human senses, for he knew instinctively when another human being was in the mood for idle conversation. At all other times he kept absolute silence.

I was disappointed in the lateen rig mainly because it was impossible to sail the *Don Quixote* single-handed with such gear and also because I saw how coming about in rough seas was a dangerous affair for the crew. It was necessary for one man to be forward and ready to push the base end of the boom around to the opposite side of the mast after we passed through the eye of the wind. During this operation the boom end would acquire a bucking motion in response to the seas and there were times when Oresté because of his light weight was nearly catapulted overboard. Other lateen-rigged boats rarely bothered to transfer the boom when coming about and simply allowed it to press against the mast making two fat balloons of the sail. But the *Don Quixote* flatly refused to sail under such casual treatment and so Oresté was kept very busy. He pretended that he heard my cautions when he went forward and once I hurt his feelings by pleading with him to use a safety line about his waist. Suddenly his black eyes burned with scorn, he turned his pockmarked little back on me, and remained sullen for the rest of the day.

In time I became accustomed to the *Don Quixote*'s casual ways, and every day, it seemed, she provided new cause for amusement. So there was continual pleasure in our relation and soon I was infatuated, as a man may become when a woman gives him frequent cause for smiling. I knew this was a dangerous stage, because overexposure to the pleasant may find a man in love.

I escaped entrapment by the *Don Quixote* only because we lived together for barely a month and because I remembered a similar affair with an enchanting craft known as the *Butterfly*. Jesús was her true owner and he kept her in Fortaleza, Brazil.

I first met Jesús in a breeze-swept open-sided cantina on the beach. It was the coolest place in Fortaleza and hence regularly patronized by crews of airplanes who were about to fly the South Atlantic or had just done so. Jesús was one of the waiters in the cantina and spoke a brand of English which was distinctly his own yet quite understandable. The word "nice" was a special favorite of his and he employed it to cover a multitude of queries and replies. He was a young man with a wispy trace of mustache, eyelids that always drooped as if to protect his eyes from the actinic blaze of the Brazilian sun, and a shriveled arm which must have been with him at birth. When I asked him where I might rent a boat he insisted I take his very own, which he called the *Butterfly*.

The working conditions for waiters in Brazil were agreeably loose, so Jesús whipped off his apron and taking me by the arm led the way to a dilapidated taxi. Once inside, he settled back into the seat and sighed contentedly. "My boat," he announced, "is nice and far from here."

Suddenly I realized we had embarked upon a journey, for Brazilians of Jesús' economic status rarely splurged on taxis. He knew the driver, a morose man whose name was Fernando, and who was called *the* Fernando because of his perpetual gloom. Such was his local fame that if you were dejected you were said to be "in a Fernando."

I had supposed we were in for a long ride to find Jesús' boat, but we had careened along hardly 3 miles before we turned toward the ocean and came to an open stretch of beach. The Fernando set his jaw and his throttle at full power. We left the last hint of roadway and charged a series of sand hummocks as if our taxi was a fullback and the goal was the sea. Neither the Fernando nor Jesús ceased his excited chattering, though at times all three of us were bounced into a weightless condition. When I was certain the taxi must collapse on the very next hummock we tumbled off it and there was the foaming ocean. And there was the *Butterfly*. I could not be sure if Jesús was joking or was simply a scoundrel who wanted to get away from his work at my expense.

"Look!" he said. "How nice?" What he was pointing at was a collection of logs lying in the sand.

There was a tin shanty farther up the beach which now exploded a cluster of people. Several children ran toward us screaming in their naked delight. There were three men, one very old, and two women. "My family," Jesús explained, just before he was engulfed by their affections. Finally when the initial excitemen of our arrival had subsided I was escorted to Jesús' "boat."

It was not a boat at all, but a raft made up of balsa logs about 12 inches in diameter. It was some 20 feet long and protruding from the sand on each side were two leeboards made of a heavy, close-grained wood which I could not identify. There was a mast also lying in the sand and a sail of musty-looking cloth was wrapped around it. There was a short, very thick and heavy oar which Jesús explained fitted in a sort of slot at the stern of the raft and was used for steering.

I tried to hide my disappointment, for I realized now that

Jesús really did intend us to go sailing in this collection of flotsam and that his interest was only for my welfare. He was almost pathetically eager to assemble the functional components of his craft and enlisted his entire family as well as the Fernando in the project.

I studied the water-soaked logs and guessed they must weigh a ton. The *Butterfly*! What an ill-chosen name. Even if we could drag her down to the water she must submerge in the first wave and never be seen again. And I had always been an indifferent swimmer.

The Fernando took off his shoes and socks and rolled up his pants in the best beach-holiday tradition. I had no choice but to do the same and together with all of Jesús' relatives we hauled the *Butterfly* down to the sea. Now, at least, she did bear some vague resemblance to a seagoing craft, for she had a mast supported by two shrouds of frayed rope, a woven fiber bench for the helmsman, and a leeboard on each side.

The naked children squealed with continuous rapture and it was a launching amid such gaiety I instantly ceased to care if this clumsy thing ever got beyond the first line of breakers.

The beach sloped gently and soon the Fernando dropped behind because the water had reached the height of his rolled pants. With him we left two of the smallest children and then the women when the water became knee deep, and then we paused while Jesús and I boarded the *Butterfly*. After waiting alertly for a smooth between breakers, Jesús shouted, the men and remaining boys gave a great shove on the *Butterfly*'s stern, and we glided into deep water. Jesús immediately hoisted sail and I was soon reminded that the quality of a vessel may no more be judged by appearance than that of a man or a woman.

At first while we were still only a little way offshore the breeze held light and we glided rather sluggishly over the sea. I took the helm and studied the sail, which was made of coffee and flour bags sewn together with heavy twine. Poor Jesús. There was a hole the size of a football halfway up the leech of his sail and I could see streaks of the glittering sea through many of the seams joining the various bags. My compassion increased as I saw into his eyes and realized that here was a moment which far transcended what little financial reward he would receive from my few hours' rental of his awkward craft. For I was smiling and he was too innocent to detect the hypocrisy behind my lips. He could not suspect that I wanted to come about at once, head for the beach and make a quick end of my disappointment.

"Nice?" he asked softly.

"Nice," I agreed, because it is a waste of breath to disagree with those who are content with next to nothing.

Now we were beginning to catch the offshore wind and the cerulean-blue surface of the sea began to shiver. Diminutive popcorn wavelets blossomed all about and when we left the shoreside haze the horizon became sharp-etched against the burning sky. It was only a modest wind, yet the *Butterfly* suddenly changed character. She was a Jekyll and Hyde boat. She shuddered as if to shake off her resemblance to a stray log jam. She emerged from her cocoon and became an entirely new individual. In a remarkable act of levitation she climbed right out of the water so that barely the bottom third of the logs was submerged. In seconds we were gliding along at an easy 10 knots with the wind and seas full on our beam. After a few seconds more I was certain we were doing 15 knots, then even faster.

Jesús beckoned toward the horizon and I eased the *Butterfly* gingerly into the wind. I sheeted home the boom until it was most inboard of the logs; and the pitiful sail, in defiance of all formal aerodynamics, drove us ever faster. Not one of the bags which composed the sail panels had the same degree of stretch, so that each ballooned in its own way. I could not see the lee side of the sail, but it must have achieved a sort of cobbled surface and all of the straining seams now passed bright sunlight.

The *Butterfly*'s deck, if it could be called that, had been awash since we first boarded her; now the top surface of the logs began to dry in the sunlight and only occasionally did we take dollops of spray aboard. Although I could sense very little increase in the wind I was astonished to see our hull speed continuously increasing. I could think of no other comparable sensation except iceboating, and I was quite certain Jesús would have comprehension trouble if I told him that his *Butterfly* sailed like a boat on a frozen lake.

Whatever explanation I might have attempted would have made little difference, for now I saw that Jesús was lost to me. He was no longer a waiter, nor just another Brazilian with just another wisp of mustache. He squatted easily with his heels jammed into the division between the two highest logs and his bare feet curving over the lowest. A small religious medallion dangled from his neck, glistening when it caught the sun, and his head was thrown back in such a way that I marveled at his suppleness. I saw that he was breathing deeply as if inhaling some powerful elixir, his attention shifted from the sail to the sea, to the horizon, and to a frigate bird which now joined our headlong flight across the wind. I saw that Jesús had left his apron-bound soul and transcended all the heritage of a puny physique and complete ignorance of power. He was a conquerer now, a guide through the little-known. He was, in these moments of rising speed and spirit, a swashbuckler, an intrepid mariner, and a paladin all in one.

I could not decide if it was Jesús' personal triumph or the tremendous exhilaration of the *Butterfly*'s grace and speed which so made me want to cheer. We were skimming over a brilliant sea which itself was dancing with life, and the sense of escape from all natural burdens was intoxicating. I doubted that many scientifically designed catamarans or trimarans had sailed faster, and certainly we would have soon left any two-million-dollar America's Cup contender far over the horizon.

Jesús turned to look at me questioningly and I hoped that if he had suspected my smile before he would now see that it was genuine. "Nice?" he asked.

"Nice."

Sailing the *Butterfly* became such an inner compulsion that I soon found myself trying to rearrange plans so that I would have at least a day or two in Fortaleza. But with all my plotting I managed no more than half a dozen sails in the *Butterfly* before I had to leave. Each time was a repeated delight and each time the routine was the same.

I would seek out Jesús at the cantina and then we would find the Fernando who would be slumping in his taxi as morose and angry at the world as ever. A half-smile for me, then some clearing of his eyes at his first abuse of the engine. The wild ride to the beach greatly stimulated the Fernando and he would change by the time of our usual launching and become positively ecstatic.

Moments later I could watch Jesús undergo his metamorphosis as the *Butterfly* picked up her skirts, and all was as it should be in God's world.

Eventually I learned that the *Butterfly* was not at all exceptional to the coast of Brazil and that her type was generally used for swift transport to the fishing grounds, where the sail was doused and the crew went to work on a stable platform. Therefore like all truly fine sailing craft her design developed from regional necessity and many years of practical experience. She was a workboat at heart and not some plastic confection designed by men more concerned with dainty interiors than nautical ability. Her initial clumsy appearance and apparent great weight were, of course, a deception. In the water the balsa logs were curved fore and aft in just the right way and there was no comparison in their weight displacement with any other natural material.

The *Butterfly*'s speed was due to her remarkable lightness, which was matched only by her financial burden. Once I asked Jesús to make an estimate of her price and he said his uncle had built her somewhat smaller than the rafts actually used for fishing and therefore could use logs that were in little demand. Jesús' mother had sewn the sail and he had gathered the material from innumerable contributors, so the actual cost was nothing. He had had to buy the sisal rope for the shrouds, sheet, halyard, and anchor and this had come to six dollars. His uncle had not charged anything at all for his labor, but he obtained the balsa logs in trade for a superior pig which would have brought some eight to ten dollars on the market. The total worth of the *Butterfly* then was about sixteen dollars which we agreed was a considerable investment.

My infatuation with the *Butterfly* was such that I tried desperately to think of a way we could see more of each other. But I could not conceive of her performing anywhere along the Atlantic coast of the United States with the possible exception of Florida. The same was true of the Pacific coast, for the *Butterfly* could not sail in her customary environment anywhere north of San Diego, where there was rarely enough wind. At last I was forced to concede that the *Butterfly* was a siren inherently incapable of being transplanted. To the South Seas or the Hawaiian Islands perhaps, but along my chill native shores she would soon wither and die of neglect. So we parted and I felt her loss for a long time.

I raise my arm slowly. It is an attempt to wave as if I am merely wishing bon voyage to my shipmates. The September dusk has settled over the Solent now and the *Albatros* is already gathering way. In a few minutes she must disappear around the point stretching north from this ferry landing and I will be left even more wretched. Then I will not wait until she is entirely gone from view. Somewhere I once heard that was bad luck. And I will not have any misfortune harm that assembly of steel and wood and rope and canvas which is more than a thing, which is in truth an inexhaustible fountain of adventure for those who dare to drink. Of all my sirens I am now certain there will never be another like the *Albatros* if only because she is the most demanding.

Go! I will not weep.

☼

EPILOGUE

One of the greatest blessings the oceans bestow upon man is a sense of everlasting permanence. The oceans *do* change, but they take their time about it and a thousand years is only an interval. Time apparently stands still for the oceans—the light and play of liquid, the sounds and scent of salt air, and the inhabitants are basically the same as they were long ago. Thus modern man needs the oceans more than ever, for the minute slice of earth upon which he dwells changes constantly and sometimes overwhelmingly. Where is the house of my childhood? Where is the building in which I found my first job, the church in which I was married, the park where the team played, the fields where we used to hunt, and the ponds where there were so many fish? Torn down, burned down, occupied by a shopping center, laid out in a housing development, polluted—all changed since only yesterday. This is very hard on normal man's deep yearning for stability. Many simply cannot endure such accelerating progress and try desperately to lose themselves in nostalgia or hurl themselves into personal tragedy. Familiarity with the oceans can do much to reassure that part of us which instinctively fears change.

Perhaps that is why, when at last I parted with the *Albatros* and was obliged to admit that I was no longer her master or owner, I sought immediate distraction in the building of a new vessel. She was to be designed specifically for research, upon the sea and particularly along its fringes. I was certain such a vessel would serve as a magnet for all manner of individuals. I wanted the new vessel to be designed as a workboat and she had best be a sailing ketch for the long oceanic passages. She must have sufficient power to handle the strong tides of the northern latitudes as well as endurance for the suffocating calms of the southerly seas. She would be built in Denmark by a small firm hoary with experience in building heavy wooden vessels of commercial design. Hopefully she would incorporate all of the qualities and inherit none of the faults of the sixteen preceding sirens. By matching the proceeds from the sale of the *Albatros* against reasonable Danish prices I could almost afford such a dream.

It had taken nearly a year to build the *Black Watch* and now another year had passed, and having come a long way, we were prowling the waters of the Aegean. We had retraced our course through Norwegian fiords, crossed the North Sea, and Scotland via the Caledonian Canal, which is one of the most delightful passages any sailor can make, and we had repeated Boswell's tour of the Hebrides with his very book in hand, and we had been hove to for three days in a September screamer of a gale off the

Irish coast, and we had been swallowed by the Mediterranean at Gibraltar and spit right out again. We had nosed into little gunk-holes the ages have chewed into the flanks of Corsica and Sardinia, and in Malta we had hobnobbed with what was left of the British Raj and met in the best clandestine style with a Maltese underground leader who vowed to overthrow the government. We had fought our way up the Dalmatian coast against an unforgiving *bora* and eventually swung about to pass through the Ionian Sea and the Gulf of Corinth to the Aegean. The summer was over and Greece in September is often a land of new rains falling on ancient ruins. The parched earth rejoices in the first scattered droplets to be sucked from the barren sky in months, and the Greek people renew their love affair with life. Ironically it was then that the terrible news found us.

The *Albatros* had capsized in the Gulf of Mexico. She had gone down so quickly it was a miracle anyone had escaped. I grieved for Sheldon, whose heavy sense of responsibility must now be torturing him. He had been operating her as a school ship and had made several highly successful cruises in that employment. The only significant changes he had made were below to improve accommodations for his students and teachers. I knew him to be a most thoroughly competent seaman—how then, after so many thousands of miles, could the *Albatros* now be on the bottom of the sea? With her had gone Sheldon's wife, our treasured friend Ptacnik, who had remained aboard as cook although he had at first intended to sail in the *Black Watch*, and four students. Sheldon himself and the balance of his company had been rescued by a freighter after spending only twenty-four hours in the two lifeboats. One report said the *Albatros* had been overcome by a "white squall," and that once it had passed the sea became quiet again. From the air I had seen the so-called white squalls, which are peculiar to the Gulf of Mexico, and I knew them to be a species of marine tornado. Although they actually cover but a small area the intensity of the winds may be as high as 100 miles an hour and a vessel caught all standing might easily be overwhelmed.

Sheldon was a man of deep convictions and honest courage. Now I longed to reach out and touch his hand, for how many times had I crept into the same after cabin and secretly whispered for mercy. There was, I knew, no wrath so dreadful as a storm at sea. It confounds the best of men, perhaps because in the wastes of the ocean he is so alone. I had flown through the interior of thunderstorms many times and my bowels were therefore accustomed to restraining one of man's primary reactions to fear, yet always we knew that the ordeal would not long endure and most of the time our radios could reach for our mental comfort to other men who stood vigil in peace and quiet. At sea the nightmare of almost any storm seems to continue forever and the total massing of cruelty may be divided by the size of the vessel.

When the *Albatros* went down something happened to the sense of permanency which I had always drawn from the sea. For a time I simply could not conceive of her not sailing somewhere in the world, if only because I had devoted four years of my life to her well-being and had striven with all my will and resource to assure her long and healthy future. I wept for a loss which was not even mine, for dreams are important to all men and Sheldon's had been viciously annihilated.

A cloak covered my spirits and I could not shake it off. The haunting sense of loss would subside for a week or more and then it would return and I was trying to learn how to be patient until it went away again.

I was so disenchanted with the sea that I could think only of its discomforts and dangers, and even the very deck upon which I stood represented a tremendous waste of time, energy, and fortune. What indeed had the life of a sailor done for me except to pay me poorly when I was paid at all, allow me to lose innumerable hours of sleep, and be so far removed from the center of things that on going ashore I must each time first adjust myself and then go about the tedious business of making new friends. I was a stranger everywhere; there were no roots in the oceans, and in little vessels such as must always be my lot there was no honest home to be found afloat. Well then, a pox on all salt water and the sooner the *Black Watch* was sold out from under me the better. There would be no more blustery days like this one when we came swirling southward before a hard and hot *meltemi,* sailed full blast through the narrow passage which separates Fournoi from an adjacent islet, and rounded up in this cul-de-sac, where we hoped for a night's sleep if the anchor decided not to drag.

There were still four of us in the *Black Watch.* When the deck gear was made up and all secured for the night I stood on the foredeck and watched the anchor chain with suspicion. The yellow light of evening was already fading, yet heat from the great cinder of Fournoi whirled down upon us, the still-hot breath of the *meltemi* augmented by hills cooked too long in the sun. The others had gone below to prepare the evening meal and I was left alone with my brooding. Our anchor seemed secure and yet I unaccountably lingered about the foredeck. Perhaps all of my movements then were a sum of delays because I was so recently advised of the *Albatros* catastrophe. Perhaps my physical cogs were slipping, because to divert my thoughts toward more rewarding fields I had deliberately become lost in Greek antiquity and my own pace had unconsciously seemed to match those more reflective times. I was staring down at the ruffled water when I first heard the singing. It was a feminine voice, thin, high, very clear and gay—the voice of a Circe or a sprite, I thought, according to a man's wish and imagination. It was a voice drifting down the wind from the ages; it was a cry of life from the fringes of the sea, of zest for all the temple of Poseidon offered.

At first I was unable to find the source of the singing, although I carefully searched the arid bowl which rose up from the sea and shaped the cove of Fournoi. There were a few white plaster houses and the inevitable goats, but there had not been a sign of human life. Yet there, as if singing for my heart alone, was the voice. It seemed so near and clear I dared not believe I had not really heard it.

I walked aft to the quarter-deck and picked up my binoculars. Again I searched the shore, then stopped in disbelief. For I focused upon a lone fig tree which was swaying violently in the wind. And in the tree was a young girl, skirt billowing, singing joyously, yet as if her very life depended on it.

I slipped below to advise my shipmates, who were weary of the wind. "Come on deck. I'll show you something you won't believe."

Perhaps three or four minutes had passed before we were all on deck. I handed the binoculars to Post and said, "That tree just there—to the left of the largest rock pile. Tell me what you see." I spoke with pride, as if the girl were mine to exploit.

"A donkey," Post said flatly. There are donkeys everywhere in Greece, so I understood her lack of enthusiasm.

"No, no. In the tree."

"I do not see the donkey in the tree. He is under it in the shade, as donkeys always are."

I snatched the binoculars away from her without apology and focused on the tree. There was no girl in it or even about it. We are looking at the wrong tree, I thought. Then one by one I inspected the few trees visible from the cove of Fournoi. They were all swinging in the wind, but none of them supported a young girl. Nor was she to be seen anywhere on the land.

"Just what are we looking for?"

"A girl . . . a young girl, singing in that tree . . ." I spoke with the binoculars still at my eyes because I sensed an uneasiness in the voices of my shipmates and I dared not risk looking into their faces. "She has a strange, haunting little voice . . ."

"Oh yes, of course, well, well . . ." My shipmates drifted away and I saw they were trying very hard not to reveal their embarrassment. When they were gone I thought that I should be more secretive about the kind of things I observed on shore.

Again I examined the tree in which I was so certain the singing girl had been. Nothing. Had I really seen a vision?

In the binoculars I saw the donkey raise his head and look in my direction. Then he brayed.

For several days afterward there was, inevitably, some badinage about my having seen a girl singing in a fig tree, and I tried to convince myself that she had been a product of my melancholy and had never really existed. Yet I could not forget her.

We passed northwestward through the Aegean as far as the Turkish coast, and the searing *meltemi* winds kept us preoccupied no matter what our course. There were innumerable other distractions, none of which succeeded in removing my thoughts from Fournoi. I had rescued a goat from certain drowning after he had foolishly decided to swim the channel at Meganisi, and I had an abscessed tooth removed on the Island of Samos by a Swiss dentist using borrowed Greek equipment. The operation had been performed before an open window which faced on the dusty street and a large proportion of the island's population was able to enjoy the afternoon entertainment. To ease my pain I thought about the singing girl of Fournoi.

On every Greek island there is a minimum of one Greco-American who has returned to his native land to rest on his social security checks, which arrive with faithful regularity from that other generous land across the sea. He is from Detroit or Philadelphia or Cleveland or St. Paul, and nothing will do but you must accept his hospitality and tell him, while he anxiously fingers his worry beads, why his favorite ball team is not at the top of the league. All of this takes a very long time and considerable concentration in the heat of the Greek sun, yet even then my memory of the singing girl simply would not go away.

A month later, running before an identical *meltemi* wind, we sailed back to Fournoi. One of the reasons for our return was punitive. My mind had betrayed me here and to chastise it I would forever prove that there was no singing girl of Fournoi. Once again we had anchored and once again I stood on the foredeck watching the chain suspiciously. I did my best to ignore the shore and finally walked aft. It was drinking time and the custom held on the *Black Watch* as firmly as on the *Albatros*.

Suddenly I halted. There . . . *there*! I dared not look around but moved quickly aft to the binocular box exactly as I had done before. I called down to my shipmates: "Come! On deck! Immediately!"

I took out the binoculars and turned them on the shore. Halfway up the side of the bowl. There! There she was singing in the fig tree, her skirts billowing in the wind just as they had done a month ago.

Post was beside me now, and Steffensen, who had also sailed in the *Albatros*.

"Yes! Yes, I hear her!" Steffensen said.

I handed the binoculars to Post, and after a moment she said wonderingly, "Yes . . . I see her now."

And Anderson, who was the last to come on deck, saw her too.

For a time we stood quietly, listening and sometimes looking through the binoculars to reassure ourselves. Except for her donkey there was again no other sign of life on the entire hillside. She sang alone then, not for us or for anyone else that we could see, a wild song to match the wind and the skittering waves of the cove.

In the binoculars we could see her head tilted back as if she sang to the sky. Her tune was difficult to classify because of the vagaries of the wind, which alternately muted and brought her voice full volume. It sounded improvised as if she sang purely on inspiration, yet her lyrics were in distinct cadence and there was nothing shy about her style. Holding to a branch of the fig tree with one hand, she would make a sweeping gesture with her free hand to encompass her audience of none. It was a regal gesture to be seen at La Scala rather than to be impressing the dry rocks on a somewhat larger rock in the middle of the Aegean. Not once did I see her look our way. She seemed oblivious to our presence; nor did she concentrate on any other sector of her view. The wind was her audience, the sky, and the sea far beyond us.

Nightfall came quickly and we thought surely that the singing girl of Fournoi would abandon her concert. Yet after dinner when we came on deck she was still there, somewhere in the darkness beyond our anchor light, singing as boisterously as before. There were short pauses which we took to be the end of things and then she could be heard again. And after a while my thoughts again followed their familiar way to the loss of the *Albatros*, but somehow my utter dejection had passed. Somehow my faith in the permanency of the sea had been restored by this daughter of Poseidon on a faraway isle in a faraway sea. And I know that I was in love again and always would be.

Soon after my mood had changed, the singing ceased and there was no more. During the night there was only the sound of the sea and the wind and in the morning the singing girl of Fournoi did not reappear.

☼

IN HARBOR

Another two years have passed and there have been times during our confinement to the harbor of Rønne when I fancied I could hear again that strangely appealing voice blown down to us on the wind. Is she still in her swaying tree, still warm from the day's sun, while here we shiver in spite of our bundled gear? Is she singing to an empty amphitheater of frying dust, donkeys and stone, or are there other sailors applauding her performance?

The Black Watch *may have returned to her home waters, but the same crew who heard the girl of Fournoi are aboard—Post, Anderson, and myself for the moment, but Steffensen has only recently been aboard. We have talked of the girl and regretted that we did not make some attempt to go ashore and perhaps thank her for just being there. And then one of us said that might have been a mistake since then we would have been positive she had really been there. This way we can pretend, if we please, that she had really not been.*

I think we can sail today. Both the wind and the sea have gone down and there is a patch of blue sky to the north as big as a Dutchman's pants. Which is invitation enough for any sailor.

Other books of interest from Sheridan House

A SINGLE WAVE

STORIES OF STORMS AND SURVIVAL
by Webb Chiles

"Chiles is philosopher, adventurer, confessor, seaman par excellence and, of course, survivor. Above all, he is a consummate storyteller who, like a true pugilist, pulls no punches but lands his blows with the sensitivity of a poet." *Yachting Monthly*

FLIRTING WITH MERMAIDS

THE UNPREDICTABLE LIFE OF A SAILBOAT DELIVERY SKIPPER
by John Kretschmer

"The book is filled with a myriad of sea stories—all eminently readable—as well as a salting of practical information about sailboats and the sea, all delivered with a wry and self-deprecating sense of humor" *Sailing* Magazine

WANDERER

by Sterling Hayden

"A superb piece of writing...Echoes from Poe and Melville to Steinbeck and Mailer. A work of fascination on every level."
New York Post

MAINSAIL TO THE WIND

A BOOK OF SAILING QUOTATIONS
by William Galvani

Over 1,000 quotes from writers and speakers around the world who have eloquently expressed the beauty, mystery and power of the sea and the unique skills of those who sail upon it.

TAMATA AND THE ALLIANCE

by Bernard Moitessier
Translated by William Rodarmor

"Told with lyrical talent, this memoir is also the story of an endless quest around the world, from his native Indochina to the islands of the Pacific and to America. Moitessier will always remain the man who rejected security to follow in perfect freedom his Robinson Crusoe destiny." *Le Figaro*

SAILS FULL AND BY

by Dom Degnon

"...like a fresh breeze after a calm, *Sails Full and By* is a grass-roots adventure in the tradition of Mark Twain and a pleasing read." *SAIL*

America's Favorite Sailing Books
www.sheridanhouse.com